The Murders of Christopher Watts

His Tragic Confessions Through His Letters

CHERYLN CADLE

ISBN 978-1-960546-40-1 (paperback)
ISBN 978-1-960546-41-8 (hardcover)
ISBN 978-1-960546-42-5 (digital)

CC Press
cjcadle@hotmail.com
815-549-6439

Printed in the United States of America

Acknowledgments

My biggest fan and my biggest supporter—my husband Ed—without you believing in me and continually telling me I was doing the right thing, I don't know how I would have gotten through it all. Thank you for helping me through the difficult times by listening to very difficult events. I love you so much! To my daughter Candace who was always there to talk things through with me, helping me to make clear-headed decisions at times when things were difficult, I love you more than you will ever know. To my two sons Steven and Michael for believing in me, and even at times talking to me about why I was writing this story, I love you both so much.

Love never dies a natural death
It dies because we don't know how to replenish its source.
It dies of blindness, and errors, and betrayals.
It dies of illness and wounds,
It dies of weariness, of witherings, of tarnishings.

—Anais Nin

Introduction

I feel called to write this book. From the first day I saw Christopher standing on his front porch pleading for his family to come home, I knew I would be meeting him and getting his story. Surprised at how quickly we became friends and how quickly he started telling me how he killed his family, I was surged on to get his entire story—a story he had not told anyone yet—the true story.

Yet, even after he told his real story, so many people questioned it. The event is so horrible that people cannot get their head around someone being able to do something like this. After the narrative of the book could not be controlled by his family or by him, they turned on me. Now I can't swear that everything I was told is 100% true but I can tell you it is 110% of what I was told by either him or his family. Not to repeat myself so many times, but Christopher told me he did not have clear memory for a while as to what happened the morning of the murders, and I can see that, but sometimes, his stories change. I have tried to decipher what I was told to come up with the truth. Many times, things he told me he had told a member of his family also. So, please know that my heart is to deliver the truth to you. It's hard to get the truth from a murderer though. I mean, if they will murder, how likely it may be for them to lie. You will also read here his story of forgiveness. Can or will God forgive a person for murdering his family? I believe he can if he chooses to, but God's law would say that Christopher should die for what he did. An eye for an eye if you will. Man's law is what saved Christopher, not God's.

I will not because I cannot go into detail about the former book. I can tell you, however, there was nothing malicious done. It was all settled for the best and so, we move forward. This story isn't about me; it's about Christopher Watts; it's about him killing his beautiful wife, unborn son, and two sweet little girls Bella and Celeste. It's about so many trying to get to the bottom and find the truth to what happened the morning of August 13, 2018.

I have to wonder if Truman Compote or Ann Rule, two of our greatest true crime writers, faced this sort of scrutiny when they wrote their books as I do in writing this one. Christopher Watts has his own fan club and women who have "befriended" him from the beginning. That is not however why I befriended him. I really wanted him to tell me how and why he did this. I certainly am not his fan like so many others who take so much pride in calling him their friend, never-mind the fact that he is a cold-blooded killer. I do understand though why some are being mesmerized by him. He is friendly, good looking, and charming. There has to be a monster or very disturbed individual that lives in his head.

The mind's delusional thoughts can make the killer feel it was someone else or he was something else at that time. Christopher was always blaming the murders on something or someone else. In watching shows on television like *I Am a Killer* or the ID shows, they all say the same thing, "I wish I had never done this." Christopher may have friends and fan clubs but at the end of the day, it is still just him and the cold reality of what he has done—the reason he is sitting in that cell. People will come and go, family members will die, others will go on to something or someone else and at some point, Christopher will be left alone to die a lonely soul in his cell . . . alone.

As you read the true story of Christopher Watts the Familia murderer, you may think you are reading about a Hollywood horror film. As I was writing, it felt more like things I have seen in a movie. However, this is a true story. Christopher Watts pled guilty to killing his pregnant wife and two toddler daughters. He killed them and disposed of them in a brutal and disgusting way. Heartless could be a good way to describe it.

After meeting him and discussing his case, he gave me very intimate detailed accounts of the things he has not been able to talk to authorities or to his family. Because Christopher is an introvert, telling his true story from the platform of this book enabled him to get the whole truth out. I ask that you please save all judgments until you have read the whole book. I'll let you then decide how you feel about Christopher Watts the Familia murderer and if you believe his account of how he coldly and brutally took the lives of the four people who trusted him the most. Also, please understand I worked hard on this project and tried to bring the true message to the many people who could not accept what had happened. No ill will or anything containing malice was put into this story. It is just the story that has been told by Christopher himself. Please ask yourself: Why can others—TV programs, YouTube videos, and other books be okay to write but this book should cause a storm that was unreal? Why? Because it contains the truth.

Christopher by law is not allowed to make any money from this book. When we discussed writing the book, he told me he just wanted to have a chapter where he can give his testimony of forgiveness and how he came to know God, and wants to help others. That would be a trade for him giving me the information.

When starting this project, I reached out to both the Watts and the Rzuceks about having a voice in the book. Sandi Rzucek declined, and that was understandable as the project started just five months after the murders. The Watts family was more than generous to help me with information. However, some is very troubling.

I want you, my dearest readers, to understand I tried to write this book as unbiased as possible. What happened to Shanann, her baby boy, and her two beautiful daughters is the most horrible of tragedies possible. None of them deserved any of this. The three children were pure souls that had nothing to do with what preceded the murders. Shanann was a wonderful mom and a trusting wife. Their marriage may have been going through rough times, but she certainly did not deserve what happened. As horrific as the murders were, the fact that they were murdered by their husband and father whom they trusted is unconscionable. This book is my account based on extensive research of what led up to and during the murders, and what has transpired since. Five lives, including Christopher's, all needlessly taken and the immense pain of many others' lives were touched by this tragedy. My information for this book was given to me by Christopher himself, along with his family and some friends.

My goal is to tell this travesty with the utmost respect to Shanann, Bella, Celeste, baby Nico, and all family members involved.

At first, I wasn't sure what there was to write about since everyone had so much information given to them through the different media sources. It did not take long, though, to know most of the information on the media sources was made-up information. Soon, I was hearing some very dark and interesting things that Christopher had not shared with the authorities. When considering my moral responsibilities, I didn't want to be the one who hurt anyone else, and this information clearly would hurt many people. However, I can't change the facts, and for the family to completely heal, they deserve to know the truth. How can I write the story any other way? I refuse to cover for Christopher or try to make things easier for him. I know Christopher's family has felt there was more to the story, and I would think Shanann's family has felt it too. He is guilty; there was never any question whether or not Shanann killed the girls. Christopher told me he only said that because the FBI agent gave him the idea during the interrogation.

As with any conflict between people, there are two sides to the story—not two sides to the murders, but two sides to the conflict that led up to the fateful morning of August 13, 2018. In this story, there are circumstances that led a seemingly devoted and loving husband and father, Christopher Watts, to decide to take the most heinous way the lives of the family that loved him. What causes a man with no history of violence or a mental disorder to take the lives of his family? Nothing can justify it and one naturally wonders what would cause him to make such bad choices. This was *his* flaw; no one else's. Most people handle things much differently and would never consider doing what he did. For some reasons, he thought this was his way out of the pain he held in his head, but what he did caused far more pain than he could have ever anticipated. The Watts family said something seemed wrong and they sensed something was going to happen although never in their wildest thoughts could they have imagined what transpired. The suffering that was put upon these people is the heaviest burden a person can endure. It has changed their lives forever in the worst way possible.

There have been other cases where the perpetrator heard voices or claimed that God or a demon was telling him to kill. There are definitely some eerie things that have happened around these murders that do appear evil. However, how is it that someone could kill anyone without it being evil? What happened that could have caused him to calculably kill his beautiful family? I sat out to find these answers from the murderer himself. It's very interesting to try and get inside his head. He guards thoughts and sometimes only tells you about things you ask him about. Therefore, I'm in belief that he still holds secrets close to him. I believe those things are the things he is keeping to protect someone else. He may deny it now, but he told me there are some things he will take to his death, and actually, I am not the only person he told that, too.

There was something about this story that was not as simple as everything looked, and I knew it. All I had to do was listen. I have a feeling if you were to ask any of the authorities who worked with this case, they would probably tell you it was very different from others they have worked on and that Christopher is different from any other perpetrator they have dealt with.

Christopher says he felt evil spirits around him for a few weeks before the murders. Actually, Christopher's story is very dark and eerie. Through research, I have found that some sophisticated psychiatrists believe that evil spirits are, however seldom, assailing humans. Sometimes, it is the patients who are deluded about demons, but careful observation by some has led them to believe that certain extremely uncommon cases can be explained no other way. The Vatican and priests have said the demand for exorcists has been increasing. In fact, in 2010, the US Conference of Catholic Bishops organized a meeting in Baltimore for interested clergy who could perform exorcisms. Assaults upon individuals are classified either as demonic possessions or as the slightly more common but less intense attacks usually called oppression. It's not exactly like the "devil made me do it."

There are many true-crime junkies that take all of this very seriously, and it all makes sense that people would hate someone who could turn on his family and kill them all in cold blood. No one really gives a criminal like this a chance. No one wants to hear excuses; they just want the truth, and in detail. I have that! I found it interesting, though, that Christopher does not give excuses. He owns up to what he has done but tells me he knows he wasn't himself. He has never talked about insanity, just the darkness he felt that came over him.

On August 13, 2018, the horrific crime was committed by a thirty-three-year-old Christopher Watts. He annihilated his entire family—his pregnant wife Shannan, only thirty-four-years-old, his four-year-old daughter Bella, and two-year-old Celeste. It would seem the very last thing on Shanann's mind would have been that her gentle and loving husband would be capable of killing his family. However, evilness seemed to hover over the house that was once so full of love and laughter as those inside were enjoying their lives. What seemed to be a normal family living in this beautiful home had secrets that were hidden in the mind of the man who was living there with his family. As he took a mistress, he didn't feel there was still room for his family.

The beautiful town of Frederick Colorado, population only 12,000 with its upper middleclass subdivisions, filled with young families enjoying the clean air and beautiful lifestyle that is offered by the best of Colorado, was on edge in August 13 and 14. This quiet, pristine subdivision could be seen in the warm evenings with families taking walks and talking to neighbors and just enjoying the surroundings of where they lived. The neighborhood was abuzz as they talked with each other about the family that lived at 2825 Saratoga Trail. However, they need not fear the person responsible for the missing of Shanann and her two daughters even though he lived amongst them; his aim was only his family. To everyone else, he was the kind and gentle friend they all loved. In the year of 2018, this was the only violent crime in Frederick. This one took four beautiful, vibrant lives. They did not realize that murderers live amongst them.

There was a black cloud that hung over the community as life tried to go on as usual. The small community where Christopher and Shanann lived became paralyzed with the news that Christopher Watts killed his family. People in town huddled in small groups discussing what had happened. Fliers with Shanann and the girls' pictures still hung in windows and businesses in town.

The tragedy seemed to have touched everyone in the small town. It touched people all over the United States as people stopped when his name crossed their television screen. As people gathered on the lawn of the Watts house to pay their respects, people who didn't even know them were emotional because of the sick way the little girls' bodies were disposed of. The story made people angry, and they wanted revenge on the man who did this. People would drive by just to get a glimpse of the house where the horrors took place. Rumors had already begun about the house having spirits and ghosts.

In August 15, when it had become clear that Christopher had murdered his family, the parents in the community that all knew the Watts were left having to explain to their children why they could not play with Bella and CeCe ever again or why they wouldn't ever be going for a visit. They had to answer questions like, "what is dead?" and "where is heaven?" and "why did Bella and CeCe's dad hurt them?" Even the parents had their own set of questions of how their friend they had to dinner last week could possibly do something like this. Some of them had even allowed him to watch their children while enjoying parties at the Watts home. All of their friends loved Christopher and thought he was one of the nicest, most gentle individuals you could ever meet. Everyone the police interviewed did not say one bad thing about Christopher Watts. How could something like this happen in such a beautiful family-oriented community to such good people as the Watts?

As I watched the crime unfold, I wanted to be able to come to some conclusion why this seemingly normal man would do something so heinous as to put his two baby girls in large battery containers of crude oil. Little did I know then that I would soon meet and come face to face with the "monster" that did this. On the first day I saw him on television, I felt I wanted to contact this man, and I wanted to write a book about his story. I thought that by writing this book, I'd be able to find out why he would do something like this. Through the course of writing this book, I started with writing him a letter. The letters continued throughout; I went to see Christopher at the prison several times, and he called me two to three times a week throughout the entire time.

Our conversations on the phone and in person were being recorded. Christopher felt it was safer and more private to send me letters with his confessions. We became sort of friends, but he knew the reason for our contact was so I could write a book about his story and confessions of how he murdered his family. Christopher does not like being called a murderer. He cares about what people think of him, and he couldn't stand that he is a hated man. However, he gave me the information and allowed me to write the book in exchange for writing and publishing his "testimony" of coming to God and the forgiveness he received. His story is moving, and it is told in his words. At times, it was difficult for him to repeat to me the things he had done and what led him up toward killing his family. In court at the day of the sentencing, he could not bear the things that were being said about him.

He told the FBI that as he was killing Shanann, he couldn't take his hands off of her neck. He wasn't himself; he says it was like something was standing behind him and making him do it. He knew if he told me he was blaming something other than himself for the murders or if he denied that the responsibility of killing Shanann and the girls fell solely on him and only him, I would not write his story. He is completely adamant the hands that killed his family were being held tight against his victims and would not allow him to stop. A person does not lose the ability to choose one's own free will and make choices. His crime is made up of several choices—all of them wrong. This story captured attention from literally millions of people. The internet was full of YouTube videos, Facebook posts, and television and newspaper updates. Still today, nine months later, there is something new on YouTube posted about his case almost every day.

When I saw the interview on the front porch of Christopher's home the day after the murders, his desperate plea for Shanann and the girls to come home screamed guilt. His body language, the way he would smile or smirk, gave the appearance he was almost relieved of something. It was clear to almost anyone that was watching that authorities need look no further. Evidently, the police felt the same because they never looked for anyone else. It clearly was a front to cover up what really happened. Begging for his family to come home when he knew they couldn't come home makes one wonder if the haughty way he was acting meant he thought he would get away with killing his family; he says on that morning when he gave the interview on the front porch that he did not have much memory of the details of what had happened. He knew he had killed his family; he just couldn't remember all of the circumstances surrounding it. The cocky way in which he acted in front of the camera was just a cover-up for the nerves he was feeling.

Christopher now says he doesn't remember much about that day on the porch and giving the interview. He has been told about it and does not understand why he would have acted that way. He told the authorities at the time that nothing made sense to him; he holds to that still today. Christopher has said the circumstances of the murders have come back to him in pieces and since that was just the next morning after the murders, he was so traumatized that he couldn't remember much about the murders. Is this because he was insane or just didn't want to remember to the point that his brain shut down? When a person experiences a traumatic event, adrenaline rushes through the body and the memory is imprinted into the limbic system. Consequently, after trauma, the brain can easily be triggered by sensory input, reading normal circumstances as dangerous. Even his father-in-law in the sentencing called him an "evil" monster. Whether it is true or not, only Christopher knows. Many do not believe he couldn't remember. Yet even though self-induced, he did suffer from tremendous trauma.

I've always had an interest in true crime and all of the big and small details that come with it. I was being warned that hearing all of the intricacies of a murder, especially one with very small children, can mess with my psyche. That warning was very correct. I myself had to have counseling after listening to the deep details of this case. I found myself not able to sleep many nights, and when sleep did come, I would dream about the case. From the first meeting with Christopher, as he talked about what had happened, I could honestly feel the darkness of it. I have always believed a person who could kill someone in cold blood must be insane. No one could possibly be sane and do this. It was confusing, however, because Christopher seemed so nice and thoughtful and sort of boyish. Even though shy and reserved, it did not take long for him to start opening up to me. I don't think I had prepared myself for what I was about to hear.

CHAPTER 1

Crossing into the Unknown

> "Out of suffering have emerged the strongest souls. The most massive characters are seared with scars."
>
> —Khalil Gibran

Before I wrote him the first letter, I thought long and hard if this was the right thing to do. However, I felt called to write this book and to get the truth out to the families, friends, and the public who had such an interest in this story. I knew that listening to the details of a murder from the murderer himself would change who I am. I just hoped I could bounce back to who I was before this. If you listen to Christopher, he is back to being as normal as he ever was, but it's hard to believe you could do something like this and not be changed forever. Reading his letters was shocking and made the hair on the back of my neck stand up. I'm sure you will feel the same when you read the first-hand accounts of what he did but did not tell the authorities all that took place. It is very hard to listen to a murderer as he tells you all of the details of a heinous crime he committed. Please keep this in mind as you judge me.

February 10, 2019

Dear Mr. Watts,

Hello, my name is Cheryln Cadle, and I am writing to talk to you about your case. I have been following your story since the day it all happened. Let me just say, the crime was horrific, so I'm not writing you to tell you how wonderful you are or that I want to be pen pals.

I do not usually follow these sorts of things, but seeing you on the front porch of your house that morning giving the interview, I knew you were in for quite a journey ahead. I have to tell you, the interview screamed guilty!

I sense also by now you must have great remorse and probably have confessed to God all of the sins that have been committed. I know you are sentenced to prison for the rest of your life, yet I feel your life still holds some purpose. If you allow, I'm sure God can still use you to make a difference in other people's lives. I would love to tell your story of redemption, and I think, in the long run, it can help you. I think also it would help your family and Shanann's family for the truth to be totally told.

I would like to write a book about your case if you will allow me to. If you will allow it, I need to know how I can contact you by phone, and I would need you to put me on your visitor's list. I live less than four hours from you, so I would be able to come and visit you.

Please write me back and let me know how you feel about this, I'm sure you've had other offers, but maybe none that are willing to publish your testimony. If you just feel you don't want to, I ask you to think about it again, and see if we can come together on it. Please write me back at the address below.

Sincerely,
Cheryln Cadle

I gave him all of my contact information.

After three times writing to him, he finally wrote me back. Maybe he thought he might as well do it for I didn't seem to be going away. He liked what I had to say, that he could still have a purpose for his life and help others. After a few back-and-forth letters, he agreed to write a book with me. He told me he had many offers from others to write a book, but he was not the least bit interested. So, when he read my letter, the first response he had in mind was "nope," but he kept feeling like God wanted him to respond to my letter. He said when God tells you to do something, well, you better do it.

I have put all of Christopher's letters into this book. They are just as he has written them.

> Hello Cheryln, March 14, 2019
>
> I'm sorry I haven't written you back when you wrote the first two letters. You have to imagine, I'm very skeptical about who I write back and when I saw you wanted to write a book, I said "Nope!" Although this letter you just sent me felt like God was giving me an ultimatum to write you back. I'm not sure why exactly because I have turned several other journalists and authors down.
>
> When the FBI and CBI came to the prison to speak with me, I had no idea they were coming. I felt like it was God telling me to clear my wife's name since so many people were confused about what happened. And well, if God tells you to do something, you do it!
>
> I'm currently on protective confinement since this last media storm, so I'm limited on telephone use and everything else; corresponding by mail is our best bet for now. Thank you for the Bible, they weren't supposed to let me keep it but they did! God's work! I have a KJV bible and I am already comparing them back and forth some words that have always confused me. I like the idea of telling people how I came to my faith, how God can turn any pain and suffering into bringing something new to be born, and recognizing when something evil takes

a hold of your life. We are attacked all day long and if people can and if people can learn to rest in His peace, joy, and love, a lot would change! I couldn't keep the self-addressed envelope you sent me, not sure when that rule might change.

I will do a book with you if you for sure will be willing to give me a chapter where I can tell about my forgiveness and coming to faith so maybe it will help someone else not to take the path I did. If I can help even one person, it would be worth it.

I hope this letter finds you in good spirits and I will close with one of my favorite scriptures.

God Bless,
Chris

"And he said unto me, My grace is made sufficient for you: for my strength is made perfect in weakness."

"Most gladly therefore will I rather glory in my infirmities, in reproaches, in necessities, in persecutions, in distresses for Christ's sake: for when I am weak then am I strong."—2 Corinthians 12:9–10

After he wrote me the first letter, he started to feel maybe I had changed my mind because I didn't get back to him quickly enough. After all, he had ignored me at first. One day, I received a call from Cindy Watts, his mother. She said it was very important to Christopher that she call me and tell me he had written me back, that he did want me to write a book with him about his story and the things he has not told until now. His mother told me she had begged him to fill in the missing pieces for her. She said he told her when she reads the book, she will understand.

Cindy Watts told me of the struggles they have had since the day of the murders. I could hear the pain in her voice when she spoke of how the son she had raised and loved was just never capable of such a horrific thing. I have no doubt her pain was excruciating. No mother would be able to come to terms with what her son had done. To make things worse, it was her grandchildren that he murdered—his very own children—flesh of his flesh, bone of his bone who he once loved, cared for, and bonded with, and they trusted him. The Watts family has come against some big challenges trying to stay out of the media's eye, and YouTubers continue to call and harass them. She said they are hated because their son did this, but never would they be okay with what happened. That would have been a good clue to stay out of the public eye. She thanked me for speaking to her and told me to please call her at any time. I found her pleasant but obviously a broken person. I hung up the phone wondering what I was getting myself into. People have been so hard on them, and it obviously shows. I wondered if I would be coming up against some of the same because I am writing with/and about a murderer who is hated by so many. Little did I know nor could have ever dreamed the path that it was going to take me down.

Christopher and I wrote back and forth a couple of times. Then, his mother sent me the papers to apply to be put on his visitor's list. The inmate has to request for a person to apply; without that, a person cannot even apply to be put on the visitor's list.

I had to go through a background check, and when I was cleared, I was allowed to visit Christopher. I visited for the first time on April 5, 2019, right after everything came out to the FBI. I had never been to a prison before, and I was a little intimidated, I must say. The building is huge and very well kept on the outside. A tidy green lawn sprawled out around the building about two blocks square.

The prison sits right downtown in the heart of a little neighborhood. Across the street and on both sides are little modest, midwestern craft-style homes. Sidewalks and big old trees line the neighborhood; although old, they're very trim.

As I walked into the building, I noticed to the public eye, everything was clean and orderly. The staff was matter of fact but helpful and not rude at all. Once I passed through the metal detector, they put a stamp on my hand. At that point, I walked through a series of seven locked doors and walked a total of about a quarter of a mile outside to get to where Christopher lives. They seated me in a visiting room where the walls were lined with vending machines. The only chance for the inmates to get a taste of something on the outside is when the visitor brings quarters with them from the vending machines and buys the inmate a drink or snack. I don't know if the feeling dulls, but they crave a taste of food that is not prison food.

I was told to have a seat and Christopher would be there shortly. Because of being in protective confinement, for him to see a visitor, they had to bring him through an area called the "hole." Therefore, the hallway unit had to be shut down or what they call "lockdown" and the other prisoners don't like that. Christopher says it's stressful being brought from his cell through that area. I noticed just being brought from his cell to the visiting room, he was shackled at the ankles and handcuffed. He was handcuffed to the table once he was seated. Three guards stood nearby. He explained that once he is out of solitary confinement, he will not be shackled and handcuffed for the visiting room. Christopher seemed to take it all in stride; I think he was just happy to see me and have someone to talk to. At that point, other than the FBI, he had not had any real communication with anyone other than phone calls to his family since August 15, 2018. I don't know what it looks like behind those walls, but for everything I could see, things in the prison ran smoothly but everyone stuck to the rules.

There were a couple of times while waiting for Christopher that I could hear the inmates yelling and making a lot of noise. It struck me what a polar opposite it was that he had come from an almost palatial home where he seemingly had all that a person could want or need. Freedom being the most important thing we have and all of the little things we take for granted like picking out our clothes, choosing what we want to eat, getting into our car and going to a movie, holding the people we love, or just walking outside when we want to are no longer afforded to Christopher as an option for his life. I can't help but wonder if Shanann didn't feel that darkness that had come over him. Christopher says she was very unsettled during that week before, but I'm sure she thought it was the marital problems they were dealing with. However, her husband was planning on killing her.

When I first met Christopher, the only recognizable thing was his voice. He looked absolutely nothing like he did during the interview on his porch or during the sentencing. During the sentencing, he looked on through shuttered eyes looking as angry as a person could, yet still hanging onto himself. He said later that he just wanted to run and bang his head against the wall. That day at the prison, I could tell he has been through a lot. He gives account later in the book some of the things he has gone through.

He immediately explained when the FBI came to the prison to meet him on February 18, 2019, they did not tell him they were coming intentionally. They told him they did not want to put stress on him, perhaps they didn't want to give him time to think about what he was going to say. He resented that unannounced visit and because of that, did not tell them everything they might have wanted to know. He had already pled guilty, was in prison for the rest of his life, and really didn't owe them anything. What he was to tell me will not change anything legally or make a difference in his conviction, but some of it will hurt the people who love Shanann and his girls. He felt like God "prompted him to clear Shanann's name" since there seemed to be confusion by some that she killed the girls. He said something hard for him to deal with is blaming her for the killing of the girls.

The FBI had some questions because there were so many unanswered parts of this case. They told him they were not going to take him to any dark places. They questioned him about his mistress Nikki, seemingly still finding out if she had anything to do with the murders. They questioned him extensively about the morning of the murders. At the sentencing, Christopher pled guilty but never gave an account as to what happened, so people were left with his first confession. In his first confession, he told the police he killed Shanann because he caught her killing the girls. Although most people did not believe Shanann would kill her girls, he didn't tell even his family any differently. Then, when the FBI came to see him, he seemingly was baring his soul. He told them in great detail how he strangled Shanann, then took her body to the oil field and buried her. Then, he smothered each of the girls with Celeste's blanket and put their bodies down the oil batteries. Later in this book, you will read Christopher's letter where he confesses the real truth, which is an extension of what he told the FBI. He left some very gruesome details out when he talked with the FBI. They promised to keep the information between them, but it was just a few days until it was all over the media.

Christopher told me personally the whole story. He is not covering for Shanann. Anyone saying he did not kill the girls based on the evidence is wrong. Christopher wants everyone to know he is guilty of killing all four human beings—Shanann, Bella, Celeste, and Nico. He said Shanann was a good mom and would never and did not ever hurt the girls in any way. Christopher said he hugely regrets blaming her. Both of them lived for their girls; that's who they were, and the girls were the most important part of their lives.

Christopher says he now lives with great remorse. The remorse is no doubt from killing his family, possibly for making the wrong decisions, and that he is in prison for the rest of his life. Christopher is hard to read; he does not seem to have emotions. Hearing the voices of Bella saying "No, daddy!" is very haunting and painful every day to him but still, there is no emotion. There are times that even though he says he is where he belongs, it seems that being in prison for the rest of his life is something very hard to come to terms with or even think about, and he hopes someday, he will be free. Maybe this is a way his mind has of coping and protecting himself from the fact he will never know any life from here forward than the depressing, unfeeling life of prison. He was living in a confused state as his mind reels back and forth in trying to make sense of it all, looking for a place to be able to find some comfort or peace in his situation. How could he ever find peace after what has happened? He claims that's the reason for his relationship with God because that is where peace and solace can be found. Yet, many theologians would say that his sentence to life in prison is man's law. Man saved him. God's law would be death, a life for a life. At times, he talks about his family in the present sense like they are right with him. He does refer to them being with him in spirit. He's had a couple of dreams that seemed very real to him about Celeste and Bella being with him in the jail cell.

Christopher objects to some of the things I have written; I believe in part because he doesn't want people to judge him. He told me there are some things he will take to his grave. Those things cause much confusion as of course, people want to know what those things are and who he is protecting. It is the belief of many that the person he wants to protect is Nikki. This story does not need embellishment. By the time I tell the whole story, you will see it has enough sensationalism all by itself. What he has told me is an extended version of what he told the FBI on February 18, 2019. I do believe this is the real story. This is the one that is the hardest for him to say. This is the one that brings out the chills. Yet, no one knows for sure as the victims cannot speak to what happened. They have no voice here. This story is the darkest of anything he has told. Maybe the darkest you have ever heard too. Let's not forget there were real lives that went through these horrible brutal murders.

CHAPTER 2

Christopher's Early Years

> "How people treat you is their karma; how you react is yours."
>
> —Wayne Dyer

The following are some accounts of Christopher's childhood given to me by his mother Cindy Watts.

Christopher Lee Watts came into the world as innocent as any other child. Born on May 16, 1985, he weighed 10 pounds and was only 19" long. He was born on a sunny warm day in Fayetteville, North Carolina at Cape Fear Medical Center. He made his debut into the world on a Thursday around 7:00 p.m. Ronnie and Cindy didn't have maternity insurance. She stated it took them 18 months to pay for his birth. He was their second child; Ronnie and Cindy's first child was a seven-year-old energetic little girl named Jamie. She was excited to welcome a baby brother into their family. They grew up close, and they still are today. He was a happy child, always respectful. He adored his father and looked up to him. Cars were their bond together. They went to places like Bristol, Tennessee and Daytona, Florida. When looking at his pictures and hearing the stories about his very normal childhood, you have to ask yourself just as his family does—how did this change? Cars were their bond together; overall, Christopher was very much his dad's son. Christopher took after his father's quiet, friendly, and soft-spoken personality. How could someone like this make such a turn from who they seemingly were and make a decision so horrible and destructive? An introvert, Christopher has never been openly affectionate or emotional. He made good grades in school and never got into any trouble with teachers or authorities. He loved sports, and Ronnie coached his little league teams. They had a good family life, better than most. His parents remain married to this day. He grew up in a modest ranch-style house. His dad worked at the dealership in their small town as a mechanic, and his mother worked in finance. Life was slow and good in the little town of Fayetteville. Summers, especially for Christopher, were easy and laid back. He liked to spend a lot of time just reading, watching television, and spending time with his grandmother; he was her favorite. She was a German lady who was not affectionate but loved Christopher and taught him many things about life. He spent a lot of time with her as she watched him while Cindy worked. Cindy and her mother did not get along; living just down the street, her mother tried to control Cindy, telling her how to raise her children. Although his grandmother was extremely negative, that didn't rub off on Christopher.

In his teen years, he never dated; he was socially very awkward. He had two good friends growing up though, and really never varied from those two friends. They remain friends today and were hurt by the tragedy not being able to believe Christopher could do something like this. When the couple of friends he did have went to school dances, he stayed home and watched television with his parents. He didn't mingle or go to parties, he never got into the usual teenage trouble, and he never drank or did drugs. He wasn't bullied by other kids; he got along well with everyone. He was known just to fly under the radar. Cindy says perhaps he was too perfect for a teenager to be true.

Christopher went to a Baptist church when he was growing up. His religious teachings made him fear he would go to hell if he died while sinning. The fundamentalist religion taught him he could not drink, go to dances, or have sex before marriage. Christopher was afraid of God and put him "in a box." He felt if he did anything to displease God, he could go to hell, but as long as he obeyed all the rules and didn't sin, God would be pleased with him. Cindy said she could hear him in the bathroom repenting over and over to God for sins he felt he had committed. Cindy said she never knew what those things were; he repeated himself in an OCD manner. Christopher and Shanann did not follow a religion. He told me he feels bad that he never asked Shanann where things were with her beliefs or how she felt about God.

When Christopher graduated high school, he went to a NASCAR technical school. His dream was to work on car engines for NASCAR. He tried to get on the circuit but never made it. He set out to work and bought his tools, and was very proud of the accomplishments. He had about twenty-five thousand dollars' worth of tools that his parents sold after he went into prison for only three thousand. That money went a long way back then. Bringing home about $2500.00 a month, he had the chance to save money for his future, which he looked forward to marrying and have children of his own. He had his own apartment, good credit, was good with money, and was always responsible for his bills. The Watts family was good with their budgets, and they lived frugally; they taught him well.

Even as an adult, he never dated much; he was still too shy. It isn't that he didn't like girls because he says he did. When his cousin told him about Shanann, he wasn't very interested at first until he saw her picture. To him, she was the most beautiful girl he had ever seen. Maybe it was because it was through Facebook, so it felt less threatening, or maybe seeing how beautiful she was, he had the nerve to send her a friend request. At first, she didn't answer his request, but his cousin, Shanann's friend, told her what a nice guy he really was. Shanann figured she didn't have anything to worry about just being friends with him on Facebook, so she finally accepted his request. They became friends and decided to meet. They hit it off and dated for a couple of years before deciding to get married. He had both sides of the family together at the beach when he proposed to her. It was very romantic, the ring was beautiful, and they made a beautiful couple. From there, it was all wedding plans. They were married in November 2012.

There are many crimes and Familia murders. Some get media attention; some are barely spoken of. What makes some noticed and others, not at all? I think in this case, we all felt we knew the Watts family. People could relate to a modern-day, upper-middle-class family. Shanann had a large presence on Facebook and YouTube. She invited us into her home to share with us all about their lives. She introduced us to her little girls, to Christopher, and even their family dog Deeter. Shanann was always positive and helpful. Some felt they lost a family member or a friend when she was murdered. Therefore, because so many people felt like they knew her, it became a popular crime; one people followed daily. Cindy gives an account that her daughter-in-law would drug the children every night with Benadryl before they went to bed and that she put the girls to bed by 6:30 every evening and down for a three-hour nap every afternoon, saying there were only a couple of hours between the time they woke from their afternoon naps until their bedtime. Shanann was live on Facebook and social media many times daily. Christopher says this was an area of stress for him. He did not want to be on camera, and many times, Shanann would put him there spontaneously. She was social and loved being in front of people and in front of the camera. He was an introvert and did not like the attention. She loved selling Thrive and helping those who were selling under her downline.

Yet, not all that a person puts on social media is really the way it is. Facebook is a place people can easily post what they want others to believe their life is, and often after posting it enough, start to believe to be true. Obviously, there are many things that Shanann posted that were very different from the way it truly was. Shanann had no way of knowing she would die and people would be able to look into her private life and know everything intimate about her. Shanann did portray them as a perfect happy family and would often brag about how lucky she and the girls were to have Christopher. Except for the financial issues, she probably really did believe it because she beamed on videos as she talked about her family, about remaining positive, and about "Everything happens for a reason." Did *this* happen for a reason? Not for a good reason.

The Rzuceks and Watts family have been treated brutally as the media harassed them, and people who must have their own set of mental issues made these families miserable for months. People became obsessed with the story. Those people took away both families' right to mourn and try to heal and get closure. These people have suffered at the hands of those who feel they have the right to know everything. They have the kind of pain that time does not heal. Every day is a struggle. They are the collateral damage.

There are literally hundreds, if not thousands of pictures that Shanann had taken to preserve the memories for the future. Little did she know those pictures would be what would help her family once she was not here. Memories that are frozen in time through these pictures—what a gift to cherish. But as the memories are frozen in time, so are their lives. They will never get to see their granddaughters drive a car, go to a prom, have their first boyfriend, get married, or have children of their own. They were cheated for being able to experience those things. Shanann will never get to experience being a grandmother holding her first grandchild or growing old with her husband. The tragedy reaches far into the future all frozen in time on August 13, 2018.

Cindy Watts keeps asking herself why she didn't see this coming and if there were signs she missed. She blames herself because she and Shanann didn't get along. They never got along from the beginning of Christopher and Shanann's relationship. The last time she saw Christopher before the murders was in August 5. He told her that he and Shanann would be separating. Cindy told him that day she hoped he wasn't seeing someone outside of his marriage. He assured his mother he was not. He was deceptive even then, but that is not unusual during an affair. Lying and deceiving others while living a double life comes easily over time.

A mother does not stop loving a child no matter what he has done, so of course, the Watts still love Christopher. The mother-child relationship is only second to God's love—an unconditional love. It's the closest human relationship there is. His mother doted on him; she was used to having a lot of control in Christopher's life. Yet Ronnie, his father, was the one Christopher looked up to, calling him his hero. Now in the judicial system, they have no say or control.

In part, his mind may have blocked out exactly what happened that morning. In trauma, one becomes anxious and out of control. Christopher brought that trauma on himself. Christopher knows he is required penitence. He owes Shanann, Nico, Bella, and Celeste penitence, but his biggest penitence is to God. He is paying for the crime for the rest of his life. He is a broken man put together by the grace of God. A couple of months leading up to the murders may put the pieces of the puzzle together for *why* Christopher did this.

It has been very important to Christopher what people think of him. He says he has always tried to be good to people and to always be kind and helpful. What people thought of him made a difference. It bothers him that people hate him and as he puts it, "judges" him. People judge what they have seen, so they hate what he has done more than they hate him. Many want to see this "evil" person in prison for the rest of his life; many also would have chosen for him to get the death penalty. It's not easy for people to let go of what happened. Maybe it's because they are trying to find a way to make sense of it. Christopher says maybe people can relate it to their lives—that they could be one bad decision away from tragedy.

CHAPTER 3

Life-Changing Realities

Shanann worked for Thrive, a direct marketing sales company that sells nutrition and weight-management products in the form of vitamins, shakes, and patches. Christopher was consuming this product daily in large amounts. He was wearing what they call DFT Duo patch which he has said caused his heart rate to speed up like he was working out all day. At one point, he said he never had less than two patches on him at all times. Besides the duo patch, he was also drinking more than one shake a day. He took two of the tablets every morning. He was loaded up. Christopher was taking so much this high-end he couldn't sleep. He says he could only sleep about three hours per night. He did say that because of living in Colorado and taking Thrive, Shanann did not have to take any medication. Shanann was doing very well selling Thrive, and Christopher benefited in several ways from it. Shanann earned many free trips that they were able to enjoy. Since Christopher worked a full-time job, he was not free to go on all of the trips and was needed at home to care for the girls. So, there were many weekends he would stay home doing special things with them and taking them to special places. That was his time to bond with them. He supported Shanann in what she had to do and when she traveled. This is how she helped to earn a living. Her goals were high, and she claimed to have more than two hundred people working under her. She had great ambition and was headed on up the ladder with Thrive.

One of the things Shanann did to help with her business was to entertain. She planned parties, some of them quite large, spending hundreds of dollars on one dinner party. It was very important to her to appear well off; appearances were everything. Some of her friends looked up to her or were envious of her because she seemed to have it all. He always knew where his place was. When they would have company or dinner parties, his place was to stay upstairs and entertain whatever children were there. He didn't mind much because he preferred to stay in the background anyway, and honestly, trying to keep up an appearance was kind of embarrassing for him. Christopher had become a background noise. It's very harmful when this happens to a person, and soon, something will have to change.

On June 22, Christopher and Shanann went to San Diego with Thrive. Right before this trip, Christopher and Nikki, a coworker, started to take flirting to the next level. The two of them made plans to meet after he returned from his trip, which he said he did not want to take. A video that Shanann posted of them the day they had just arrived in San Diego shows Christopher trying to stay away from the camera. He obviously was not happy about being there. The two girls, Bella four and Celeste two (almost three), stayed home with their Papa, Frank Rzucek, Shanann's father.

Arriving home early on June 26, Shanann took the girls and left later that afternoon with her dad for a five-week family visit to North Carolina. Even though he never told her he didn't want her to go, he joined them a month later for a week-long family vacation. Shanann told her friends that before she left, he couldn't keep his hands off of her. He now says if she had not gone, he does not think he would have had an affair and none of this would have ever happened. If she had been home, he probably would not have met Nikki at that park or ever went out with her, he says. I want to be careful about this statement he made that it does not sound like it's Shanann's fault he had the affair or that he killed her. Neither was her fault. She was probably tired from her early pregnancy. She got a lot of help from grandparents in North Carolina; it was probably a welcomed break for her.

It was just before the trip that Christopher learned of her pregnancy. The video that Shanann posted online shows he was not happy about the news of their third child. The very same week he had started to see Nikki was when he found out Shanann was pregnant. He was caught off guard by the announcement because it had taken Shanann much longer to get pregnant the last two times. He said it made him feel more guilty because he had just decided to have a more serious relationship with Nikki. He always wanted a son, but this was a big stressor for him even though he was part of the decision and at the time, it felt right to have another baby. He did not know what was just around the corner—that he would meet someone that would sweep him off his feet and make him regret he ever had a family. Now, he felt he was not ready for this baby because mentally, he was with Nikki.

Once Shanann and the girls left for North Carolina, Christopher was free to do whatever he desired, and he desired Nikki. He and Nikki's relationship escalated fast. He said that as much as he tried to take things slow, Nikki was pulling him. Christopher was caught off guard because he had never had a woman pursue him before. She lured him with lewd sex and sent nude pictures of herself on his phone. Nikki was definitely chasing him; she knew he was married and had two girls, but, in fairness, she was told by Christopher that he and Shannan had *both* decided to separate. She most likely knew about Shanann's pregnancy because she spent time looking up Shanann on Facebook and the internet. She possibly wanted Shanann's life. Shanann had many YouTube and Facebook videos that Nikki had most likely saw. Christopher says really bad things went on in Nikki's house—things he is very ashamed of—some of the things Christopher says he will take to the grave with him.

Shanann was beautiful, lived in a beautiful home, had two beautiful children, had it all, or at least it appeared. She had all of the things that would make a mistress jealous. It seemed Nikki stalked Shanann at least on the internet, if not in person. Even though Shanann dealt with health issues, she seemed like a person who accomplished a lot. Nikki, watching from the outside, was very unfair to Shanann. Nikki knew her competition, but Shanann never knew hers. Nikki went to the police early on to let them know she had been seeing Christopher. As far as it appears, her accounts of the relationship were not truthful. She went to them early on to make herself not look guilty. Her feelings were more than she would tell the FBI; some things she told them were blatantly not true.

But Christopher was drawn to Nikki and enjoyed being with her: she cared how he felt about things. She cared about what he thought and would ask his opinion. He was not used to this. Since this was what Christopher needed most, it wasn't the sex for the most part that pulled him in. He was much more in love with the way she treated him and made him feel like a man again. She validated his masculinity and gave him the feeling she adored, looked up to him, and valued what he had to say. Respect is what he felt from her. He did not want to let that go; at all costs, he determined to hang on to someone that caused him to feel like he had never felt before. Possibly, she knew how to play him and played him like a piano, but he felt like he had a voice with her, which he did not have with Shanann. He had been afraid to be himself around Shanann; he never offered his opinion and was rarely asked how he felt about anything. He commented he could not hang something on the wall in their house by his own decision without Shanann getting mad about it. Probably Shanann had always been that, but then, Nikki came into the picture. He says her control and being so bossy seems to have led him where he could not even talk to her about things that were vital to their marriage. Being deeply loved by someone gives you strength while loving someone deeply gives you courage. Christopher's deep love he thought he had for Nikki may have given him the courage he needed to get rid of his family or to live the life he felt he deserved. Christopher said he had never even considered having an affair or that there was anything wrong with his marriage until he met Nikki. He wasn't looking for an affair, but Nikki was too much for him to resist. They felt a common bond, and he chose the wrong path.

Nikki was playing a dangerous game, and it seemed she pulled out every stop to seduce and intoxicate him. Christopher spent almost all of his time with Nikki in July. He practically lived at her house and had almost no time to think about what he was doing. When he was with her, he did not even think about his family, as though he did not have one. When he did think about them, he felt very guilty. Nikki knew this and is the reason Christopher, in his words, had to "talk her down off the ledge" more than once. She became the injured party in her eyes instead of seeing it for what it was. She then tried pulling the last punch by telling him she wanted to give him a son. She knew she could get Christopher to feel bad for her by telling him they didn't have any first together. She's trying to steal someone else's husband, and she is sad she doesn't have any firsts with him. She'd shared his first affair with him but that wasn't enough. Did she think Shanann was ruining *her* life? Christopher feels this is when the idea to take the lives of his family began. He didn't want to but knew it was going to happen. He did nothing to fight those feelings. Nikki had a group of friends he says were involved in some very dark things. He can pinpoint a time that he could feel himself get darker on the inside.

In asking what Nikki was really like, he suggested reading Proverbs 7:5–27, and I would see Nikki. These verses in the Bible show a very sexual woman who does not care that she is married.

"Wisdom will save you from that other woman, the other man's wife, who tempts you with such sweet words. One day I was looking out my window at some foolish teenagers and noticed one who had no sense at all. He was walking through the market place and came to the corner where a certain woman lived. He then turned up the road that goes by her house. The day was ending. The sun has set, and it was almost dark. Suddenly, there she was in front of him, dressed like a prostitute. She had plans for him. She was a wild and rebellious woman who would not stay at home. She walked the streets, always looking for someone to trap. She grabbed the young man and kissed him. Without shame, she looked him in the eyes and said, I offered a fellowship offering today. I gave what I promised to give, and I still have plenty of food left. So I came out to find you, and here you are! I have clean sheets on my bed—special ones from Egypt. My bed smells wonderful with Myrrh, Aloes, and Cinnamon. Come, let's enjoy ourselves all night. We can make love until dawn. My husband has gone on a business trip. He took enough money for a long trip and won't be home for two weeks. This is what the woman said to tempt the young man, and her smooth words tricked him. He followed her like a bull being led to the slaughter. He was like a dear walking into a trap, where a hunter waits to shoot an arrow through its heart. The boy was like a bird flying into a net, never seeing the danger he was in. Now, sons, listen to me. Pay attention to what I say. Don't let your heart lead you to an evil woman like that. Don't go where she wants to lead you. She has brought down some of the most powerful men; she has left many dead bodies in her path. Her house is the place of death. The road to it leads straight to the grave (Proverbs 7:15–27 ERV)."

On August 5, when Christopher was visiting his family, he had already started to plan what he was going to do to his family when he got back to Colorado. To make Shanann look bad, he told his family that if he ended up dead, they should have the authorities look at Shanann. His sister told him to put that in writing. He wrote a letter stating such, and that letter has hit the media.

CHAPTER 4

The Watts' Side of the Story

> "Love is giving someone the ability to destroy you, but trusting them not to."
>
> —Unknown

Several stories were highlighted in the media about Shanann and Christopher's family problems.

When Shanann and Christopher got engaged, they decided to have an engagement party. During the planning of the party, Christopher's sister Jamie offered to help. Shanann had a list of things that needed to be done. Jamie offered to address and mail out the invitations. On the day of the party, most of the friends did not come. The next day, Shanann made some phone calls and found out her friends never got an invitation. So, Jamie was accused of never mailing them out; Jamie says she sent them.

Shanann had asked Jamie to be a bridesmaid in her wedding and for Jamie's daughter to be a flower girl. The week right before the wedding, Shanann made an appointment for all of the girls in the wedding party to have their nails done at a spa. I was told that because of Jamie's work hours, she was unable to meet them at the spa. She says Shanann told her that both Jamie and her daughter need not be at the wedding but the dresses were bought and the money had been spent. So, because of this, Cindy, Ronnie, Jamie, and the rest of her family did not attend the wedding. Although they finally moved past it, this is a reason for the hurt that never completely healed. Cindy says, however, they have always regretted not going to the wedding. Christopher said he forgave his parents but it deeply hurt him and Shanann that they chose not to come.

One of the big things that happened just before the murders was a huge falling out between Shanann and her in-laws. During her five week visit to North Carolina, Shanann's plan was to spend the weekends at the Watts. The second weekend, she was there on Saturday when the ice cream debacle, what Cindy calls "nutgate," took place. Sandi Rzucek, Shanann's mom, has refused to comment. Cindy Watts wanted to tell her side of the story of what she calls the "nutgate."

During the investigation, Cindy was blamed for trying to "kill" Celeste. According to Cindy and Jamie, it happened on a weekend when Shanann was at the Watts house during her five week-visit. The only people there were Cindy, Shanann, Ronnie, and all the grandkids. Jamie had dropped her kids off on her way to work, so she said she was there when the ice cream issue came out. Yet, the story told was she was not only there, but that she also came into the house and put out a bowl of nuts. Cindy and Jamie said this did not happen. Ronnie was there also and said he was caught off-guard with how the argument escalated.

The story Shanann's mother has told is not exactly the way Cindy and Jamie tell it. The oldest granddaughter, which is eleven-years-old, went into the kitchen and got ice cream from the freezer, which Cindy says was one of the small vanilla cups. They had to be careful about ice cream because of the factory it was made from. Two-year-old Celeste was allergic to tree nuts, which are almonds, pistachio, pecans, walnuts, etc. It was not a peanut allergy. Peanuts grow in the ground, so that is not one of the nuts she was allergic to. Christopher said the allergic reactions Celeste had from tree nuts were rashes and breathing problems; also, each reaction can get worse. With her already having breathing problems, I'm sure Shanann was afraid of her having a bad reaction where she would have problems in breathing. Any mother would be careful about any allergy her child has. The granddaughter went to the freezer and took out an ice cream cup. She sat next to Celeste, was eating ice cream, and was not made to move while eating it. The tree nut allergy was something newer, and Christopher said he doesn't think Cindy really believed she had an allergy to nuts. Cindy says she did not know her granddaughter had gotten the ice cream out. This made Shanann angry, and she did not hide her feelings. Christopher's nephew who was ten told Bella that they would probably not ever get to see them again. That was a prophetic word as that was the last time any of them saw Bella, Celeste, or Shanann. Things had been so bad for so long between the Watts and Shanann that Cindy asked her to leave until she could calm down. Cindy then took her daughter's children and left the house until everything had a chance to deflate.

Something Shanann had only just realized and was willing to fix was the breach between her and her in-laws. She could see how seriously Christopher was taking it. She sensed a difference in the way Christopher was treating her for the first time since she knew him. She shared with a friend maybe she had gone too far this time, and he was tired of having her pit him against his family. He knew his parents weren't perfect, but he didn't like the demands Shanann put on him to not see his family or not to allow his kids to see their grandparents. He didn't like what Shanann had done to him in making him shut his parents out of their lives. He said she had flat out told him he could not call or see his parents again. In the past, this may have worked, but now, Christopher was simmering and getting up the nerve he needed.

Christopher did cleave to his wife during the times of trouble between Shanann and his parents. After a while, he had missed his family, and he longed for things to be good between them. He didn't see any real reason they couldn't all be family.

Cindy and her daughter-in-law did not get along well, but that certainly does not make her a murderer. Not all personalities get along, and that's okay. Cindy says she did not interfere in their marriage. Christopher said he knew from the beginning that Shanann did not care for his mother and his sister, and they did not care for her. He says he let it go on for too long; he should have confronted it but never did. He always sided with Shanann because he knew if he didn't, there would have been trouble.

On a daily basis, the Watts family deals with people who hate them for the crime their son committed. Thinking their daughter-in-law had just killed their granddaughters, of course, they were not happy with her. At that time, all the information they had was what Christopher had told them—of how he killed Shanann because he caught her killing the girls. That is what Christopher told his dad and the FBI agents at the time of the confession. What people don't realize is that this is the last time they saw their son or talked to him until the day of the sentencing. When they saw him, the only thing he would tell them is he was pleading guilty for a reason. Going into the sentencing, they still had no idea as to what exactly had happened. Ronnie and Cindy did not know what to think; their heads were spinning. Just as Shanann's parents knew she wasn't capable of hurting her girls, the Watts family questioned how Christopher could be capable of this since he had never shown any sign of violence.

The Watts did not go to the funeral, and this was huge for them. Ronnie made a phone call to one of the family members and was told it might be best if they did not come. They were told the media was everywhere and if they came down, most definitely, they would have been attacked by them. This was not told to him in a malicious way; just in a way to watch out for everyone.

The Watts family say they did not want to make a scene or make it harder on anyone, so they decided to stay away. However, they did have a service of their own with friends and family. They had their pastor say some words, and they sang *Amazing Grace.* It was beautiful and very sad at the same time. What did it take not to go to the funeral and graveside of their daughter-in-law and three grandchildren? It was heartbreaking for all of their family. They had no way to tell them goodbye. Unfortunately, the last visit with Shanann and their granddaughters ended in discord. No one can possibly know how hard this would be or how one might feel, but it would have been nice if the two families could have put their differences aside and held each other up during this time. It was totally heartbreaking for all.

There are many things between the Watts family and Shanann I have chosen not to write about. Some of the things that have been said about Shanann are cruel and filled with hate. Christopher agreed with me not to say these things about her; she does not deserve it.

It is very unfortunate because they are both good families. They both were hurt and had the most unimaginable loss when they could have been a strength for each other. Hopefully, true and complete healing will come between them someday. They loved and adored those grandchildren, and there are hundreds of pictures and videos to prove it. They were very blessed for what time they had with them. Those baby girls are their shared bond, and hopefully, someday, they will be able to look past their hurt just enough to help each other try to heal and get past this.

CHAPTER 5

All the Money

> "One of the deep secrets of life is that all that is worth doing is what we do for others."
>
> —Lewis Caroll

It is hard when writing a true crime story because you only get one side of the story. These accounts are what I have been told; please keep in mind Shanann is not here to defend herself. I have been told that Shanann controlled all the money that came into the house. Christopher says he recalls a time when he sold a four-wheeler and didn't get enough money to pay off the loan. Shanann never trusted him thereafter, and she never allowed him to have anything to do with the money after that. It's unclear to him if that's the real reason she didn't want him to touch the money or if it were because she didn't want to answer for what she spent. The girls were enrolled in a $25,000-a-year school. Shanann liked to shop, sometimes spending most of her check without having paid on her obligations. Christopher said they could not afford this. She would sometimes turn around and put a lot of the money that she made back into Thrive. She also had Christopher withdraw $10,000 from his $401K to catch up on house payments they were behind on. Christopher believes that's what she did with it but does not know for sure. He said she was the kind that could always find a way. The way things were going, they may have lost their house before they could sell it. According to Christopher, she controlled everything in the house.

This was a pressure point for Christopher. He worked all the time, but they were constantly having money issues. They were living way beyond their means and way beyond their needs. They had filed for bankruptcy once and were headed that way again. He would not talk to Shanann about how bad things were financially and how he didn't want the household money to be abused that way, and he felt enough money was coming in to afford the house. He feels now they needed to find a more affordable school. Since Shanann worked from home, maybe daycare/school should not have been a full-time option. The girls should not have been taken to daycare from 7:15 a.m. to 4:30 p.m. five days a week. Celeste was not even three, and Bella was just four. There is more to the story but Christopher thinks much was kept from him. The girls going to a $500.00-a-week daycare was something Christopher was not allowed an opinion on. He now knows there were many things with their finances that were kept from him. These are some of the truths that have been hard for the Watts family to understand. The girls' records were sealed by Christopher right after the sentencing even though he does not remember signing them. No one seems to know why. He says it was a stipulation for his plea agreement; he was not clear-headed and he says he still does not remember everything that happened during that time.

Money could have been managed better, and he knew this. Shanann was used to all the best money would buy. She did make great money; she had to put a lot back into her business. Money became a big stressor for Shanann also. However, they also had a lot of medical bills and ongoing medicines to buy, so this affected their budget hugely.

Christopher realizes he didn't take charge of his family, but he says that's what's worked for them. By his own admission, he knows that Shanann wanted a husband to take charge, but he didn't have the confidence to do that. Christopher is the kind of person that has always just done whatever he has been told to do. Also, by his own admission, he had a hard time telling the people who worked under him to do something; he found it easier to do it himself. He felt emasculated and found it hard to take the lead. According to research, a man who has been emasculated concedes leadership decisions to his wife. They become men that cannot make a firm decision without second-guessing themselves and run from relational conflict. Emasculation is said to reach what is called malignancy level; hence, resulting in even killing if something devastating or bad happens to him. Many a man turns to alcohol. This alone can build resentment to the point it is not talked about and could come out in a dangerous way. It's not known if Shanann knew Christopher felt emasculated if, in fact, he was. Yet, if he was such a quiet personality, how would Shanann know he was a simmering pot? Obviously, he was afraid of her, and that's why even up until the end, he did not tell her about Nikki. Under normal circumstances, a man would tell his wife it is over, and he is divorcing and moving on. It has happened millions of times. Maybe he thought over it. In actuality, Shanann's reaction after the initial shock may not have been so bad, but even if it was, why couldn't he handle it? He never learned coping skills or how to be assertive.

When asked about why he never spoke up, he said he didn't realize at the time it was so bad; it's just what worked for them as a family. It was their normal until he started realizing it was just not working for him. He realizes now it was building up and getting ready to implode. Yet, there were times she was going off on him that he could purposely not say anything but only smile to himself as he thought about how he really felt. He knew better than argue unless he wanted to go through a big ordeal. The last time he challenged her during an argument and tried to hold his own, she got very angry and screamed, "Get out of my house!" He says she kicked him out and wouldn't even let him come home overnight. He said he had to do some huge "Please forgive me's" to get back in the next day. He says that gave him the fear of going up against her. So, he decided after that, he would not ever argue with her again but just take it. He is quick to say, though, that it was not like this all the time. Christopher shared that one time, when the sign of trouble was everywhere, neither of them stopped to notice what was happening to them. They allowed their relationship to suffer and never stopped long enough to fix it. There were many happy times; many more happy than sad. He dwells on those happy times now as he longs just to be with his family one more time. He says he loves Shanann,

Bella, and Celeste, and he knows he would have loved Nico, too. He only has himself to blame. He longs to be able to hold Shanann and the girls, he craves to feel their touch, and he would so love the chance to hold his baby boy. Shanann had told her friends before that she wanted a man who could make decisions and be more assertive, but this was not Christopher. Yet, their problems are problems that many families face. Until just before the murders, they weren't so bad that working on them and concentrating on making their lives better wouldn't have worked.

CHAPTER 6

The Mistress

"Birds sing after a storm, why shouldn't people feel as free to delight in whatever sunlight remains to them?"

—Rose Kennedy

Christopher has not told the FBI, but as soon as Nikki told him she wanted to have a first with him, he started planning how he could kill the baby so he could give Nikki their first together. How very sad that Shanann was excited to be able to give him a son. He was planning to take that baby's life before he had a chance to come into the world. This baby boy was the son he always told Shanann he wanted. This would perfectly complete their little family. Shanann had thought if Christopher could get excited about their baby boy, then he might start feeling differently about their family. At first, Nikki had told Christopher she did not even want children, yet telling him she wanted to give him his first son was her way of keeping him. He was not wanting to get rid of Shanann's baby because he thought it was not his; he wanted to get rid of the baby because it *was* his and he did not want it. However, Shanann was the only one fighting for the marriage; all the while, he was trying to destroy it. He would not give his marriage another chance, would not even talk to her about their problems, and would not be honest with her. He let her be the only one in the marriage that had a desire to save it. Christopher did not try one time to talk to Shanann about their problems until the morning he killed her. He just couldn't confront her.

As soon as the girls all left for North Carolina, he had a new sense of freedom. Nikki latched on very quickly even though he was married and with two girls. She wanted him to stay with her every night. She had not yet included Christopher in her friend circle but was ready to right before the murders. In the past, she had been in an abusive relationship, so when it was over, she deleted most of her social media. Her mail went to her father's house like she was hiding from someone. She took medications but never told Christopher why; he suspected she was bipolar. She was in Christopher and Shanann's house twice—July 4 and again on July 14. Christopher was off to work on July 4, stayed the night at Nikki's, and slept late the next morning. When he was up and checked his phone, there were many missed calls from Shanann. He knew she was going to be really mad. He went outside to call her and she was beyond pissed—absolutely furious! He decided to just go home for the rest of the day. He went back inside to let Nikki know. Now, it was Nikki's turn to be angry. Weren't they going to do something later on that day? He told her no, he was just going home for the day. For the first time, she realized that she was not the number one in his life. Christopher must have been having second thoughts. Had she left him alone for the rest of that day, he may have turned around. Later on, she showed up at Christopher's house with the ruse she wanted to help him build a healthy protein diet plan. She didn't look around the house much that day. She felt she couldn't allow him to be alone. She knew if he was alone in that house with all of the memories and pictures of his family that he might decide his life was too good to give up. Or maybe, there was love deep inside him for his family that could be brought to the surface again.

On July 14, Christopher and Nikki were headed home from Shelby Museum and decided to stop at his house before getting something to eat. There, Nikki played with Deeter the family dog, which led her upstairs. This time, she could see what things were like in their life and all the pictures of Bella, Celeste, and Shanann. She came downstairs with the most frozen, dazed, confused look on her face. She realized for the first time the life he was living and the family that would be broken into pieces because of their affair. He saw the look of despair, and he put his arms around her leading her to the couch. As they lay on the couch, she said to him, "You have all this, more than most people, and we are doing this? Why are we doing this? Are you willing to give all this up? Is your relationship with your wife that bad?" He told her that he and Shanann had drifted apart, and they didn't talk anymore. He was not even sure in his own head that he believed that fully. Yet, he could see the deficit in their relationship. He then told her that before he started seeing her, he and Shanann had actually decided to have a baby. More signs that he was having second thoughts. She freaked out completely and started yelling "what the fuck are you doing with me then?" He saw something in her he had not seen before that made him take notice. "Your relationship couldn't be that bad if you and Shanann were trying to conceive!" Even though he tried to get her to stay and talk to him, she left the house, went out to her truck, and sat there for thirty minutes texting him. Whatever he said to her as he was texting back to her had worked. In his words, he "talked her off the cliff," and she wanted him to make her feel better and to come after her, but he didn't. As he thought about it, he realized this is one of the things that turned him on about her. She allowed him to calm her down by telling her he did not want another baby with Shanann. He withheld the information that Shanann was already pregnant. He told her the plans to have another baby were before he had met Nikki. It had been a way to possibly save their marriage but it wasn't working. He really doesn't think Shanann was looking at it that way. I believe she was thinking they decided together to have a third baby, and they were blessed it was going to be a boy.

Nikki came back into the house. She told him he was the only man she ever met who tried to fix problems, smooth it over, and talk things through. He thought, ironically, he never tried to do that with Shanann. He knew she probably wouldn't listen to him, yet he realized he didn't give her a chance. They had never really talked about things. He had always just let her make the decisions. Nikki asked him then to come over to her house as if nothing had ever happened. They went back to her house and made love. She tried for it to be hot, passionate love and did some of the things that would normally turn him on, but this time, their lovemaking felt different. He felt the guilt rush back to him, and he really didn't want to be there. When they made love, Nikki even felt it was different. They normally would have had sex three to four times a day. After that happened, she said their sex was down to only one to two times daily. "When they were finished making love, she told him, 'I got mad because I thought I could give you your first son. When you told me you and your wife were trying to have a baby, that made me really mad, and it scared me.'" That made him much more confident in his relationship with her. After all of that, Christopher and Nikki went to the Bendamare races on July 21 and camping in the mountains on July 28 and 29.

CHAPTER 7

The Last Family Vacation

"Although the world is full of suffering, it is also full of overcoming."

—Helen Keller

The following couple of paragraphs have some lightly touched on things the FBI does not know. Trust me, there is much more to come in the following chapters.

When Christopher was at the airport leaving for North Carolina, Nikki sent him a text telling him to "Take this time to fix the issues with your wife and enjoy time with your family." This gave him a warm feeling of no pressure and loved her for it.

The first night Christopher arrived in North Carolina, Shanann needed something for a really bad headache, so Christopher told her he would get her something. *Thinking she was taking an over-the-counter pain reliever, he gave her 80 mg of Oxycodone.* He said the pill made her sick, and Shanann was up vomiting most of the night. He didn't help her because he wanted her to lose the baby. He felt he had given her a large enough dose to miscarry. He texted Nikki that he wouldn't be able to call her, just text her. She replied to him with "why not, are you with her?" *He thought she wanted him to spend time with his family.* That put the pressure back on him. Obviously, she wanted him to spend time with her no matter what. Christopher was used to trying to please the woman he cared about; for the next eight days, he ignored his wife. At night when she would want sex, he would leave the room. He was not intimate with Shanann during that entire week. He felt he had to do this so he could disappear and talk to Nikki for hours on the phone.

When he returned from Colorado, he went to Nikki's using his work truck. That day, Nikki gave him a key to her place. She withheld from the FBI that she ever gave him a key to her house. It told him that she was ready to take the next step forward in their relationship, so he told her he was moving forward with the separation. He promised Nikki his relationship with Shannan was going to end even though he had not yet talked with Shanann about a separation. Shanann, in the hopes they could still fix their marriage or at least work on it, ordered a book and had it mailed to him hoping he would read it before she came home. When he got it; he didn't even open it, he just threw it in the garbage. *Christopher realized that day that he could not have Nikki and his family at the same time. It was the first he realized it.* It was time to get rid of what was standing in the way of his and Nikki's being together, and he could make that happen. He had his nerve up, but the nerve he had was not to talk to his wife about their problems—it was about killing her.

While in North Carolina, they had made plans to have a little family vacation at Myrtle Beach. The week he'd met Shanann and the girls in North Carolina, Shanann may have thought if they got away together for a few nights, they could talk things out and make things better. She tried to do that; by his account, she really wanted to talk but he wouldn't give her any time to talk or try to come together. Christopher was not willing nor did he have any desire for things to work out between them. The only reason he was there was for the girls, not Shanann. Even the girls were on his nerves; he had very little patience with them. It was blatant. Anyone around him would have noticed he was aloof and unfriendly, which was very out of character for Christopher. But even his three- and four-year-old girls' spirits noticed the darkness in him. Their pure spirits could see or sense his dark spirit, and they did not have much to do with him. They did not want to hold his hand or walk and play with him on the beach. Normally, they loved playing with their dad, and he loved playing with them. Not during these days, however; they basically didn't want anything to do with him, and he really didn't want much to do with them. The first time ever, he felt like that way about his kids. Children can see things sometimes that adults cannot. They are innocent and pure. It's a belief in the paranormal community that infants and small children are much more sensitive to someone that is evil or has evil intentions. It's believed they have a more open mind as they don't have the mental barriers adults have developed. In order for a spirit to be seen by a human, the human needs to be open and non-judgmental; that describes children. The world hasn't touched them yet; maybe to some point, they still belong to that sweet, sinless spirit world from which they come. They probably did not sense he was going to harm them but just his spirit being opposite of theirs, and not necessarily something to fear.

When he left Nikki's that first day back from North Carolina, he had to hurry to meet Shanann for an ultrasound. What should have been a joyful time for them was met with almost a hatred for her and the baby. As they were doing the ultrasound, he could see a new life moving. He felt indifferent and cold toward Shanann and the baby. He did not let the event register in his mind: here was his son, the son he has always wanted, but he felt nothing for him. Shanann reached out to take his hand in support, but he pulled away. He wanted no part of her or this baby. He wanted a different life.

Christopher went back to work and things carried on as they had before they left. He tried to act as usual around his co-workers. Shanann believed they were better or at least taking small steps toward getting better. When he met Shanann later that day for her ultrasound, Shanann was excited. She gave a friend the envelope that revealed the gender of the baby and had invited friends over for the big reveal. Christopher was obviously not happy, so since it would have been awkward in front of all their friends that they were not the usual couple they had always been, she canceled the party. A day or so later, she asked that friend to return the envelope, and she texted Christopher. He texted back that he would like to find out with her the gender of their baby. When he answered "Yes," she texted back she loved him so much. He did not respond. Later, she asked him to hold her or hug her; he refused. Christopher was cold and shut her out. She said they were talking some, so she thought things were a little better since he found out the baby was a boy. However, he was trying to make things work to his advantage. He was thinking about killing her and the girls. At what point does a person allow their fantasies to change to reality? In this case, it changed soon thereafter.

Later that evening, as they were getting ready for bed, Shanann brought up how cold he was when she wanted to hold his hand. He told her his head was just not in the right place, and he couldn't deal with her right now. He told her he would be sleeping on the couch. She said to him, "whatever is going on or whoever she is, know that you will never see these kids again, so make sure she is worth it!" With that, she slammed the door with him on the other side. He waited until he figured she was asleep and called Nikki. He slept on the couch that night. The next night, he stayed in the basement to call Nikki from there. He had decided his marriage was over but had not told his wife.

Shanann knew that the fight between her and Christopher's parents had really affected him. So, she sent pictures of the ultrasound to Ronnie and Cindy introducing them to their grandson, trying to start rebuilding what had been torn down. They said they did not respond to her.

Nikki was excited about where things were going and started to tell her friends about Christopher. He decided he needed to delete his Facebook. He knew that her friends might see that Shanann was pregnant. Taking down his Facebook was a further signal to Shanann that something was wrong. This was a definite red flag. It was still important that she save her marriage, so she did what she knew best. She booked a couple's weekend in the mountains. She found someone to watch the girls, and Christopher agreed to go but already knew he would not be going. He said he went along with it to satisfy her for the moment. He was already planning how to kill her and the girls and was daydreaming about getting rid of his "baggage" and starting a new life with Nikki. With this new life, he would be able to dump all the things of the old life—the house mortgage, his big bills, and his family. This was not logical or normal by any means. Why was he not able to see that none of this was real but has huge consequences? Is it possible that being wrapped in the web of lies because of this affair kept him from looking at things logically? Yet, of course, not every affair ends in murder.

Shanann had thought about canceling the trip to Arizona with Thrive. She was going to a Thrive convention with some of the girls on her downline. Her heart was just not in it since they had just been apart for so many weeks and things had not gone well. Yet, Christopher did agree to go away with her the next weekend; just the two of them. And she had told a friend they seemed to be headed in the right direction. Christopher did not want her to cancel. He saw an open door to be able to see Nikki. So, he told Shanann to go ahead and go on her trip, and they would talk when she got home. This gave her a flicker of hope that things may be getting better, so feeling somewhat relieved, she decided to go ahead and go to Arizona for her job. The weekend was hard for Shanann; her pregnancy, morning sickness, and marital problems were all she could think about and he wouldn't even touch her. She loved their life and didn't want it to end. She didn't want to raise these three kids alone. Shanann was a person who seemed to love life and the people in her life and she wasn't ready to stop fighting for her marriage, but unfair as it was, she didn't know what or who she was fighting.

With things being stressful and confusing while living a double life, Christopher felt God gave him three chances to turn around from the affair and the things he was planning in his mind. He had those chances to turn everything around, and none of these things would have happened. One evening, on his way to Nikki's house, he felt God urging him to turn around and not do this, but he kept going. Knowing the whole way there, he should turn around and not go to her place. All of a sudden, his car started to skid like it was going to run off the road. He almost lost control, knowing immediately God was trying to turn him around. There was no other explanation for why he started to lose control of his car. He knew this was the first chance God gave him to get out of the situation. Christopher put it well when he said we always think something new feels better than something old. It didn't take long for Christopher to find out the old was much more appealing and comfortable than the new.

When Christopher talked to Shanann during that five-week period that she was in North Carolina, he became more and more distant with her. As much as possible, he would ignore her calls and texts and come up with excuses for why he didn't answer her. He was building that wall between them so it was easier to forget he had a family. She didn't understand and started to question the distance being put between them. He had always been so good and attentive to her. She even told one of her friends that before she left, he couldn't keep his hands off of her, and now, he would barely talk to her. I think she realized how much she loved Christopher and wanted to make things right between them. Had she taken the girls and gotten on a plane and gone home, it might have changed everything. Yet, his actions were so different than anything he had ever shown before.

He was either trying to rid himself of guilt by going to Nikki's or he didn't have any guilt at all, which is very possible since he did not feel remorse or guilt after he killed them. He was falling out of love with Shanann, and in its place were only the thoughts of trying to get rid of her and his kids. He now thought he had fallen in love with Nikki or was he in love with the way Nikki treated him? Nikki was not like anyone he had ever met. He loved her touch, her conversation, her beauty. He thought she brought out the best in him, yet she actually was bringing the darkness out of him. He had an addictive craving for her when he wasn't with her.

Shanann was not one to coddle him or give in to his actions, but she knew this was not the Christopher she had always known and loved, so she did try to be kind and more attentive to him. Something had drastically changed between them, and if it wasn't someone else, she could not figure out what it possibly could have been. With this looming over her, she must have felt such a heavyweight over her. She was about to be blindsided even though she was being warned by her friends that she should find out if he was seeing someone. Her friends urged her to ask him if there was someone else, and later that month, she did start asking him. She asked him daily several times. Her insecurities were coming out. She had never worried about Christopher cheating on her or making her feel anything but important to him. He would only answer he didn't know what was going on in his head, but no, there was no one else. He kept making excuses for being tired or would say he fell asleep early. It seems the last thing she considered was his having an affair—no, the last thing she considered is him murdering his two daughters and her. She trusted him and believed he had always been truthful with her. She even told a friend Christopher didn't have a game. She did not think it was possible for him to love anyone but her. That's the kind of trust she had in him. That's the way he had always made her feel, and she made him feel the same—she thought.

CHAPTER 8

The Week Before

> "So much of what is best in us is bound up in our love of family, that it remains the measure of our stability because it measures our sense of loyalty."
>
> —Daniel Long

As with anyone having a premarital affair, the lies got bigger and the deception grew. Christopher during this time says he felt dark; he felt that he had definitely changed and not for the good. This may sound like a ruse and may sound like he is blaming the murders on something else, but he says that is not the case. Darkness would have to fill a person who could plan to kill his family because he has a mistress he wants to be with.

Darkness enters through a person's mind and makes one feel it's fine to plan and carry out dark things. The individual reasons away from the good and makes the bad choice. It empowers the person to feel he is commissioned to do whatever he wants to do. Was Christopher temporarily insane that morning or oppressed by a dark spirit? Whatever it was, it prevailed.

Knowing what was to happen, in hindsight, it's hard not to look at it as a darkness that was hovering over their home that fateful morning. Shanann did not know, and she may not have felt anything unusual.

His plan is lurking over his home. He must have felt empowered, knowing all things are going as planned. Much has been posted on

YouTube about the spirits and sightings that were left in the home. If spirits can dwell in an empty house, that spirit could still be there which would make sense why things have happened since no one has lived there. The person buying the house next should definitely have the house blessed. Consider Matthew 12 in the Bible. When an impure spirit comes out of a person (later, Christopher will tell you when and how that happened), it goes through arid places seeking rest and does not find it. Then, it says, "I will return to the house I left (ERV)." When it arrives, it finds the house swept clean and put in order. Then, it goes and takes with it seven other spirits more wicked than itself, and they go in and live there. If there were spirits in that home, they are not the spirits of Shanann, Nico, Bella, and Celeste. They aren't hating and mad. They are in the most beautiful place there could ever be—heaven! Sandi says her experience was beautiful and did not feel like a haunting. Any kind of spirit that haunts is evil. Christopher talked about how eerie his house was after the murders.

How is it a man's love for his children isn't more powerful than the act of murdering them? The forces of evil are not greater than the forces of good unless we have allowed that evil to take deep root. Christopher had read that fathers do not kill their children, but he did. Why was Christopher not able as a grown man to see the consequences? No one can imagine the conflict of good and evil that must have gone on in his head, yet he says when his mind went to getting rid of his family, it stayed there. This is one of the things Christopher did not tell the FBI. The thought of killing the girls did not just come into his head the morning of the "rage." This is something he had been fantasizing about for a while. He planned Shanann's murder, and he planned the girls' murders. When he was distant and withdrawn from her, in his mind, he was planning how he could kill her. He said he had been having these thoughts for a couple of weeks.

He keeps saying he knows had he not chosen to have an affair with Nikki, he would not have killed his family. Christopher does know why he killed Shanann, Nico, Bella, and Celeste. By his own admission, he wanted to be with Nikki no matter what even if that meant he needed to kill his family so he could be free to be with her. That may not be a big surprise to many people, but Christopher until now has not admitted it. His mother kept asking him why, why, why? He would not tell her. He ended up telling her she would find out when she read this book. However, there is still a lot of denial by his family that Christopher killed his family.

The Watts family came home on August 7. The day Shanann and her girls left North Carolina would be the last time they would ever make that trip. It's the last time she would hug her family goodbye. It was the last she would ever see her family. The little girls so innocent and trusting waved goodbye and left to face a horrible death; for Bella a horrible, violent death.

Things were very strained between the two of them. Shanann kept asking Christopher if he was having an affair. Her friends kept telling her she needed to find out, but he kept denying it. She only had six days left of her life. Does a person have feelings of death leading up to something like this? A mom may have a sixth sense about her children but in this case, no one saw it coming. Cindy Watts said she doesn't understand why she didn't see it coming. She has repeatedly said there were no signs there was anything wrong. Through some of the videos Shanann posted, you can feel the excitement she had for life, for her home, and family. She shows how she loves her friends and was willing to help them find the joy for the life she had. It was very hard to read the texts between Shanann and her girlfriends about Christopher's cold and hurtful behavior. He was building walls between them, and this is disturbing knowing what he was planning, but this was something she had no control over.

CHAPTER 9

The Weekend of the Murders

Shanann left for her trip to Arizona and Christopher and the girls stayed home. That Saturday evening is when Christopher told Shanann he was going to a game with the guys but in fact, had a date with Nikki. He hired a babysitter and the two of them went out. Christopher had never gotten a sitter and gone out while Shanann was out of town. This is something she normally did not feel comfortable with. Christopher and Nikki went out for dinner at a bar and grill. Christopher usually used gift cards for their dates that he got from work, but all of those were used. This time, he charged the meal on their personal account; it was over $62.00.

Saturday afternoon, one of Christopher's friends had tickets to a football game. He asked Christopher to go with him and have a guy's night out. Christopher did think about telling Nikki he could not get a babysitter and go to the game with his friend. This was chance number two that God gave him. As we know, he did not take that chance, he went out with Nikki instead.

He, as usual, let Shanann know how much he had spent. It seems that Christopher wanted Shanann to just find out so he didn't have to tell her. To use their credit card and then tell Shanann was the closest he could get toward telling her about Nikki. Immediately, when she saw the amount, she knew something was not right. That was way too much for one person's meal at a bar and grill. She knew Christopher would not have had more than one beer, two at the most. She looked up the menu online. Christopher had told her he had salmon and a beer. She shared with her girlfriends, and they agreed that was too much money for one person.

The average time an affair usually lasts is six to eight weeks. Christopher was well within that time frame. Had it been under normal circumstances and had he been left alone by Nikki, even a little, he would have turned around. Guessing, she probably would have forgiven and put their marriage back together had she been given the opportunity to do so. Nikki was worried that Shanann was back home, and Nikki had to dig her nails in a little deeper, and so she did.

Why was killing on Christopher's mind? Are six weeks really worth giving up everything? Of course, that has happened that way, but usually, no one is ready to give up family and the life they've built for a six-week love affair. His family was everything he had ever wanted in his life and he knew he loved them, deeply. He could feel himself going back and forth in his head about killing them. No one knows, not even Christopher, he says. Obviously, a scenario not thought through finally played out. Why did Christopher felt he could not leave Shanann and have a girlfriend? Perhaps, in his mind, it didn't follow the rules. It didn't make sense to him, but did murder make more sense? He ruined his own life and everything he had ever wanted, and he threw it all away (literally). He knows that had he made a different decision, it could have changed everything. What was putting that roadblock in his head and why could he not think normally?

There was never a toxicology test or a psychological exam done on Christopher. The toxicology test wouldn't make sense because they did not arrest Christopher until a few days after the murders, but a psychological exam is usually done automatically. It would have made sense to have a complete workup done on him; otherwise, who knows what was wrong with him? Christopher was told at the time by his attorneys that if he let them do an exam, anything he said could be held against him, and the courts would hear everything he said.

Since he pled guilty, that should have mattered to him unless it had something to do with the future, but for some reason, that meant something to Christopher and he did not want a psychological exam done. Now, if he wants a psychological workup done, it would be at his expense. He has no money; therefore, he would have to depend upon his parents to pay for it. They would be willing to pay for one, but Christopher still says he does not want one. As to the reason why he wouldn't, one could only guess he's afraid of what he might hear. Is it worse to find out you are insane and realize you do not live in reality or you are not insane but have the capability to murder your whole family? How does a society imprison people without knowing the difference? It says society has no patience or responsibility to the criminally insane. They are misfits of society who can basically be put away without any thought as to why they are sick.

We know a normal thinking person does not think about and plan to kill his family. Yet, we know there are many times this has happened. Christopher Coleman's case from 2007 is almost parallel to this story. He murdered his wife and two sons. He was a bodyguard for Joyce Meyers. He received four life sentences and weirdly, he is in the same prison as Christopher Watts.

Still another case in Channahon, Illinois: Christopher Vaughn murdered his wife and three children by shooting them in the face at close range with a shotgun. He talked later about how there was real darkness and evil around him. Right after the murders, he had no remorse. When the police were questioning him later, he refused to even look at the pictures of his family. They said there was such a darkness in him that it was scary. He would not put the names of his children with their pictures for the authorities. He would not even use his wife's or children's names. He is also spending life in prison. What evil lurks ready to put this into someone's mind and why are some people susceptible to it and others are not?

Christopher has a hard time looking people in the eye when talking to them, and when asked why, he says he has always been that way. His mother verified that by saying when he was a teenager, he asked her why he couldn't look people in the eyes when talking to them. She thought it was a sign of shyness. How much of it was a lack of confidence or social anxiety? Others will say when a person can't look you in the eye, it's because they are hiding something.

Still today, he wants to follow all rules at the prison and not upset anyone. He is said to be a model prisoner. He won't ask for anything or complain about anything. Christopher says he never felt the emotion of anger until the morning of August 13. That does not seem possible or normal. He went into a rage at the time of the murders and could not stop but that was his first confession. In his own words today, he says that he was not in a rage that morning. He said Shanann made him angry, but when he killed her, he was not in a rage. As he explains the murders today, he wasn't in a rage until he got to the oil fields. If he had been planning the murders, then he did not suddenly go into a rage. That's how the DA put it—that he calculatedly planned the murders. Later in the book, you will read this in his own words. Is this a learned ability to kill a loved one or is it genetics combined with the path taken as a younger person? How could the idea have even come to his mind to kill his family? All things start in the mind; however, is it insanity to have it come into your mind and entertain the thought? How is it the crime scene was so sloppy at the oil fields, especially for someone that planned the murders ahead of time?

His family feels he pled guilty and was pushed through the system and put in prison as quickly as possible. The feeling that he was guilty, they say, looks like he was sentenced and just thrown away. Uncanny because that's what he did to his family. Does society want to know what causes another human to do something like this so maybe it can watch for signs to prevent it? We don't even know if there were signs. Christopher hid it well, as do most who plan something like this. Yet, he has a family—mother, father, sister, aunts, and uncles—that is left in the wake of what has happened. Maybe it would help Shanann's family to understand what disconnected that morning and caused an otherwise normal father, husband, son to do something so horrific. The Rzuceks loved Christopher like he was their son, and trusted him to care for their sweetest and most valuable treasures, and they would like to know why he would do something like he did. Christopher says he would like to have some of the questions answered himself.

Christopher does not show much of any emotions. I'm not sure as I've said that he is capable of real emotions. He is called by many a narcissist. The definition of a narcissist is a person who has an excessive interest in or admiration of themselves.

There is a spectrum of narcissism but Christopher does not fit the common narcissist. However, there is narcissistic rage. Narcissistic rage is a reaction to narcissistic injury. Narcissistic injury is a perceived threat to narcissistic self-esteem or self-worth. Narcissistic injury is a cause of distress and can lead to dysregulation of behaviors as in narcissistic rage. The injury is usually caused by one of three things: challenged confidence, injured self-esteem, or a false sense of self. The fact that Christopher was usually so quiet may mean he has the fortitude of both forms of expression—silence and rage.

He did think of others besides himself. By the praises of so many people, he was a loving father, husband, son-in-law, and friend. Christopher cared for his little girls' daily needs. He picked them up from school, played with them, gave them baths, fed them, and read them bedtime stories. These are not the usual traits of a narcissist. However, if his life was considered a threat to who he really is, it probably built up until he blew. A simmering pot ready to explode, and explode he did.

CHAPTER 10

The Night Before

On Saturday night, August 11, Shanann had less than 36 hours to live. Did she start to feel her life was almost over? Research has shown, people do not have a clue. Shanann's friends all have said she was sick all weekend and was throwing up. Her friends talked about how she just wasn't herself; she was down, not fun-loving as usual. Shanann was usually the life of the party, but not this weekend. Little did she know she was about to step into eternity, and everything she had done in her life, every friendship she had made, and everything she had accomplished were about to come to an abrupt end. Soon, the reality and sadness would set into her family as they realized she is now a memory. As we could look around her house and see her things—her closet of clothes and shoes, her furniture, even her pantry—all these once belonged to a vibrant young woman who thought she had the world in front of her. She was someone who planned on living, not dying. Shanann seemed to have touched the lives of so many people. She struggled with her own health issues but kept going. Now, she is gone and all that's left are memories, good and bad, but the one true thing that remains is the insatiable sadness. What she thought was a perfect life at one time and the thoughts she shared about Christopher being the perfect husband were about to be all taken away by that perfect husband. He was someone that his family loved, adored, and trusted.

Sunday on August 12, 2018: A good day by all accounts. Shanann was in Phoenix, Arizona at a Thrive weekend convention.

Christopher was with Bella and Cece who for the last couple of weeks had steadily gotten on his nerves. He didn't remember any other time the girls were bothering him so much. He would have rather been with Nikki, and she's all he could think about, causing him to feel the girls were rubbing his last nerve. One thing he can't explain is how he feels so pulled toward her when he wasn't with her.

The birthday party was nice, but he really couldn't concentrate on anything that was going on around him. He was in a fog. Yet, it was helping to pass the time, and it kept the girls occupied. Shanann forgot to tell him there would be water balloons and the kids would be playing with water, so he didn't bring their swimsuits and towels. They had a lot of fun anyway. They laughed and squealed along with the other kids. This was the last party and the last playing in the water they would ever have. While they were playing with water balloons and squealing in fun, he watched them, but it didn't even register to him. He planned to kill them the next morning. He's said he really didn't want to but knew he would. The plan to annihilate his family and dispose of them was not a well-thought-out plan—one that would include hiding evidence. Christopher did not even try to hide all the evidence. When asked about that, he said he didn't know what he was doing; nothing made sense.

It didn't help things that day that Nikki kept texting him telling him she wanted him, and she wanted to see him. It kept his mind active with thoughts of killing his family, clearing the slate, and starting over. How could he think he could do something like this, just get away with it, and start over like his family never existed? This part of his thinking was all an illusion. We can see how all of this does not make sense. Christopher has an IQ of 140. The Binet-Simon Scale of Intelligence says a genius or almost a genius is 140 or over. Possibly, his genius brain did not afford him common sense.

After they came home from the party, he grilled some chicken breasts, even packed his lunch for the next day, and cleaned the kitchen. He bathed the girls, read them bedtime stories, and put them down for the night. He spent the next hour and a half or so talking on the phone with Nikki. According to Christopher, they had phone sex. The police records show this call lasted for 111 minutes. "She had a hold of me, pulling me into her, I couldn't escape. She was like a drug that you get hooked on, and I couldn't get enough." He didn't want to stay with Shanann and the girls another day. "Nikki was all I could think about." Christopher was that close to Nikki, and yet the night before the murders, when he clearly was planning on killing his family the next morning, he didn't say anything to her about it. Had he planned on what he was going to do or what he was going to say to her to make sense of what happened to his family? *When he tucked his little girls into bed that night, he said he knew it would be the last time he would tuck them in.* Again, he said he didn't want it to be but knew it would be.

Wouldn't a person know he can't create a life with someone and then after a while, decide he is bored and just throw them away? The pain and destruction of divorce are awful. None of that though is as destructive as killing the entire family. There has to be something evil that could cause a man to disregard his family to this degree. As those babies went to sleep that night, hopefully, their minds didn't feel any differently than any other night. Usually, once they went to bed, they stayed in their beds and went to sleep. They had an early nap that day and a busy day afterward; they should have fallen asleep quickly. However, Bella kept getting out of bed, wanting to know when her mommy was coming home. To snuff out the innocent lives of two little girls makes no sense at all. They are two little girls that loved and trusted their daddy to protect them from harm but the latter would be the very one to snuff out their lives. In talking to Christopher now, he would be the first to tell you how senseless and unjust it is. Christopher will say today that if a friend had been there to tell him he needed to come to his senses, wake up, stop this affair, and put his life back together, he would have probably listened to them. Of course, no one knew about his affair, and no one knew the extent of his double life.

On the morning of August 13, Christopher checked out of his mind and allowed the thoughts he had been entertaining to become a reality. What was inside of him seemed to have taken over. The monster that had been growing needed to satisfy its craving for a human soul—several human souls. Now, it was too late, and the most unbelievable and dark act was about to play out on 2825 Saratoga Trail in the beautiful little town of Frederick, Colorado.

Shanann texted him that her plane was delayed. It would be very late before she would be home. This was disappointing to Christopher since he wanted to talk to her about everything and felt he had his nerve up. He had played it over and over in his mind. When he thought about talking to her, his heart would race. He knew he was going to kill her but said he did not want to. Why, if he didn't want to, would he have chosen to anyway?

One can only imagine the conflict of a mind contemplating doing such a horrible thing. What torment it is to plan the killing of your family. Christopher says this is just not who he has ever been, and does not know what could make him do such a horrible thing. After blaming it on Shanann, he confused everything and made it worse. This was not fair to Shanann's or his own family. It is possible he did not have a good memory of what happened, not at first anyway. Most likely, the trauma could have caused memory loss. He says after he killed Shanann, he trembled all the way to the oil site. As we have seen on the neighbor's video camera, he looks scared and guilty. It seems as though he knew that the camera was pointing to him.

Research shows that physical and emotional trauma can directly affect a person's memory, a condition causing temporary memory loss to help a person cope with the traumatic event. If the brain registers an overwhelming trauma, then it can essentially block that memory in a process called dissociation or detachment from reality. It is similar to being "lost" in the middle of a good book, daydreaming at work, or playing a video game, all of which are experiences of a common form of mild dissociation. However, over time, severe trauma can change the brain. The area that controls memory (hippocampus) becomes smaller.

The night before the murders, Christopher knew the next morning was going to be the day he would rid the life of his family. He thought it would free him to be with Nikki.

Shanann was leaving the Arizona airport and leaving her group of Thrive friends for the last time. There would be an empty place at the Thrive conventions from now on. The empty seat would be missed as many of them were the downline to Shanann. In the months ahead, it would be her father and brother that would stand on stage at the Thrive convention and accept the award that would have been hers as she had worked tirelessly for it. The business she had built and the friends she made would be gone in an instant for only about six hours from the time she left Arizona.

CHAPTER 11

Home for the Last Time

Death Ends a Life; Not a Life Relationship

The weather report for early morning on August 13, 2018, in Frederick, Colorado: Clear skies, temps in the middle 60s, light winds 15mph.

Quiet Monday

Following in the footsteps of the past weekend, this week begins with calm conditions remaining across the state of Colorado. A cut-off low-pressure system had developed across southeast Colorado and will slowly move northeastward over the next few days. The ridge, while centered near Las Vegas, has eroded and weakened significantly.

In the middle of the night, Shanann and her friend left the airport on their way home after a trip to Arizona with Thrive. To Shanann, this probably seemed like the weekend that would never end. She probably thought if she could do it over, she would have stayed home.

As they pulled into the subdivision where the Watts family lived, it was about 1:48 a.m. How could Shanann have known this would be the last time she would take this street to go home? She was tired, feeling sick, and probably wanted to get home to her family and crawl into bed. What was weighing heavily on her mind was how she was going to save her marriage. She must have wondered if she was facing life as a single mom and how she would do it. She just wanted to be home though in the safety of her family. She probably felt grieved as she thought about having to give up her home and the life she had built with Christopher. Most likely, she searched her heart and mind as to how to repair the way she had always treated him and taken him for granted. As Shanann got out of her friend's car, she opened the back door and pulled out her bag. As she shut the car door, she could feel the night air in her face, about 66 degrees with a breeze of about 15mph. This would be the last time Shanann would feel the Colorado clean air—the last time she would wave goodbye to her friend. Thinking about the finality of that gives one some chills.

It was a beautiful night. She could hear the crickets and the summer nighttime bugs' noises. The neighborhood slept, having no idea what was going on right next to them. The nighttime sky was lit with millions of stars; the moon was almost blackened out with only 8% showing; so, the only light to light her way up her driveway and onto the porch was the outside lights that Christopher had left on for her. Leaving the outside lights on for your wife (husband) signifies "I'm glad you're home safe/I'm waiting for you." Many spouses have used this for years as being a sign of love for each other.

The darkness that had hovered over her husband and her home was waiting for her on the inside. The video from their doorbell camera shows her walking up to the door. Knowing what we do now, it's chilling to watch her walk up and into her death. It was the last time Shanann would ever walk up the steps to her beautiful home, a place she had felt safe and that she and the girls loved. As she walked through the front door, the shadow that waited for her will follow her in and cover her like a heavy blanket. That shadow welcomed her as she walked in the front door, and slipped off her flip-flops. Doubtful, she had any feeling this would be the last time she would come in their front door, and up the stairs that would lead her to the "evil monster." When the police officers entered the Watts house for the first time, they saw there Shanann's flip-flops sitting by the front door. That tells it all that this truly was the sign of a mother who came home and never left.

She had made it a home, not just a house. In better times, Christopher said she always made it feel like love dwelled there. She would have never even considered the evil that actually was lurking there for her, just waiting for her to walk in the door and into the hands of the evil that lay ahead and beyond that door. She probably looked in on her babies without having any idea that would be the last time she would see them on this earth. She undressed, put on a T-shirt, too tired to even take off her makeup, and slipped into bed next to Christopher, the "evil monster."

Had she known that would be the last time she would see her babies, she probably would have gone to each of them, lain next to them, and sweetly kissed each of them, telling them she would see them in heaven in a few hours. As these gentle, pure souls were sleeping, they were totally unaware that their father whom they loved and trusted would be doing the most unspeakable things to them in just a little while. These happy trusting little girls were cuddled in their beds, looking forward to seeing their mommy when they woke up, but they never saw her again; not alive anyway. It hurts to think they would be aware of what happened. It's the worst thing anyone could possibly go through, let alone such innocent little souls. His plan was to quietly rid them from his life. It might have been symbolic of his own silence. His victims (his children) became surrogates for his rage and a means by which to exact his revenge, but Shanann became the first object of his rage. No one would suspect the anger he harbored inside.

On February 18, 2019, three agents from the FBI, CBI, and Frederick Police Department showed up at the prison where Christopher was and an inmate in Waupun, Wisconsin. He was not expecting them and was not happy without the notice. He needed to clear Shanann's name, he said; he told them the truth about his killing the girls himself but did not give them the other details surrounding it all. At the time, he did not tell the truth about how he killed Shanann even after they questioned him several times about how he killed her. Obviously, though, there was more to the story.

A couple of months after first approaching Christopher, he decided he would tell me the truth about what happened during the morning of August 13, 2018. When this endeavor began at some point, he would give me his true confession because somehow, I knew there was more to the story. Since he had already pleaded guilty, it would do him no harm. Yet, I wasn't really ready for what I was about to learn. That's one of the reasons I want you to read it in his own words. His confession in the letter that follows is a huge and shocking surprise.

Below is a letter that Christopher wrote to me, telling in part what he never told the FBI. Warning for those who are affected by the details of these murders, the following is very hard to read. I spent much time trying to decide what was the best thing to do with the information I have. Finally, I decided that if this were my family, I would want and deserve to have full disclosure about the matter.

> Dear Cheryln, April 23, 2019
>
> Hello again! I hope you are doing well! It has been awesome talking with you on the phone, but I know the 15-minute time frame is a pain. Sometimes I can get right back on the phone but right now there are other inmates that like to be on the phone as much as I do, so I respect their time as well. How's your dad doing, I've been praying on that every day.
>
> Yes, that petition really blew my mind that people really want to make me suffer like that. Even if they did ever take my pictures, they can't take my memories. An inmate from another institution wrote me about that subject and said, "If they take your pictures, they would need to take the pictures from the other 500-600 people that have their family pictures up on their cell convicted of the same act."
>
> Do I feel like I should be incarcerated? For the act I committed, I most definitely think so. Do I imagine myself ever doing anything like this or be a danger to society? I most definitely think *not*! If I were to ever be released, I know I would go straight to a ministry and start going to jails/prisons and help inmates. If God led me to be ordained, I would go that route as well; possibly even be a chaplain. Maybe the laws will change one day. My attorney team could see I was different and knew that this was a one-time occurrence for me. They told

me that in Europe, the law is I would serve 20 years or so for homicide, and in California, after 25 years of imprisonment on a life sentence, you can be released if you've had good behavior. So, there's hope for everyone to live outside prison walls. I know physically I'm behind these walls, but my spirit is *free* with Christ!

If God keeps putting it on your heart that there is more to the story than what I told the FBI has, you're correct. I don't like saying stuff like that over the phone because I'm never certain when they screen my calls. I know I already told you the vision I had before August 13 when I was lying in bed and all the lights were on in the loft and downstairs, and I felt so alone. That's exactly what happened April 14 when I was lying in bed.

I don't know if you want this in the book or if God does but here are the things I left out. 1) August 12 when I finished putting the girls to bed, I walked away and said "That's the last time I'm going to be tucking my babies in." I knew what was going to happen the day before and I did nothing to stop it! I was numb to the entire world. I had literally taken my kids to a birthday party, played with water balloons, had an amazing time, sang songs all the way home, gave them bath a shower, ate dinner, read bedtime stories and sang bedtime songs, and still nothing registered! When Shannan had to be somewhere, I always enjoyed taking the girls to places or playing outside because it was our opportunity to bond, and still the night before, I couldn't stop myself from what I knew would occur the next morning. 2) August 13, morning of, I went to the girls' room first before Shannan and I had our argument. I went to Bella's room, then CeCe's room and used a pillow from their bed (to kill them). That's why the cause of death was smothering. After I left CeCe's room, I climbed back in bed with Shannan and our argument ensued. After Shanann had passed, Bella and CeCe woke back up. I'm not sure how they woke back up, but they did. That made the act that much worse knowing I went to their rooms first and knowing I still took their lives at the location of the batteries. 3) The reason the medical examiner found oxycodone in Shanann's system is because I gave it to her. I thought it would be easier to be with Nichol if Shanann wasn't pregnant.

I don't know if this was a spiritual visit, but I had a dream CeCe was dancing next to the chair in my cell. When she was dancing, all of my folders on the chair started moving and I thought she was in trouble, so I said, "Watch out, get away, watch out!" Then I woke up. I'm hoping she comes back! I hope everyone comes to visit me. I'm trying to see if I can clear my head better before I go to sleep to help.

I like that John 10: 10 passage you sent. I wish I could've had an open ear to hear the Lord calling me back in June/July/August. If we run after sin, we won't hear our shepherd calling us. I couldn't discern between the good spirits and the evil spirits and that eventually lodged me into a deep pit I couldn't climb back out of.

Take care and God Bless!
Chris

After receiving this letter from Christopher, I had many questions as you can imagine. These are the things he told me after I had received this letter.

I asked him about the oxy. He told me first that he gave it to her twice. Once at her parents' and the second time was right before he killed her. At that time, he told me that's the reason she couldn't fight back. Later, when I questioned him about it again, he said he only gave it to her once. I asked him where he got the oxy, and he told me that is one of the things he will take to his death. The oxy was crushed up and given to her in a Thrive shake. If you notice in one of his letters, he states that Shanann did not take oxy. This is a contradiction from what I had been told by one of his family members. However, I do not believe she took oxy. Shanann seemed to be responsible to be hooked on an opioid.

"One minute, we would talk about downsizing the house and getting something more affordable in a more affordable town, then we would go back to me telling her I was going to get an apartment and move out on my own for a while. Shanann started crying because she did not want to separate, telling me she loved me. I hate so much that I came back to her with 'I don't love you, and I'm not compatible with you anymore.' As she was crying, with her mascara running down her face, she told me she couldn't make it in Colorado by herself with three kids. Isn't it weird how I look back and what I remember so much is her face getting all black with streaks of mascara? There was no feeling coming from me as I told her I could help her, and she would make it. What kind of a man or father could callously say that to his pregnant wife who is almost begging to keep her family together? Then, she became very angry and was very upset and told me if I left her, she would not allow me to see the kids. She was used to getting her way and when she saw she wasn't, she would revert as always to anger and threats to get what she wanted. This time though, I was not giving in to her demands. That's when my anger for her began. It had been years of her telling me what to do and what not to do. Keeping me from my own family for sometimes months at a time was over; keeping me in the background was over. All the weeks of me thinking about killing her, and now I was faced with it. When she started to get drowsy, I somehow knew how to squeeze the juggler veins until it cut off the blood flow to her brain, and she passed out. It was even easier than the girls. She lay there and didn't fight back. I held the juggler for what seemed like a very long time. I watched my hands and thought I should take them off her neck but I couldn't. I knew if I took my hands off of her, she would still keep me from Nikki. They asked me why she didn't fight back; it's because she couldn't fight back. Her eyes were filled with blood as she looked at me, and she died. I knew she was gone when she relieved herself.

I was wrapping her up in the bedsheet when the girls came walking into the room. I don't know how it could be possible but they were both up and walking around. I knew if Nikki and I were going to be together, I had to kill all of them.

I wrapped Shanann in the sheet and Bella kept asking me what was wrong with mommy. Both girls started crying. Both girls looked like they had been through something. I knew it was because of being smothered. I could not comfort my girls; I had no desire to. I think I told her mommy would be okay, she just didn't feel good. I tried to carry Shanann down the stairs, but I lost my grip on her twice and she was too heavy for me to carry. She fell to the floor, and I ended up kind of sliding her down the stairs. The girls were just kind of running around the house and watching me with scared looks on their faces. Bella started to cry and when she did, Celeste started whimpering. What a nightmare this was. This is the reason I killed them first so they did not have to witness any of this. I wanted to take them peacefully and make it so much easier for them and for me. Now, I didn't know what I was going to do. I got Shanann down the stairs and laid her by the back door. I ran outside and backed my truck up in the driveway. As I was moving the truck, I realized that everything I had thought about was about to be completed. I was angry with the girls that they were up and awake, and I felt anger for Shanann that I could have killed anything that got in my way.

My hands were shaking so hard, and my knees were buckling under me. I felt like I was seeing through a dark screen. It was too late. I was in this nightmare and it wouldn't let me out.

I realize now the girls getting up and walking around may have been God's third attempt to stop what I was doing. It was too late though; I couldn't stop. Something had taken me and I couldn't pull back from it.

I gathered the things I would need, such as my lunch, a shovel, and rake from the garage, and something wanted me to take the gas can from the garage. I still do not know why I took the gas can. The FBI asked me if I was going to take my own life, and I told them I thought about it, but honestly no, I was not going to take my own life. I got Shanann out to the truck by mostly dragging her. Once at the truck, I lifted her in the back and laid her on the floor. I went around to the other side and pulled her across the back floor. The stench of her relieving herself was so strong that to this day, I can smell it and it makes me sick. Now, I'm not sure if it's the stench of her relieving herself or if it was the stench of death. At some point, I grabbed a couple of garbage bags and put them around Shanann's feet and around her head.

I ran back in, cut some lights, and told the girls to follow me. I was shocked when later that day, I was standing in the neighbors' living room looking at their security camera video and thought everyone could see the girls walk up to me and I put them in the truck. I loaded them in the back seat. Bella said they couldn't ride with me because they didn't have their car seats. I remember telling her this time, it's alright. It hurts but I remember being so mad they were still alive. The girls sat curled up with each other. I noticed they were consoling each other. Kind of whimpering, but not really crying. The only thing they talked about was why did it stink in the truck. I could not believe that they came back to life. Now, I had this to deal with for the second time plus Shanann. I was still shaking and in a sweat, and my heart was pounding so hard in my chest. I didn't know what to do next. I didn't know what I was even doing; nothing made any sense to me. I had not planned this out carefully enough. I remembered just feeling so angry, feeling an emotion I had never experienced before.

It took me an hour to get to the site, and I had not calmed down at all. The rest of the story, you know, I dumped Shanann on the ground, then I walked back to the truck, and with the blanket that Celeste was holding, I put it over her head and smothered her. I carried her up the stairs. I opened the hatch, and I was surprised how small the opening was. I lifted her up and down into the hole. She went in pretty smoothly. I remembered as I was lowering her body that I would never see her again, but instead of the love I had always had for her, numbness was in its place. I could not feel anything for her. I couldn't believe how easy it was to just let her drop through the hole and let her go. I heard the splash as she hit the oil.

Then, without blinking an eye, I went right back to my truck and went over to Bella. She asked me if I was going to do to her what I had just done to Celeste. I don't think I answered her, I just put the same blanket over her head and smothered her. I could not believe though how much of a fight she put up. Little quiet Bella had a will to live. Nothing registered in my head for her. Out of all three, Bella was the only one who put up a fight. I will hear her soft little voice for the rest of my life, saying Daddy, *no!* She knew what I was doing to her. She may not have understood death, but she knew I was killing her.

I was so empowered at the time I had the strength to climb those stairs for the second time and put her little body through the hole in the next tank. Bella was harder to get down the hole. Her arms and shoulders did not want to fit through the hole, so I had to force her through the hatch. They told me they found a tuff of blonde hair; I would suspect that's when that happened. I did separate them purposely. I was trying to get them as far away from Shanann as possible. I guess I put them in the tanks to make sure this time, they didn't get up.

I don't know why except for the anger I felt. You asked me why I was so angry with Shanann, it was a couple of reasons. I was angry that she kept me from my family and I was angry because she was standing in the way of me being truly happy with someone I wanted to be with.

Had I not killed them, when I got home that afternoon from work, Shanann would not have let me in my own house. She would have locked the doors or had the locks changed to show me she was in control still. I would have had to make a scene which is something I did not want to do for the neighbors to see. I had to put the girls in the tanks so they wouldn't get up the second time.

I then went and dug a hole for Shanann. The dirt was loose and I remember easy to move. When I dug the hole, it seemed a lot deeper than it was. As I pulled on the sheet, she rolled out and into the hole. I think she had given birth. She landed face down. I remember being so angry with her that I was not going to change how she landed. I didn't think about if the hole was deep enough or if I had the hole in the right place, or if I had made sure to pick everything up so there was nothing left lying around. I realized I had just murdered my daughters twice. I still don't understand how that happened because I know they were dead the first time.

My entire life lay there on that oil site. All I could feel was now, I was free to be with Nikki. Feelings of my love for her was overcoming me. I felt no remorse. The darkness inside of me had won, it was still in me though. I thought maybe permanently. I felt evil, swallowed up by this thing inside of me. I felt like I could kill anything and be justified for doing it. I didn't feel any remorse for what I did; I didn't feel bad for killing my entire family. I really didn't feel anything. My mind went to the dog . . . did I remember to put him in the cage?"

What possible horror could have been going through those precious little minds at that time? Not understanding, but understanding enough to know something was horribly wrong without even being comforted by their mommy or their daddy. Having hopes in their little minds, I'm sure that mommy was going to be fine and they would be back home in just a little while. They had no concept of what was truly happening or lying just ahead of them just as Shanann had no idea what she was walking into. I believe they were probably very afraid.

After Christopher killed his family and drove away, Nikki texted him to look up the song by Metallica band called "Battery." I challenge you to look up the full lyrics of this song. I find it interesting that we should believe it's only a coincidence.

After Christopher wrote this letter to me, I asked him if he really put the girls in the oil batteries so he could make sure they didn't get back up the second time. He replied, "yeah, it seems."

Christopher went back to work that day like it was a normal day. Later when interviewed, his co-workers said he acted like it was a normal day. They noticed nothing different about him at all, except they said his clothes were not as neat as normal. They mentioned how he usually came to work looking very well put together.

CHAPTER 12

Later the Morning of the Murders

"For light restores what darkness cannot repair."

—Unknown

Later, on the morning of August 13, 2018, Shanann's friend who had dropped her off the night before came over to the Watts house. She and Shanann were supposed to go look for a car for her to rent through Thrive. She had not heard from Shanann that morning after she had texted her several times. She contacted another friend who also usually heard from Shanann every morning. That friend became very worried when she heard others had tried to contact her but also to no avail. Shanann had not reached out to anyone and was not on Facebook all morning, which was very unusual. Her friend was concerned that maybe she was sick and passed out. She knew the girls were too young to get help.

She tried to get in by the front door code but that would not work either. A latch on the top of the door, and she let the door open only a few inches. She could see Shanann's shoes that she had worn the night before sitting by the door. That was even more upsetting because Shanann wore those shoes every time she left the house. She was convinced there was something wrong. Thank goodness, she was persistent or it may have been days long before the police could have pieced everything together. This just shows how good it was that Shanann was connected to a lot of people—what a benefit that ended up being.

Two of Shanann's friends were at the frantic stage and both called Christopher, telling him he needed to get home. Most likely, it seemed to them, Christopher wasn't taking them seriously; in actuality, he was hoping they would believe his story that Shanann was at a friend's house and leave it alone.

In his mind, he could not believe how quickly they had found out she was gone. That was not something he had thought about ahead of time. He had to be called the second time. He told them he would be there in a little while. Shanann had a doctor's appointment at 10:00 a.m. and Shanann's friends knew her well enough to know she would never blow off her doctor's appointment. The girls' first day of school was that day also and they were looking forward to going, yet they had not shown up for school. She drove to the doctor's office to see if Shanann had been there. They told her she had not shown up for her appointment. She also knew that had Shanann's plans changed, she would have let her know. Now, she knew something was definitely wrong.

Christopher said he believes she called the third time. By then, he was on his way. Instead of acting like he was a concerned husband and father, he acted detached. When she called the last time, he told her not to call the police as he was not far from home. However, she did not listen to Christopher, and she did call the police.

While waiting for the police, she pulled her car into the driveway and had her son stand on the hood and look through the garage window to see if her car was in the garage. He could see not only the car but also see the car seats still inside. This meant to Shanann's friend that Shanann had to be in the house. She knew Shanann well enough to know there is no way she would have left the house and gone anywhere without the girls being in their car seats.

The Frederick Police Department dispatched an officer to the house.

On August 13, 2018, at approximately 1:40 p.m., an officer was dispatched to 2825 Saratoga Trail on a well-being check. The reporting party had called about her friend, Shanann Watts. She stated she had dropped Shanann off about twelve hours earlier at around 1:48 a.m. after returning from a business trip that took place in Arizona. She stated Shanann was fifteen weeks pregnant and had not been feeling well during the trip.

Upon arriving, the officer checked all the windows and doors including the back-slider door, and discovered all of them were locked with no way into the house. The officer called Christopher Watts and asked for the outside garage door pad combination. Christopher told him it did not work, but he was only five minutes away. The officer also called for back-up from the Police Department.

When the second officer arrived, he noticed Shanann's white Lexus in the garage. Christopher exited the front door and introduced himself. There was also a brown Ford extended cab pick-up truck parked on the street in front of the house. The officer asked if there was any kind of a note left in the house, and Christopher told him, "no, there was none."

When Christopher arrived, he allowed the police inside the house in an attempt to locate Shanann and the girls, but they were not in the home. He told them he was going to go for a walk around the neighborhood to clear his head while they went through the house. They asked him where he works and what hours he usually works. He told them he worked for Anadarko, Monday through Friday. They gave Christopher a form for him to sign to allow them to search the house in its entirety and told him to ask if he had any questions. He read the bottom of the form and signed it, waiving the right to have a warrant to search his home.

Christopher told the officers they had free reign and to do whatever they had to do. Christopher put Deeter on the back deck and told the officers that's where he would wait for them to get done after he took a short walk.

The police officer found Shanann's purse on the kitchen counter, and it was open and her wallet was out. There was also a black phone lying next to her purse. As the police searched her purse, they saw her driver's license for the state of Colorado, some cash, and a bottle of nausea medication in her name.

As they searched the house, they did not find anything that looked as though there would have been a struggle. The house was very well organized and well-kept except for her office where they found a large baggie with medications on the corner of the desk.

The medications were inhalers and nebulizers. There was another medication for Celeste.

The police searched Shanann's Lexus and found there were two car seats in the back. Keys were lying on the center console and a garage door opener on the visor. They also saw two car seats sitting on the garage floor. As they moved to the basement, they found it also very well organized and saw an unmade bed in the corner of the basement. There was a Disney sheet hanging over the window.

Upstairs, they found that the bed in the master bedroom was stripped of the sheets, which were lying on the floor. They checked them for foul play but did not find anything. In a subsequent search, a top sheet and pillowcases from the bed were located in the trash in the kitchen, but the bottom fitted sheet was missing. In the loft upstairs between the master bedroom and the children's bedroom was a sofa. Located between the cushions of this sofa was a cell phone that Christopher identified as Shanann's. The pink and white I-phone was taken into evidence. Lying on the couch also was Shanann's pink I-phone watch.

As they walked through the kids' bedrooms, they noticed the beds were unmade but there were sheets and blankets on the bed. There was a Jack and Jill pink bathroom between the two bedrooms. They noticed there was no water in the toilet, and actually, the door to the bathroom had been locked. In the laundry room, there was a load of clothes in the dryer, and the washing machine had a couple of items that looked like children's clothing.

There was a well-organized playroom with kids' toys and books. Another bathroom was next to the playroom. It appeared that's where the girls were bathed as there were shampoos and kids' bath wash in there.

As the officers walked out the front door, they noticed a latch-up high on the door—the kind found often in a hotel room. It kept the door from opening unless it was unlatched. Shanann's flip flops were by the front door, and at the bottom of the stairs was a small suitcase.

Once back outside, the police checked the outside door pad. Christopher told them it had not worked for some time. He told them all of their family lived in North Carolina, but Shanann had friends in Frederick, Aurora, Parker, and Erie, and he had called them to see if any of them had heard from Shanann.

The police asked Christopher if any money had come out of their bank accounts. He said he wouldn't know because he can't get into the bank accounts. He said Shanann took care of all finances and he wouldn't even know if there was a stash of cash in the house. The officer told him to call the bank and see if Shanann has taken money out of the account. He said he'd check for activity on the account and inside to get the information to call the bank. When coming back out, he said there was a charge for a taxi cab that was posted to the bank on the 12th.

Christopher told the police Shanann arrived home around 2:00 a.m. from a trip to Arizona for her work. He told the officer he woke up around 5:00 a.m. and initiated a conversation with Shanann where he told her he wants a separation. He stated it was a civil conversation but emotional. Shanann had told him this morning that she was taking the girls and going to a friend's house today and would be back later in the day. He didn't know which friend.

Christopher told them he'd backed his truck up to the garage door around 5:27, loaded his tools, and left for work. He said Shanann was in bed when he left. Christopher told them he works for Anadarko Oil and left for a job site near Hudson that morning to check on it.

A neighborhood canvas was conducted for several hours later that evening by officers and a well-being check was issued statewide. A search of the surrounding areas was also conducted.

One of Shanann's friends that lives out of town talked to the police. She was with Shanann the weekend before in Arizona. When she saw Shanann on Sunday night, she thought Shanann looked really sad. She told her Christopher had gone to a Rockies game with a bunch of guys. While he was out, Shanann talked with the babysitter to check on the girls, that Christopher told her they went out and got food after the game, and that he had salmon and a beer for $62.00. She knew that was expensive for just him. She also told the officer that Christopher had deleted his Facebook account, which was unusual since they used social media for their business.

The officers stopped by Christopher's house to meet CBI agents and do another search in the house. As they walked in, there was a strong odor of cleaning chemicals. They remarked the house was spotless. The carpet had noticeable vacuum lines.

As they walked through the kitchen area and into the back living room area, Christopher had a sports show on television. The deputy walked over to the back-sliding glass door and noticed two pairs of little girls' shoes. He asked Christopher about them who said they were the shoes the girls had worn to the pool party on Sunday. They had gotten wet, so he sat them on the back porch to dry. The officer commented to Christopher that he can't imagine what he is going through. Christopher did not seem to have any emotion and did not seem to respond in an appropriate way. His facial expressions did not seem to change and when they did, he would smirk or smile inappropriately, showing a lack of empathy, especially when speaking of his girls. His voice remained low and even-toned and his nonverbal cues were very apparent. Christopher had an erect and tense posture with his arms crossed most of the time. He lacked eye contact and kept looking around appearing nervous. After doing this investigation, the agent put Shanann, Bella, and Celeste on the Missing Person's List.

CHAPTER 13

The Days After

> "You will never meet a murderer that isn't afraid of a ghost."
>
> —Unknown

The evil force that he thinks was pursuing him was also living in his home; Christopher feels this was a force that kept causing him to have a reoccurring dream. In the weeks leading up to the murders, this disturbing dream made him realize there was something that was coming after him; he realized it had been chasing him until it caught him.

He would dream he was lying on their bed asleep. He would wake up in his dream and all of the lights in his house were on. They were upstairs and downstairs. Then, in his dream, he would realize he was all alone, that his family was gone, and it was just him. The dream gave him an awful feeling; somehow, he knew that dream was going to come true. Was this his mind preparing him? Or was it God's warning?

Sure enough, the night of August 13 after he had just killed his family that morning, he said he turned off all the lights and went to bed. He woke with a start and realized all of the lights in the house were on. He knew he had turned them off before lying down. The first thing that came to his mind was he was all alone and his family was gone. Wow, what a reality check! This was his dream exactly! He laid downstairs for the rest of the night. He was so crept out; he could feel the spirit in his home. Who turned on all of the lights? He said he did not, and was convinced for sure there were evil spirits there. We know this is true, because in one of the police reports, they said an officer sat outside all night and he made a note in his report that all of the lights in the house were on. Could Christopher have been sleepwalking and turned the lights on or was this the work of what he says was in his home? It's said that sometimes, a dark spirit will follow a person around for a while.

On the morning of August 14, Christopher woke up very early to find himself lying on his bed feeling totally alone. How could he explain the lights were on in the house when he knew he had turned them off? He was completely creeped out by this and went downstairs to lie on the couch to rest until morning. He was not feeling sad or remorseful; he just wanted to be able to get on with his life. His dream came to him, but the difference this time was he realized it wasn't just a dream—he really was alone. He thought to himself how he can justify his family being gone and the only feeling he has is a relief. As he looked around his house, he was wondering how it was that he didn't miss them or wish they were back. He looked at the pictures on the walls but it still did not register. It did not bring back memories. He realized he had a headache and went into the kitchen to fix himself something to eat. He opened the refrigerator, took out a couple of eggs, and scrambled them. When he sat down to eat, the phone rang. It was the police wanting to know if he had heard anything. It was hard to explain the family disappearance. It's not like he'd cleaned out a room and threw away something important. He had cleaned out his house and thrown away his family. Did he really believe he and Nikki could be happy after he had done something like this? What could possibly have been going through his mind?

The police immediately requested a press release be issued and requested the help of the CBI and FBI. A missing person's alert was put out for Shanann and the two girls. The two-day search revealed Christopher was involved in an affair that he had denied in previous interviews.

Christopher was at home trying to decide if he should go to work. That seemed very odd to his family that it would even be a consideration. When he made a call to his boss, he was concerned and told Christopher not to worry about coming to work that day.

On August 14, the day after the murders, Shanann's friend who still didn't know what happened to Shanann and the girls reached out to the media for help. She didn't ask Christopher how he felt about it at first. She called them and then told him they wanted to do an interview. Christopher did not want to do an interview and sought advice from a friend. His friend told him it may not look good if he didn't do the interview. So, he agreed to meet them if they would come to his house. Meanwhile, the FBI had plans to bring in their K-9 to search the house for scents that could aid them in finding Shanann and the girls. In actuality, they were there to determine if there had been any struggles or a dead body in the house. These dogs are very smart and well trained in their field. As the K-9 units arrived, Christopher was about to do the interview with the television station. As the police opened the door, they saw the cameraman and the interviewer in the living room filming Christopher. They took their equipment and moved to the front porch. Christopher had no way of knowing at that time that the interview on the front porch would end up being his demise. As he stood there hugging himself looking smug and cocky, he had a hard time not smiling, and he showed no emotions about what had happened to his family. He only seemed concerned about himself and what it was doing to him.

The morning after the murders on August 14 is when the first search with K-9 dogs took place. As the police officer was with the dog handler, she wore a body cam recording the search as seen on YouTube. Christopher had spent time the night before doing some cleaning. As they walked into the house, they saw a beautiful well-decorated home. Some things already looked familiar from the videos Shanann had posted. First, the living room furniture and even her throw pillows are seen on the body cam video. As they walked straight ahead, they passed an empty dining room with its tray ceiling painted a dark purple. There were toys that lined against the wall that belonged to Bella and Celeste. Toys without children display an emptiness that yelled out and cried for the little girls who should be there playing with them. They passed then into the kitchen and an open neatly organized pantry. Everything had a place and everything was in its place. Moving on into the family room which was open directly off the kitchen was a family room. A blanket that belonged to one of the girls lay on the love seat and again, there were toys that stood against the walls. We could see the three-foot princess doll that was on one of Shanann's Facebook posts all covered up except its feet. After the murders, that post started a bit of a controversy as to who posted it. Christopher took a picture of the doll while Shanann was in Arizona. *This is one of the things he did during the time he was having thoughts of planning the murders. He sent the picture to Shanann.* It was posted to be funny but ended up being prophetic, eerily so. The dog moved downstairs to the hall that led to the guest bathroom, and the fifth bedroom that had been turned into Shanann's office. Next was her office with all of the things she most likely needed to attend to after being gone for so many weeks. Just a few weeks earlier, she posted a video from that office, bragging about how lucky she and the girls were to have Christopher.

The handler then opened the walk-in closet door. On the left side of the closet hung Shanann's designer purses. They hung all along one side of the closet. On the right side of the closet were many pairs of shoes—one for every occasion and some of every style and color. All were very well organized. On the floor of the closet were odd and ends, a few toys, and coloring books. As the dog walked into the closet, it seemed apprehensive. About that time, there was a little girl's voice giggling. It startled the dog and the handler as they immediately backed out of the closet. The police officer had heard it, too, and she went in to find where it was coming from. There was no toy or anything else that could have made the noise. It gave both the police officer and the handler a very odd feeling, and they decided to close the door and move on.

From there, they moved upstairs. The house was immaculate but showed a family lived there. Upstairs, they went into the laundry room, which, like the rest of the house, was very organized and clean. As they checked each of the bedrooms, it was all the same—just a very organized home. It is weird to watch an invasion of someone's privacy. Is it right being able to look into a family's private things without their permission, the things everyone all has that belong in private spaces? It was a sad feeling that Shanann's private things were on the internet, but she didn't have a say in it. Supposedly, the dogs were to find if there had been a dead body in the house. Then, later it was said the dog would be able to sense if there had been a struggle. The report stated there was a struggle or something that happened at the inside back garage door. This would have been the door Christopher brought Shanann through.

Christopher talked with Nikki that day, and in their conversation, she asked where his family could be. Of course, he denied everything, but somehow, she could tell by his voice that something was not exactly how he was saying it was. When they got off the phone, she cleared all of his text messages and phone calls from hers. She was concerned it would appear she was involved, so before the police found her, she decided to go to them. Her first encounter with the police sounded like Christopher was a casual friend whom she was not very fond of. In actuality, he was much more than that. Nikki always wanted to downplay their relationship with the authorities. The police were not looking for that yet but it was given to them by the mistress herself. She showed up at the Police Department ready to bear her soul to make it seem she herself was a victim. Listening to the interview, it was one-sided, and the police would want a more thorough interview at another time. Right now, their focus wasn't on an affair; it was on finding Shanann and the two girls. They would get back with Nikki later.

The police were watching Christopher's every move that day. There was an unmarked car that sat down the street; the undercover agent logged all of the comings and goings of Christopher and any visitors. The police knew he was the one that killed his family before they needed the evidence to arrest him.

Later that day, a big storm blew in, seeming to have come out of nowhere. The wind was blowing hard, and when the storm was over, there were three of the neighbors' empty garbage cans lying in his front yard. Seemed symbolic for "throwing his family away"—did it mean one can each for Shanann, Bella, and Celeste? It really hit him hard when during the sentencing, Frank Rzucek made the statement: "You threw them all away like they were garbage." Was this another coincidence? A crime to this magnitude affects a lot of people. When planning the murders, he didn't consider this would take his life along with the lives of everyone around him. In many ways, he took all of their families' lives too. The fall out is so huge, and they are all the collateral damage.

He talked with Shanann's parents. They sensed his story was not true. He wasn't sure how they knew or exactly how to handle them. His parents also did not believe Shanann was just missing. They thought she had just taken the girls someplace and was hiding from him for attention. As time went on, however, they realized something must be wrong, and Ronnie decided to fly out to Colorado when Christopher called and told his dad he needed him to come. Christopher had never asked for anything, and the sound of his voice had a real urgency that sounded desperate. Cindy still thought Shanann and the girls missing was Shanann's way of dramatically getting attention. Still, they never considered in a million years Christopher could be involved in killing his own family. When they found out the police were questioning Christopher, it came as a total shock to them.

August 15, in the early morning, the police called Christopher and asked if he could come down to the police station sometime that day. Trying to appear even more confident and nonchalant, he seemed even more suspicious. The biggest reason is he had no emotion for not being able to find his family. What if Shanann couldn't find Christopher and the girls? She would have been so emotionally upset, crying and calling everyone she knew. She would not have been able to function until she found them. Nothing and no one else would matter until she could have found her girls. This is the way most people would be.

Christopher got to the police station around 8:00 p.m. that evening. At first, they just lightly discussed the missing status of his wife and children, but as the conversation continued, the questions were tougher, and Christopher would have to think about more ways to answer that did not give him away. It became more and more difficult for him to answer the questions. Obviously, he was starting to squirm. He used the word "like" in most of his sentences, multiple times. Somewhere between 11 p.m. and midnight that evening, they ended their interview. Christopher promised to come back the next morning to take a polygraph test. He says he was willing to take the polygraph because he did not realize all that happened and was hoping it would jog his memory.

When he was done that evening, his friends were waiting outside to take him to their house still unsuspecting that he was the one that killed his family. As things progressed, they were devastated by what they would learn.

Earlier that day, those friends had stopped by his house to see how he was doing. They asked him to spend the night at their house. They felt bad for him that he would be home alone with his family missing. These kind folks were good friends of the Watts—like a family—and never did they expect Christopher would ever do anything to harm his family. They had watched how he was a doting father and husband, doing everything he could for them. He accepted and slept at their house that night. Christopher was totally freaked out because of what had happened at his house the night before and was happy to accept their invitation.

CHAPTER 14

Interviews

Nikki went to the police on August 15 to tell them she had been involved with Christopher and their affair began in June. Simultaneously, investigators learned that the GPS on Christopher's work truck showed he had driven to an oil battery, known as CERVI-319, in Roggan, Colorado on the morning of August 13.

There were dozens of interviews conducted during this investigation, way more than could be put into this book. Here are some of the interviews. This information is pulled from the discovery that was done during the investigation time frame.

The police interview with Nikki, the mistress

On August 16, 2018, two CBI agents met with Nikki at the Thornton Police Department to speak with her regarding this case. She had already met with the FBI; however, it had not been video recorded. She asked that she be given a ride to the police station and was picked up by two agents. Her father met her at the police station, and he had agreed to speak with the CBI also.

The agents noted that she was very tired during the interviews and that she stated she had not slept very much over the last five days. Prior to the interview, she gave the agents pieces of clothing that belonged to Christopher that she did not want in her home.

She said she deleted all of the text messages between her and Christopher. They had met at work in May or early June. He was not wearing a wedding ring, never mentioned he was married, and did not initially mention he had children. Then one day, he told her he had two children. She thought that was cute. He mentioned he had a significant other, and they were in the process of separating.

Nikki was a contract employee at Anadarko Petroleum in Platteville, Colorado. She worked in safety in the office (Nikki no longer works for Anadarko).

She first met Christopher at a park near her house sometime at the end of June or the beginning of July. This was the first time they met outside of work. From that point, they talked every day. She said Christopher was always kind when he talked about his wife. She said to this day, she didn't see any red lights.

Nikki told the agents Christopher is an introvert. He is reserved around people, so he enjoyed talking to her because he could get out of his shell. Around most people, he did not feel like he wanted to talk. With her, though, he was a little more outgoing. He was very relaxed all the time when he was with her. He never got worked up.

She said they never argued, never had lost his temper, and never saw him mad or upset. He was very open-minded and rational. He was very open with communication, not closed off, and always very kind.

She thought they had a lot in common as both of them were into fitness and healthy eating. They both love cars so they had a lot to talk about. He always was very interested in what she had to share with him. She never got an indication he was having any issues.

They spent a lot of their time together at her place or they would go out. She was at his house only twice. Both times were brief; she did not feel comfortable there knowing it was someone else's life and existence, so she did not want to be there. She respected that as their space. She went to his house once very early in their relationship. Their house was right off the highway in Frederick but she didn't remember the name of the street. Christopher told her he was living in the basement; she could tell others lived there. He told her they were getting ready to sell the house.

The first time she was at his house was July 4. She had gone to help him set up fitness apps on his phone.

He made lunch, they ate, and she left.

She was at his house the second time on July 14. At that time, she saw a picture of his wife and girls. She questioned why he would want to leave all that he had. They talked about him working on his relationship with his wife. He said they had tried working on their relationship, but it was not working. He described his relationship with Shanann as a contractual agreement and not emotional. She felt bad, having not waited for him to be completely divorced. He was reluctant to try and work on his relationship with Shanann. Nikki backed away a bit, so he would try to fix his relationship with Shanann. She thought he had a beautiful life going on and she wanted him to try and fix it (All signs indicate this is not true.).

The Police Interview with Ronnie Watts

Just minutes after Christopher had confessed to murdering Shanann, the agents interviewed Ronnie Watts.

Ronnie knew he was being recorded for this interview. He told the agents that he has never known Christopher to use any drugs. He's never shown any kind of mental illness and does not have any violent tendencies. He never took any kind of drugs for mental illness either, and when he was in school, he was a strong student. When Christopher was in high school, he played a lot of sports. He really loved sports. He prioritized between his sports and school though so he continued to make good grades. He took care of his school work and sports over dating. Christopher was asked to the prom once by a girl instead of him asking someone. The program Shanann was promoting called Thrive is how Christopher lost a lot of weight. Ronnie said he felt that Christopher did not want to be on the program but Shanann was forcing him. In his opinion, he does not believe Shanann or Christopher wanted a third baby. Ronnie said Shanann was extremely bipolar and had paranoid tendencies toward Cindy Watts, the grandmother of their children. In one instance, Shanann accused Cindy Watts of trying to kill their granddaughter by exposing her to nuts that she is allergic to. The last few weeks, Shanann spent time in North Carolina where it became very contentious between them. She spent most of her time at her parents' house and refused to allow Ronnie and Cindy to see their granddaughters.

Toward the end of the video, Ronnie showed the agents a video of his wife playing with their granddaughters.

The police interviews with Frank Rzucek, Shanann's father

According to what Frank told the police, Christopher was a great father. He played with the girls, bathed them, and took care of their general needs. He could not have asked for a better father or a better husband for his daughter. He had never witnessed any kind of problems between them. He had noticed recently though, Christopher was sterner with the girls than he had been, but he does not think he would have ever hit them. Christopher always took care of himself physically; he recently had lost a lot of weight. Recently, Shanann went back and forth with the girls between his house and the Watts house but Shanann had problems getting along with Christopher's mother. She felt Shanann had taken Christopher away from them. The whole story of the nuts came up and even more was added to it by saying Cindy Watts had nuts all over the house and one of the kids was eating ice cream with nuts. When Shanann called him and asked him to come and pick her and the girls up, it was the day of the nut debacle. They never saw Shanann or the kids again.

Something that Frank observed in Christopher is that he is always quiet and never shows any emotion. The week he came out to North Carolina, he and Shanann never let on like anything was wrong between them. He did feel though that it was odd on August 11 when Christopher got a babysitter and left the girls while he went to a baseball game. He had never left the girls while Shanann was gone before. On Sunday night, Frank called the girls on FaceTime, and Bella was eating cold pizza and candy. That was the last time he saw or spoke to the girls. He had not spoken to Shanann for a few days because when she is traveling, he usually does not bother her. On the morning of August 13, his wife told him Shanann was missing. Sometimes, Shanann would not respond to her mother. Sandra did call Christopher and told him that she was not responding to any of her texts or phone calls. She told him that she was very excited about today being Bella's first day of school, yet they had not shown up there. She was always a stickler to be on time wherever she went. Christopher told Sandra that he and Shanann had a small fight and she was in one of her moods where she would not answer texts. His mother-in-law was still worried and told him he should call the hospitals in the area to make sure she was not at one of them. About that time, the friend that had taken Shanann home and watched her walk in called Sandra and told her the police were at Shanann's house and they could not get in because of the security lock that Frank had put on the front door. The door would only open about three inches, and she could see Shanann's favorite shoes sitting by the door but no one appeared to be home. She had called Christopher and he was on his way home. Frank said he called Christopher several times and asked where he was at and he assured Frank he was hurrying. The next-door neighbor told Frank he had a video of Christopher backing his truck into the driveway that morning. He said that Christopher never pulled the truck into the driveway because Shanann did not want oil in the driveway. He had lived there for over a year and had never seen the truck in the driveway. The next-door neighbor also said that while Shanann was gone, Christopher took her SUV out of the garage and parked it on the street. Rzucek's said that both of these pieces of information were concerning him because it was vastly different than what was the norm. Frank knew something was very wrong when Sandra talked to Shanann's friend and they had found Shanann's purse and telephone. Frank knew his daughter never left her cell phone behind as she had it with her twenty-four hours a day. He said he did not believe his daughter would ever hurt the girls; they were her life. He did not know anything about their financial problems; they never talked about their finances. He said they never asked to borrow any money from him.

Shanann did not ever discuss her and Christopher not getting along. His daughter suffered from lupus, migraines, and fibromyalgia, and about a year ago, had surgery on her neck. The Thrive she was using helped her to stop taking her lupus medications. They met in North Carolina, got married there, and moved to Colorado because the weather conditions were better for Shanann's medical conditions. Christopher quickly found a job because he was a master mechanic and moved out ahead of Shanann because she had a house to sell. They moved to Colorado four or five years ago. When he heard that Shanann's phone and epi-pen had been left in the house, he immediately knew something was terribly wrong and Christopher had something to do with it.

The visit in August was the first time they came and stayed that long. He and Sandra would take their vacations around when Shanann and Christopher would take trips paid for by Thrive. He felt that when she came to North Carolina for six weeks, it gave him time to think about what he wanted to do and he does not believe he killed his family in the spur of the moment. Frank and his wife were worried about her being pregnant again because it was difficult for her, but she didn't suffer from post-partum depression. Christopher also did not have any mental issues and does not think he ever went to a psychiatric doctor. On August 12, when he had FaceTimed the girls, he knew Celeste was there because he could hear her, but he didn't see her. He remembers the girls asking about their mommy and Christopher told them she would be there tomorrow. After the nut incident, Christopher's family had deleted all of them on Facebook.

CHAPTER 15

Two Texts with Shanann's Friends

On Saturday night in Arizona, as Shanann was with some of her friends, she expressed her fear that Christopher was cheating on her. One of the friends called their house for Shanann and talked with the babysitter since Christopher was not home from the baseball game yet. There was a charge alert that came across Shanann's phone for a place about fifteen minutes from their home. It was over $60.00 and she thought that sounded like a bit much for a bar and grill meal. An hour after she got the charge alert, Christopher still was not home. Her friends told her their opinions were he was cheating on her. Once back to her room, Shanann did talk with Christopher but she decided not to drill him about it.

Shanann's friend said that Shanann is not the type of person to be able to hold her emotions in. She said that Shanann did not say there was any mention of her and Christopher separating before she left for Arizona. They agreed to counseling while she was in Arizona.

Her friends said that Christopher is a great guy, but there are no others to be concerned about regarding Shanann's disappearance. One of them recalled Christopher's voice when he was telling her not to call the police; not to get them involved.

One of them said that Christopher refuses to pull his work truck into the driveway. One of the friends and her husband stayed with Shanann and Christopher at the end of May 2018. She offered to park her car on the street to allow Christopher to park in the driveway, but he declined. He said that he never pulls in the driveway because he did not want any oil from the oil fields messing up the driveway. She learned from another friend that he backed his truck into the driveway on the morning of August 13. She said that when she was staying at their home, he never backed his truck into the driveway to load and unload anything. Their friends were there from May 24–May 28, 2018. She saw him come home from work Thursday evening and he did not pull into the driveway. He left for work Monday morning, Memorial Day, and his truck was gone before she left.

Her friends all knew that Shanann would flip out if Christopher opened the garage door in the morning because the girls were light sleepers and she did not want the door to wake them. He used the front door to leave for work in the mornings because she said the garage door woke the girls.

Shanann's friends told the FBI that their gut told them Shanann and the girls were not alive because it is not possible given her pattern of life.

Below are screenshots her friends sent the FBI that are pertinent to this case.

The text between a friend and Shanann:

- 07/09/2018 Friend asks Shanann about a post about Celeste and is concerned.
- 07/09/2018 Shanann replies to explain a disagreement with her mother-in-law regarding her children and allergies.
- 07/09/2018 Shanann says they (her mother-in-law) have had it out for eight years.
- 07/09/2018 Shanann says she is different when her hubby is around and her daughter.
- 07/09/2018 Shanann says her daughter is the golden child and so is her kids.
- 07/09/2019 Shanann says Christopher was chopped liver his whole life.
- 07/09/2018 Friend suggests Christopher confronts his mother.
- 07/15/2018 Shanann says she got home from Celeste's birthday party and the in-laws were no show.

- 07/15/2018 Shanann says they are out of her kid's life now.
- 07/15/2018 Shanann says she wants to block them.
- 07/15/2018 Friend says she would keep them on Facebook, but would not talk to them or make it a point to be around them for anything.
- 07/15/2018 Shanann says she does not ever want to see them again.
- 08/03/2018 Friend asks Shanann if she got all of her messages.
- 08/03/2018 Shanann responds that she did and that it has been a rough day.
- 08/03/2018 Friend asks why it was rough.
- 08/03/2018 They then discuss (possibly) a home and friend say they do not want to be in their home for any longer than a month as they do not want to put them out.
- 08/03/2018 Shanann says they would not put them out and that she cannot explain on the text and it is not a good time.
- 08/05/2018 Shanann sends texts that she said she sent to Christopher about the incident in North Carolina between her and his parents about their children. Shanann is not sorry for what she said to his mother and says that she loves her kids. Shanann then also addresses the distance between her and Christopher in the text, *"From the day I left. You never said I missed you before I said it. Something changed when I left. You may be happier alone and that's fine. You can be alone! This pregnancy you have failed to acknowledge it or to acknowledge how I'm feeling. The first trimester is the scariest and most dangerous yet we can lose this baby at any point till delivery. I'm not going to be treated this way for having the balls to protect our family and kids. I should get a gold fucking medal for handling it the way I did. Because I had a lot of choice words, I wanted to say to her and your dad for his stupidity. No one stands up to your mom and dad for that. He's just as guilty by not doing anything. I have nothing to do with him stop sharing memories of his grandkids. What does that have to do with me, I am their mother and I will protect them.*

I have enough to worry about with the world out there I'm not going to worry about family. I'll just remove it.

- 8/05/18 Shanann told a friend that is what she texted Christopher in the middle of the night. Her friend asked what Christopher said and Shanann said he said nothing and then she said he replied that he loves the kids. He asked Shanann if the kids could see his parents and she told him no. She said she is standing her ground. They have not made contact in four weeks, no-show for her party, and said nothing for her birthday. Friend replied that she is shocked that Christopher had not said a word about what she said to him, that he needs to open up and talk to Shanann about everything, clear the air and work on it, and then work on the issue with his parents. Shanann says she has been trying to talk to him for four days and he has not said anything in return. Shanann says it's okay. Friend asks if that is really what she and he want. Shanann says it is not, but she also is not going to live like this. She is not going to be ignored and not loved.
- 08/05/2018 Shanann says he is going to his parents tomorrow.
- 08/05/2018 Friend suggests they talk with someone when they get home as throwing away what they have together is not okay.
- 08/05/2018 Shanann says she cannot and will not fight alone. She needs a man that has the balls to protect his family even when it comes to his own blood. She says he is completely different from the guy she has known for eight years. She said she would not change a thing and calls herself a saint for not telling his mom that she is a narcissist, stupid bitch and just said they were done and never coming back.
- 08/05/2018 They discussed they will see each other on Friday and they will split the room.
- 08/05/2018 Shanann says she is dizzy, lightheaded, and nauseous. She then says she has not pooped in weeks due to constipation.

- 08/06/2018 Shanann sends a screenshot of her flight itinerary: 08/10/2018 . . . 0700 Denver to Phoenix 0750 hours . . . 08/12/2018 2045 hours depart Phoenix.
- 08/06/2018 There is a "Do not disturb while driving" text from Shanann to friend. Shanann replies that Christopher is driving, not her. Shanann said they were headed to see his grandma and then, she was taking the girls as he goes to his parents. Friend asked if he was going to talk with them about the issue and work it out. Shanann replied, *"Who knows. You can't protect someone you're not in love with anymore. He doesn't have the balls."* Shanann tells her friend that his parents do not love him the way he loves them and that he is wanting their love and attention so much and they do not give it. He is seeking their approval according to Shanann.
- 08/06/2018 Shanann tells friend that he is so cold and not the guy she has been with for eight years.
- 08/06/2018 Friend tells Shanann that she talked with her husband and he wanted to try to talk with Christopher but won't because he is not supposed to know what is going on.
- 08/06/2018 Shanann texted, "I told him I don't know who this person is but the person I left seven weeks ago would have answered differently. Why are you married to me? Because we love each other! (He said that's all he can think of to say at the moment. I told him why I married him and why I'm still married to him. I said you love me because I'm the mother of your kids. You're not in love with me. I told him I think he enjoyed single life too well. And that I think he may realize he prefers to be alone. He's not in love with me. A person still madly in love can find a way to say. He responded, 'I don't want to lose the kids!' I walked away in tears since I couldn't take it anymore. If you are done, don't love me, don't want to work this out, not happy anymore, and only staying because of kids. I *need* you to tell me.) There was also a screenshot of the text from the right side (apparent sender—Shanann), "I don't know how you fell out of love with me in 5.5 weeks or if this has been going

on for a long time. But you don't plan another baby if you're not in love. Kids don't deserve a broken family. I left, you could not take your hands off me. You show up and I have to practically ask you for a kiss in airport. Being away from you, it's not the help I missed because I handle that. It was exhausting, but with school, that's not hard. I missed the smell of you, watching TV with you. I missed staring at you, I missed making love with you. I missed everything about you. I couldn't wait to touch you, hold you, kiss you, make love to you, smell you, laugh . . ." Shanann said she texted him that the previous night after she could not take anymore. She told her friend that she knows he is not good with conflict and avoids it at all costs, and is better at writing his feelings than talking with them at times. Shanann planned to see how he was that night. She told her friend that she told him life is about making tough choices and he cannot fight for someone he does not love. She told him he was going to have to step out of his comfort zone and defend and protect his family. Shanann said all he said is that he knew.

- 08/07/2018 Friend asks Shanann how Christopher was after he was with his parents' house. Shanann texted it was a long story and she was on her way to the airport. She said she will call her friend tomorrow.
- 08/08/2018 Shanann texts friend a photo of a house for sale and they discuss mortgage issues as friend has a foreclosure on her history. Shanann shares that Celeste is thirty-seven pounds and Bella is forty.
- 08/08/2018 Friend asks how the ultrasound went.
- 08/08/2018 Shanann replied, "He said we are not compatible anymore! He refused to hug me. Said he thought another baby would fix his feelings. Said he refused couples counseling!"
- 08/08/2018 Friend said that was a load of shit and Shanann said she cannot take it anymore. She said he said that he had a lot of time to reflect on his feelings and that he said a few months. Shanann did not get it. She said that he has never called her Shanann until this week. She told her

their other friend knows. Shanann said she wants to know what fucking changed and there were no signs of anything wrong—zero. There was sex all the time, talking, going to places, and doing things. He just says he does not feel it anymore. Shanann asked her friend how she can make him feel compatible again. Friend asks if there is someone else and she replies, "He says no." Shanann asks if she should call Mark to talk with him, stating that he talks. Friend tells her she can. Shanann apologized and said that Bella came into her bed and did not even ask where Chris was. She thinks Bella senses she is in pain.

- 08/12/2018 1338 hours Colorado Time. Shanann sends a list of counselors to friend.
- Monday 08/13/2018. 0900 Colorado time. Friend texts Shanann asking how she is doing—no reply.
- Monday 08/13/2018 1003 hours Colorado time. Friend texts Shanann that she is worried—no reply.

Group texts between Shanann and two friends:

08/08/2018 9:52 a.m. Colorado time

A friend texts Shanann and another friend and asked if they would still be her friend if she lived in Boulder. After six texts about that, Shanann asks one friend to tell her the gender of her baby, saying she needs happy news. They arrange for her to tell Shanann in person and the other friend wants to FaceTime it with them. Shanann tells the friend to come early and that she is up at 6:00. The friend asks what time Christopher leaves. Shanann replies, "Dude I need sex," "6," "Come whenever in the a.m. just not 11." Friend asks "why not 11" and Shanann replied, "Too long" with a laughing emoji. They agree to meet around 7:30–8:00.

Shanann texted one of her other friends to let her know the reveal party was canceled. She tells them to not slip on Facebook as she does not want anyone to know right now because then, Christopher will know and she wants him to want to know. One of the friends replied "Fuck him! Yep I said it!" Shanann replied, "Please no. He doesn't deserve to know. He doesn't even want it. Jack ass.

He's such a fucking liar. He said I think it would be great having another. He wanted this. He started the conversation. You don't get me pregnant and not love me. What's that going to do." Friend encourages Shanann stating that she is one of the strongest people she knows and knows she will get through this. Shanann replied, "Fuck him. I am nowhere near perfect but I love unconditionally; I give my all; I do so much as a mom and wife. More than 90% of women out there. This fucking suck so bad because I do love him and his fucking flaws." Friend encourages Shanann and Shanann replied, "This was a total slap in the face, stab in the heart. I can't afford 3 kids alone in Colorado." Both friends encouraged Shanann and she told them both she loved them. They started talking about friend and her husband moving into the house with Shanann. Shanann said the house is in Christopher's name. They discussed the courts would make them sell it before he would just get it. They encourage Shanann further. Shanann replied that masturbating is an awesome stress reliever with a laughing and "I don't know" emoji. Shanann said that when she asked him for a hug and to hold her tonight for a minute, he said he couldn't right now. Shanann said he's not there right now.

Shanann sends a screenshot of what appears to be her texting Christopher.

Today 6:09 a.m. "Do you want to find out together with me tonight on the baby's gender?"

Christopher replied "Yes" and Shanann loved his reply with a heart emoji. Shanann replied, "Please take 5 minutes today to tell me how you are feeling! I love you Christopher more than you know."

Shanann texted that she offered it to him this morning and told her friends, "I need us to work. And if he's wanting to know with me, I'm willing to wait. Can you put it in another envelope? I'd love to still see you."

CHAPTER 16

Christopher's First Official Interview

"I will not say do not weep, for not all tears are an evil."

—J. R. R. Tolkien

He felt a lot of anger, something he says he never felt before, but that was the only emotion he felt. He said he did not feel remorse. Originally, when talking to the CBI and Frederick Police, he said in his confession that he killed Shanann in a blind rage. Christopher now says there was no rage. He was angry with Shanann over her not allowing him to see his family. When talking to the authorities, even when talking about his children, he felt nothing for them. He says it did not register with him that his family was gone. It's not normal that a person never felt anger in his life, but Christopher says until that morning, he never felt the emotion of anger. While growing up, he said he never got into fights and never was in any kind of trouble. Christopher shows signs of Alexithymia, the inability to express emotions or to understand other's emotions.

On August 14 around 7:00 p.m., the police conducted their first official interview with Christopher. Sometimes, Christopher's answers were not really coherent. Yet, this is the actual interview.

This is the preamble for a consensual recording at the police station with Christopher Watts. Time is 7:08 p.m., Thursday, August 14, 2018.

The agent introduced himself; Christopher said hello and introduced himself.

Agent: Hey, good to meet you. Thanks for coming in. I'm from the FBI.

CW: Okay.

A: Um, just saying thank you for your willingness to help start from the beginning. Please include everything that you can remember. And tell us what happened.

CW: Okay.

A: Um, so this way you write it down, we have it forever, we can say hey, um, you know, where do you think they would go and you're going to be like well, I don't know, and we'll say oh well wait, is it possible that, you know, we sit here, something we can look at later so we find it to be very, very helpful.

CW: Okay

A: Um, so do you mind writing everything down for us?

CW: Yeah.

A: And then I'll give you, um, as much time as you need . . .

CW: Okay.

A: In fact, I'm going to go give these to a few other people while we're doing that, if that's all right?

CW: Okay. But the . . .

A: You'll be all right here alone?

CW: Oh yeah, just like just start from like when she got home that . . . okay

A: Yeah, um.

CW: Times and everything?

A: Yeah, just yes. Everything . . .

CW: Yeah.

A: You can remember

CW: Gotcha

A: Yeah, um, and then I'm going to let you do this, is that all right?

CW: Yeah.

A: Cause.

CW: Can I put my name up here?

A: Yeah, yeah, please

CW: Feels like I'm in high school again.

A: Name, date, uh, yeah. Um, I'm going to make sure that we get these to as many people as we possibly can.

As Christopher wrote out his account of the morning of August 13, the FBI agents sat face to face to ask some questions.

A: Okay, Chris, let's get started, we have just a few questions for you now. Thank you for your written statement.

CW: Okay.

A: Why was it such a big deal to Shanann's friend that she wasn't available?

CW: Because if she doesn't get back to her people like the people she works with direct—direct sales. So, if she doesn't get back with them, that's strange.

A: Is she the type to answer the phone?

CW: For them, yes . . .

A: Uh, like . . .

CW: . . . like all the time. Yeah. It . . . for me, it's just like hey, you can wait, we'll see you later. Um, so about 12:40, a few more efforts from her friend to reach Shanann while she's there like outside the house. And at 1 o'clock, that's when I left and I was like all right, I'm . . . I'm on my way down there. Uh, 2:00 o'clock when I got home, uh, 'cause they could they couldn't get un because the front door had a top latch to keep the kids in.

A: Who's they?

CW: Uh, her friend and the police officer that was there.

A: Okay, Oh . . . oh right . . .

CW: And . . .

A: . . . okay gotcha.

CW: Yeah. Um, so they couldn't get in because the top latch of the car. . . I mean top latch on the front door was hinged and the keypad on the outside does not work to get in the garage, so they had to wait 'til I got there so I can get the remote opened. Uh, three o'clock, um, right up t-the police officer, detective, came.

A: Uh, yes.

CW: Um, asking Shanann's friend and I questions about where she could have gone or who she could be with. Um, at about four o'clock, police officer that was there, he was checking the neighbor's security footage, um, at 5:00 pm, uh, the same-same police officer, detective and then a sergeant, another officer, they showed up and they searched the house again. Um, about six o'clock, they'd been calling around to anyone that-that could-that-that may know something . . . called hospitals and hotels. Uh, 7:30 is my friend showed up to show support and from then on, just friends are showing up. Uh . . . At ten is pretty much when I laid down, but I didn't go to bed until about like 2:00 a.m. just 'cause I was fielding texts and call all night . . . and I was just hoping that . . . I mean I left all the lights in the house. I was just hoping that I'll get a knock on the door but . . .

A: Yeah. She's back.

CW: Yeah, but nothing happened.

A: What do you think happened?

CW: At first, I really thought maybe she was just at somebody's house. Just decompressing.

A: Just blowing off steam.

CW: Yeah. But after today like with the onslaught of all the cars—I mean all the police cars, all the news, all the K9 units, it's making me lean the other direction about someone took her. But this is—if someone took her—it would have to have been someone she knew. Because there's—there—there's no sign of anything like being disturbed or broken. But like that's the way I'm thinking now. At first, I thought for real she was just decompressing somewhere—even though everything in the house was left there. But now, it's just—after today—with the news crews and everything, it just—it feels more the other direction and it's freaking me out. Because I have no idea where a—where they are.

A: Okay, if you could think of anything that we could do to find them, what could it be?

CW: I mean everything that I've exhausted so far is like people that have car seats because she left the car seats. And she would never just—I mean—I mean Bella could sit in a—in a regular booster chair, that would be—because she's about that time. Celeste is—isn't quite there yet, but. All the people that I know that have car, I mean they've contacted me. I mean unless it's—I mean there's—they—there's definitely a chance of somebody I don't know, or being a guy or a girl, I don't—I mean. She has plenty of friends through like direct sales that I . . . I've never met that could have a k . . . could have a kid that she—that they come and just say hey, you know, let's go. Like just back—open the back, put them in, let's go. But I wouldn't have a name. I wouldn't know who they are. And this is like that's what's driving me nuts like when I told the news crew was like if she's out there, like please come home. Like who are—I if someone has her or like not just have her, but if she's at somebody's house and she's just decompressing, it's—it's time to come back with—not it—this is real. This has gone to a different level.

A: Absolutely. Okay. Um, do you have any inkling of if it's good or bad?

CW: Yesterday, I . . . I would have thought that she was safe and she—it was good. That she would have been—that she'd come home. Today, it's more of on the other side. It's—I don't think that she would let it get this far if she was just decompressing somewhere. I mean she's not talking to anybody. As far as—I mean I—of people that have reached out to me that I haven't talked to in like y-year . . . that are friends with her. Like one of her like best friends, uh, lives in Florida, she's—works in the Police Department down in Miami. And she called me today. Like that's one of her friends she would confide in. So.

A: And—and she hasn't heard . . .

CW: Nothing.

A: And nobody's heard anything?

CW: Mm-hm. Like her parents, I mean she doesn't like talking to her mom, but still would—her mom calls her enough that she would at least answer once.

A: Yeah. And if she—I mean I'm married; I know how it is. If she's hacked off at her husband, would she call her mom?

CW: She would call one of the friends that's, uh, contacted me. At least one of them because she has—she has her close-knit group. But then the fact that none of them know anything is very strange cause one of them would have said something by now. Seeing what this has escalated to.

A: Is it possible that her close-knit group isn't close with you and there is somebody who knows where she is right now?

CW: I don't think so because I mean her friend that was at the house looking for her is v—she's very close with her. And the way she was acting right now, as far as how emotional she'd get, there's no way like she knows.

A: What does that mean?

CW: There's no way li-like she wouldn't know like where she is. If she knew.

A: Oh, so you're saying if her friend knew.

CW: Yeah, she knew like the way she's acting right now, she's—she's as freaked out as I am. So, there is no way like she would know where she is if she knew, uh . . .

A: Do you know—do you know her friend that well?

CW: Decent, she's been over m—our house a good amount of times.

A: Oh, okay.

CW: Yeah.

A: And so—and you obviously spoke with her friend.

CW: Oh yeah.

A: And don't have any weird feelings from her?

CW: No she was—she was there at the—at the house, okay, she was—she was the one that was ringing the doorbell trying to see what was going on.

A: Okay. Um, do you have a sense that the police here or the FBI here—do you have a sense that we have a good enough list of people to call and check with?

CW: I . . .

A: So . . .

CW: I think so cause I've—I've gone through my entire phone. I know her friend that was there has gone through her entire phone. Anybody that lives here that knows Shanann. They pretty much have the same contact list. So, if there's somebody that's not on that—on my phone, it's on theirs.

A: Okay. Has somebody, uh, I think the police have her friend's phone uh, I'm sorry, your wife's phone, right?

CW: Yes

A: And I don't want to s—pronounce her name wrong—Shanayne?

CW: Shanann.

A: Shanann?

CW: Mm.

A: Okay, so the police have Shanann's phone.

CW: Yeah.

A: Do they have your phones, have they looked at your phones?

CW: I don't think so.

A: Okay. Can I run that out and have a look real quick?

CW: Yeah.

A: Okay. Is there any password that I'm gonna run into?

CW: Uh, 3387.

A: 3307?

CW: 3387.

A: 3387.

CW: Um.

A: Is there any other phones we can check?

CW: Mm-mm.

A: Okay. When they look at this, what's the best thing that they can do to, I don't know, to say, um look for these contacts, look for this, uh, Instagram, look for this Snapchat, you know.

CW: So, like the only thing on here that I would say is gonna be weird because our contact list is the same.

A: Oh you guys have a shared contact . . .

CW: Yeah, like every . . .

A: like, through Google?

CW: Yeah. Like it's like I—like all the, uh, I—what drove me nuts is that when she like got all into the cloud, it multiplied or duplicated.

A: Oh I hate that, I hate that, yeah.

CW: Yeah, so this—it's the same person over and over again.

A: Ten people over. Oh, okay.

CW: So, we had the same contact list.

A: Okay. So, I'm gonna run this out.

CW: Okay.

A: Um, so 330 . . .

CW: 87.

A: Eight—3387. And I really want them to just not physically rip this phone apart, but really dive in.

CW: Okay

A: And—and are you okay with that?

CW: Yeah.

A: So, let's continue on . . . There's a whole shoe closet, I . . .

CW: No.

A: . . . she's preparing for this type of activity. Okay. Um . . .

CW: And the girls—the kids' clothes too. There wasn't e-enough that was there that I saw missing.

A: Okay. So um, all right. So, I know it's hard to talk about, um, you mentioned that there was a hard conversation the two of you had about uh . . .

CW: Separation?

A: . . . your marriage and separation. Now that you've had a little bit of time to think, looking back on that conversation, um, can you connect the dots between both of you being upset and crying and here we are now, she and the kids are gone? What do—what do you think about?

CW: I think about like that I caused this. Like did I make her feel like she needed to leave? And like did she really feel like the things she was saying; did she really feel the same, did she really feel like, right, did this connection, did she really feel all or that or she's just saying it? Like maybe like us falling out of love, did that—was that really registering with her at the time or did it register after I left to go to work? And then she's just like, you know, I'm just gonna leave. It's like and I'm not—sh-she laid back down, she was still there when I left. But it's like maybe she sat there and . . . and thought about it like do I really need to stay here right now? He doesn't love me. Maybe I should just go.

A: Can you really get into that conversation with me? Like what I want to know is, um, you obviously had a very deep relationship with her, she's your wife. But it's gonna be easy for me to listen to what—that was said and maybe think that there are some clues about—I mean she had just laid down and—and cried a little bit longer and something happened to her or maybe she did get frustrated and she left. So, let's—can we recreate that conversation?

CW: Mm-hm.

A: So tell me what happened.

CW: So I crawled back to bed.

A: So sorry, let's start . . .

CW: Mm.

A: from um, she gets home late at night.

CW: Mm-hm.

A: Okay. Let's start from that point.

CW: Okay. So, she got home about 2:00 am.

A: And you were already home?

CW: I . . . I was—I was passed out. Yeah, so like I g—I felt her get in the bed, that was about it. At about 4:00 am, that's when my alarm, uh, that's when my alarm went off to go to work. That's when I got ready and everything. And . . .

A: So, she gets in at 2, alarm goes off at 4:00 okay.

CW: Mm-hm.

A: And—and you're sleeping the whole time?

CW: Oh yeah.

A: Okay. So the conversation hasn't started.

CW: No. So, uh, when my alarm goes off, that's when I try and get ready for work, I crawl back in bed and we have that conversation.

A: So you wake up at 4.

CW: Mm-hm.

A: From—at 4:00 then what until you start the conversation?

CW: I get dressed, get my clothes on, brush my teeth, get a drink, all that kind of stuff.

A: Okay. Shower?

CW: No.

A: Okay.

CW: Shower like, yeah, the night before.

A: What do you do for a living?

CW: I work in the oil and gas.

A: Okay. So, then it doesn't matter if you go to work without a shower? Okay.

CW: Doesn't really matter. It's gonna be bad anyway.

A: Yeah. So then, you wake up, you get ready. I'm sorry I interrupted you.

CW: You're fine.

A: Um, so then—so then what time are we talking about when you're ready to talk with her?

CW: About 4:15 or so.

A: Okay. And so, she was asleep from the time she got in from 2:00 to 4:00

CW: Mm-hm.

A: Or 4:15. You wake up at 4:00, 4:15 you're ready, okay, and at 4:15 you start talking.

CW: Mm-hm

A: Why did you talk at 4:15 in the morning?

CW: I felt like I needed to talk to her face to face . . . because like I wanted to say something much—I'm—I—like when she was in Arizona like I didn't want to do it through text, and I wouldn't do it through a call. Like I got back in bed and like I needed to—I needed to talk to her about it. Cause she told me—she told me like when she was—when she was giving to fly back that she wanted to get up with me so she could take a shower. She wanted to get the airport off of her.

A: What do you mean when she got back?

CW: When she flew back in.

A: From Phoenix?

CW: Yeah.

A: Okay, okay. She told you let's have a talk?

CW: No. She wanted to get up with me so she could take a shower to get the airport off her. Because she was . . . like her flight was delayed.

CW: Her flight was supposed—was supposed to get in at 11:00, but . . . it didn't leave until 11:00

A: Okay. And so, did she call you or did she text you?

CW: Think there was a call. On that one.

A: All right. And then so at 4:15, what happens?

CW: That was when I crawled back in bed, I was I . . . I woke her up. And then obviously I talked to her about how I was feeling, about how I felt like what's been going on with us for the last what—what she's seen in like the last six weeks cause we were—she was in North Carolina and I was down there just the last week, but from what—just being apart and just like figuring out who people are. It's like the best—honestly like the best way people really find out who they are is to spend time apart.

A: I agree.

CW: And she kind of just like you need to see yourself. And all—and then on the last week, that's when I went back to North Carolina and I was there for the last week there. And when we were together, we could feel like it was—it wasn't there, that spark. I know that's kind of cliché, but that spark . . . wasn't there anymore. And, on the night, I told—I told her that morning, early that morning . . . I told her like the disconnection, it's—it's there, like it's not going away. Like the connection we had, when—in the beginning. It's not there anymore. Cause like I don't feel like the love we had was there any more. And it was just like I don't feel like—I mean if we want to stay together for the kids. I'm not sure if that's going to work.

A: And that is what you told her?

CW: Yeah. Like having another baby, bring this into a relationship, do you think this is going to work? With us being together or separation I think is going to be the best possible route for us. And that's when like all the crying and everything proceeded and it was just—it was very hard just—just to talk—talk about that. But I needed to do it face to face. And I needed like—I needed to see her face like while the—I couldn't uh, text . . . phone, whatever. I needed to be face to face and be able to see her and know that she was gonna be at least reciprocating back to me.

A: Oh. What did she say?

CW: She said that it was—I mean it was—she wants—she wanted to kind of work on it. But if that's the way I was feeling, then she respects that. And she said that most of the time when you have kids and you have a relationship where people like they don't—they don't love each other, where they fall out of love, disconnection, that having kids, even bringing a new baby into the—into the equation doesn't always work as—a keeping like, you know, the couple happy and the kids happy. It's like it almost is like better if . . . it was different. Different sides.

A: Different side.

CW: Yeah, you don't want to spend your whole marriage just like each other faking for the kids. I mean y-you don't want to be—you don't want to be the people parading around with like a mask on when their kids are around and then when the kids go to sleep, you just go your separate ways. Like that's what I don't want. That's why we were talking about the separation that night. And that's why I got so emotional right there.

A: Okay. Emotional for you too?

CW: Um . . .

A: What did you say about the house?

CW: Like we needed to sell the house, like, there's no way like we can stay in this house and have another kid. And being able to just keep everything afloat. And she was like, well where do you want to move to? I was like, well, we could move to Brighton, we could move uh, whatever area. Okay. So, thing it was Brighton, we can move Longmont, we can move like, you know, wherever. So much cheaper. And she was like well—'cause she had already contacted the, uh, realtor the week before her email. To see like what she thought. And that's like I . . . I actually contacted the realtor that day, like well—like pretty much probably about eight o'clock that day. And that's we're like if we can get the ball rolling, like see what she thought.

A: So, you said your wife called the realtor the week before?

CW: Emailed her.

A: Okay. So then, this conversation early in the morning wasn't a shock to either of you . . .

CW: No.

A: . . . or a surprise, it was the next step.

CW: Mm, yeah. Yeah it was—this was on like a—it's like way—like a big thing that we had like it was—just like this was. It would hit—that's why it was just an emotional conversation. Like 'cause it wasn't just like oh it come out of nowhere, left field type of thing. Like, we know like something wasn't—we knew about we want to do with the house. We knew like what—what's going on with it really, we knew something was . . .

A: Okay. Is it accurate to say that then, the time when you were away from each other when she was in North Carolina, the time that she was in Arizona, maybe the two of you knew that that could have been time you were talking and so when you finally get together, it's "we can't wait another second, we're gonna talk."

CW: Mm-hm.

A: Is that right? Okay. Now tell me if it's wrong.

CW: No, no, you-you're right.

A: Okay. Okay, so then, uh, the conversation starts at 4:15, you talk about each other and your marriage, you talk about the house and then what?

CW: That's when the conversation ended and we talked—that's when she said she's going to take her friend—or take her friend, uh, to take her and the kids to a friend's house.

A: Okay. Um, so let's you know, if we're gonna play the DVR let's r-rewind five minutes, so we're at the house, you're talking about the house, you're saying this isn't going to work with the kid, we're going to have to sell this house. Then how do you remember what led to her talking about the kids?

CW: As far like taking her to friend's house?

A: Yeah, like what—what conversation did you guys have?

CW: That's when I rolled out of bed and that's when she—she pretty much told me, like, I'm taking the kids to a friend's house. And I'll be back later. I'm not sure why she had to go somewhere. But that's what she wanted, like maybe she didn't want to be in the house after what we were just talking about.

A: Fair enough, you'd just talked about it, yeah. It's no longer, um mentally, emotionally her house then. Okay. So, let's focus on I'm going to take the kids to my friend's house What does that mean?

CW: Hopefully, someone that she trusts. Hopefully, it's someone that she knows pretty well and hopefully, maybe they had a kid that Bella and Celeste can play with. That's when I went downstairs, uh, make my protein shake, get my lunch, everything ready. 'Cause I gotta go to work.

A: And this is somewhere around 5:00?

CW: 5:25. And then that's when I go out, do my truck, load everything in it, and 5:30 I'm . . . or about—what the neighbors think, at about 5:26, I'm gone.

A: And this conversation happened upstairs? In the master bedroom? And you're sure that she didn't come down?

CW: Like once I was in the garage, I was in the garage, I didn't see anything after that. And when I left, her car was in the garage.

A: I'm just trying to determine this. I need the times she d-disappeared. And then, so from 5:30, then what?

CW: That's when I . . . I went to work. And then 7:40's the next time I texted her. I was like I hadn't heard from her and I was just seeing if she knew like where—if—or just seeing where she went. And asked her if she could tell me where she was taking the kids.

A: Okay. Uh, then all the way, what happened between 7:40 and noon?

CW: I was work—I was outside working.

A: Okay. Uh, noon, texted Shanann to call me and that's going to be in your phone too? Okay, 12:10 doorbell visitor.

CW: That's when Shanann's friend was at the door—at the door and it pinged on my phone.

A: Okay. What's she doing there then? Uh, then ten minutes later, you call the friend to see what was going on and she told me she couldn't get a hold of Shanann either and that her shoes were next—whose shoes? Shanann's shoes?

CW: Yep.

A: Were next to the door and her car was in the garage next to the door inside or outside?

CW: Inside. She—there is like a little—like a little, small rectangular window next to the door. You can see right in there.

A: Okay, So you—you see what we're trying to do? We're trying to be like did she walk out or was she taken out? Then it makes sense that her shoes are still right there. But she's obviously not wearing those shoes. Okay? All right, keep going. Looking. 12:40, a few more efforts by her friend to reach her, how do you know?

CW: Because that is when I was—she was still at the front door and I was trying to reach her at the front door.

A: Okay. Uh, 1:00 pm. I'm now on my way home to check on my family. Uh, is that 'cause you're worried with—based on the conversation . . . And the police had contacted you by then?

CW: No. She said she's going to contact the police though. Her friend was freaking out. I mean like sh-she like for her not to get back to her friends like that, like that's not normal 'cause like she'll get like tons of text messages throughout the day from . . . direct sales. Like if she doesn't get back to me, I . . . I just assume that she's busy.

A: So you get in the house. Shanann, Bella, and Celeste are not in the house. Shanann's wedding ring is in—on her night stand. Her phone's on the couch. Her purse is still here. The medicine for the kids is still here. The car with the car seats is still here. There is no sign of them anywhere. Frederick police officer and detectives are asking her friend and I question about where she could have gone or who she could be with. How did that go?

CW: Uh, n—we tried to go through, from what we could, uh, what we could gather like where she could have gone. As far as I could—what we saw in the house didn't really make sense. But that's when we were—that's when we were just like calling, started to look through the phone and just kind of called around. Once we found the phone and her friend knew what the passcode was, I can see what—what transpired and obviously, there was like 50 something text messages that had come—that was like all through. Because her phone was off. Why was it off and why was it not with her?

A: It's weird right? Because if you're saying that she does a ton of exiting, marketing and sales, and calling certain people back, okay. How would it turn off?

CW: You' have to turn it off.

A: Is that right?

CW: Yeah.

A: And . . . and I'm . . . I'm walking myself through this, you tell me no, no, no, that's not what happened.

CW: No, I mean like sh-she—like for her not to get back to her friends like that, like that's not normal 'cause like she'll get like tons of text messages throughout the day from . . . direct sales. Like if she doesn't get back to me, I . . . I just assume that she's busy.

A: Okay. I'm now on my way home to check my family, 2:00 p.m., I arrive home, open the garage door. How?

CW: I have my uh, uh, button. It's in my truck. Shanann's wedding ring is in . . . on . . .

A: On her night stand. Her phone's on the couch. Her purse is still here. The medicine for the kids is still here. The car with the car seats is still here. Shanann's friend says she's going to call the cops. Okay. All right. Now so it sounds like her friend is pretty worried. More worried than you.

CW: I was—I—once—once she couldn't get anything out of her and nothing was going on at the house, I was like I . . . I got to go home. I wasn't as worried because like if she doesn't text me back, I'm just like she's busy, like I understand that. Sometimes, that happens. But for her not to get back to her gr—direct sales group. That's very unorthodox.

A: So, uh, now let's talk about her phone. Did you turn it off or did she?

CW: I don't know like I guess she did. Because it was the—at like 50% or so I think.

A: Are you sure? Okay. And it was on the couch?

CW: Mm-hm. So, usually it's not right by her night stand. That's where it usually is, on her night stand. It's weird that it was sitting like on the couch cushion, like right there.

A: Okay. So, can we back up a tiny bit? You come home, no one had been in the house? Okay. *No* one could get in the house, is that right?

CW: Yeah unless you had a garage door . . . opener. When I got there, the police were there. Shanann's friend and her son, and the police.

A: Okay. Is there anything weird about the friend and her son?

CW: Not that I really think of.

A: Do you think anything about your wife not being around has—has anything to do with her friend and her son?

CW: I . . . I would hope not. I mean like she is one of her good friends. I don't think they could have done—like I don't think they could have done anything like as far as like helping her get out and then being so emotional when they couldn't find her. I don't think like they d—I don't think they'd be capable of that.

A: Okay. So, then they're—they're home, um, police officer's there.

CW: Mm-hm.

A: Um, then walk me through that.

CW: So as they go through the house, we're all . . . Uh, like I open the garage door, I just—I just go into the house. I'm—I mean I'm looking for a—as I go in the garage door I'm not looking. Uh, I just—I go up there, shake his hand, and I'm like opening the garage door at the same time. And then, I go through and then, they're waiting at the front door, I go and open that up and then, they come in. They went in the garage, but they didn't come in the way I did. I run upstairs; I look in the bedrooms. I go into Bella's room, go into Celeste's room, playroom, master bedroom. I'm looking everywhere like bathroom, and nothing. Like found the night—found the wedding ring right there on the night stand. She only takes it off if she colors her hair. Actually, she had colored her hair like the week before so, um, that was probably a result of our conversation. I would think. And then her friend's son finds her phone on the couch.

A: And why did he find her phone on the couch, what's he looking for there?

CW: I . . . I don't know, he was—he was looking. Uh, for clues—looking—was looking around too and he's happened just like to run across it right there on the couch and . . . right on the cushion. Saw the, um, so that we just told the officer that we found the phone, we turn it on. Her friend knows the passcode in 'cause it was a four-digit passcode before it was six digit, this one, this time, so . . .

A: And that's 013119?

CW: Yeah.

A: How did she know?

CW: Maybe she knew it over the weekend 'cause I'd never seen a six-digit passcode on her—on her phone.
A: Is that normal to you?
CW: No.
A: She might share her passcode with somebody?
CW: I wouldn't think so.
A: That's—do you know her to have done that before?
CW: No 'cause only—she's only told me her passcode before or like her—I mean her phone's her lifetime, so . . .
A: All right, so now we're at finding the phone. She unlocked the phone then what?
CW: Waiting for the—everything to load up and watching all the text messages pop up, phone calls, phone-missed calls, phone-missed calls pop up and went from there. They were just people call and as—and asking like "are you okay, where are you" type of things.
A: Okay. Does your gut tell you that Shanann and the kids walked out or that they were taken out?
CW: Yesterday, I would have said they walked out. Today, I would have said, um, I'm leaning the other direction.
A: Okay, All right. Who called that evening to check on her? Did anyone call?
CW: See, her mom talked to my parents, talked to my sister, talked to or texted with another friend she lives in New Jersey. Uh, who else? All of our friends.
A: Okay. All right, um, can we talk about something that's kind of hard to talk about? Um. So, when I work investigations like these, I like to keep an open mind. On everything. And part of keeping an open mind is listening to you talk about your wife and your marriage and the day she goes missing is the day that you guys have marital discord. Okay? So, you can understand . . . what I'm thinking about you. What do you think about that?
CW: Uh, I—makes me sick to my stomach, honestly. Like I know like I talked to a few of my friends like, you know, this does not look good on you, I'm like "I know." It's like people that—if people knew that we were having marital issues, they're gonna look at

me. Especially with the way everything looks. And it honestly just makes me sick to my stomach because this is something every vantage point; this is something I would never do to my kids or my wife. At all. I'm not sure like what I could do to like to make people believe that just because it—they—they—they knew we were having marital discord they au-automatically look at me. But there's no way I'd harm anybody in my family. At all. I know we were having marital discord and we had that in my family. At all. I know we were having marital discord and we had that conversation that morning, as in she goes and—we have no idea where she is. Or the kids. I promise you that is not—I—had nothing to do with any of that.

A: Are you telling me the truth?

CW: I am telling you the absolute truth.

A: Why should I believe you?

CW: Cause I'm a very trustworthy person and people that do know me, they know how I am a calm person. I am not an argumentative person. I am a person who is—that's never gonna be abusive or physical in any kind of relationship. I would never harm my kids; I would never harm my wife. And you can talk—I mean and—you can talk to any of my friends. Any of her friends. They know me. They know I'm a lowkey guy that's quiet, I'm—I'm not about confrontation. I'm not about anything that elevates to that level. I mean you can't—like if someone yells at me, screams at me, I just take it and I just try to get by the wayside and get it back to where it's cool and just a cool conversation to where like none of that—nothing that gets to that height. Because I am not that person. I've never been that person.

A: Uh . . . Okay. Would you take a polygraph?

CW: Sure.

Christopher came back the next morning after he picked his dad up from the airport. He took the polygraph test and failed it.

CHAPTER 17

Polygraph Test and Interrogation

On August 14, 2018, at around 5:45 a.m., the police called Christopher to see if he had heard anything from Shanann or the girls. He told them he had not heard anything. At 7:00 a.m., the police decided it was time to call in some extra help. They issued a "be on the lookout" and gave a press release. The CBI called the police to say they saw the press release and would issue a Missing Persons Alert, also asking them for extra assistance in finding the Watts. They agreed and said someone was en route to assist them and were given all of the specifics on the case. When the FBI and CBI gathered, the police gave them all the information that had been gathered by interviewing Christopher, Shanann's friends, colleagues, and they had made numerous searches of the Watts house.

At 6:45 p.m. on August 14, the police called Christopher asking him to come to the police station so they could ask him some questions. Christopher arrived at the police station around 8:00 p.m. and the police turned him over to talk with the CBI agent. The agent told Christopher there had been a possible sighting of Shanann and the girls at a Walmart store in Longmont. The photos were of an adult female and two female juveniles within the store. They showed Christopher the photos, and he confirmed it was not Shanann and the girls. They met only briefly at this time, but he did agree to return the next day for more interviewing. He left the police station around 11:00 p.m. that night.

Christopher also agreed before he left the police station that evening that the police could conduct another search of the house the next morning. He was staying that night with his friends, so they could come into the house as early as they wanted. They arrived at his house at 6:00 am. on August 15. They conducted a thorough search of the Watts home. It was noticed there was a sheet in the kitchen garbage can. Why would Christopher, if he had been planning this, be so careless as to leave a sheet in the kitchen trash? It's either he wanted to be caught or he had something major going on in his thought process. They noticed there was just one fitted sheet and one pillow case. The pillow case had some sort of residue on it that looked like glitter.

At 11:00 a.m., on August 15, Christopher arrived at the Frederick Police Dept. The plan was to do a polygraph test which Christopher had already agreed to. The door to the interview room automatically locks from the inside, but there was a key inserted into the lock that could be turned to open the door. They explained to Christopher the door was shut for privacy, but he was not under arrest and could leave at any time. He said he understood. The agent was not wearing a gun, badge or handcuffs, magazines, or any other police insignia during the polygraph and interview. CBI's polygraph procedures were explained to Christopher. He was read his Miranda rights and explained to him that he did not have to talk to the agent. He signed the Advisement of Rights stated he understood his rights and wished to continue with the interview and polygraph. Christopher also signed a consent form indicating his willingness to undergo a polygraph examination. During the pretest interview, Christopher told the agent the following. At 4:00 p.m., the polygraph test was over and Christopher was advised that he had flunked the test. He still denied having any knowledge as to what happened with Shanann and the girls. The FBI agent told him he needed to be truthful with them. The only thing Christopher would admit to was having an affair with Nicole.

Prior to Christopher disclosing the events surrounding their deaths and the location of their bodies, Firestone Police investigators located via a drone equipped with a camera the missing fitted bedsheet and two black plastic bags in a field adjacent to the CERVI

3-19 oil tank site. They also discovered an area of freshly moved dirt near the cleared driveway area of the site.

The police identified the freshly moved dirt and went about extracting Shanann's body from the clandestine grave. During the extraction, the agents bagged Shanann's hands and also placed a clean sheet at the bottom of the cadaver bag in an attempt to preserve any evidence that may have been present but not visible at that time. Due to decomposition, it was difficult to recognize the body from photographs but it was presumed based on Christopher's admission that it was Shanann. They removed her body from the scene around midnight.

A polygraph examination was administered using a recognized directed lie comparison—Utah 3-Question Test. The examination utilized a Lafayette computerized instrument that continuously monitors and records respiration electrodermal activity and cardiovascular functioning. In addition, a motion sensor pad designed to record peripheral behavior activity and cooperation during the examination was utilized. The instrument passed internal self-calibration prior to the exam.

The FBI agent asked Christopher a series of questions before the polygraph test. She asked him to give her ways that a person could cause the disappearance of someone. He started with "you can hire somebody (like a hitman). I'm just being honest." She asked him to think about all the possible scenarios in his head and he said he could hire someone or a person would use someone they knew to "do it." At that point, Christopher giggled and told her it was a hard question to answer because he had nothing to do with the disappearance. He said he didn't like to think about it.

The agent explained to him that a person could physically cause another person's disappearance by murdering them. He agreed with that statement. She asked Christopher to list all the physical ways a person could cause someone's disappearance through murder. He stated, "Stab someone, shoot someone, hit em' with a blunt object, um, what else is there, I mean, use a weapon of like a gun or a knife." Christopher appeared to be thinking so she said, "You could smother someone." He repeated what she said and she immediately said, "You could strangle someone." He said, "You could hand som—yeah, you can—all that kind of things . . . I mean, it's hard to even think about that kind of stuff right now." She continued by telling him a person could drown, shock, or burn someone to death. She asked him if he could think of other ways to murder someone. He said, "Lure them into a trap . . . I guess." The agent asked him to explain and he said you could have someone waiting around the corner and an accident could happen, such as getting hit by a car. She told Christopher that a person could kidnap another person, and he agreed and said someone could take a person somewhere and torture them and leave them without food or water. He then stated that a person could poison another person or beat them to death as a way to make them disappear. She asked him if he would have an issue with that question on the test and he said he could definitely pass that question.

The agent explained to Christopher that she wanted him to make sure that she only wanted to know if he "physically" caused Shanann's disappearance. She told him that sometimes, people can feel guilty for causing someone to leave, such as telling a spouse you wanted to be separated. Christopher said that's why "I feel like a jackass right now." She reiterated to him that the test was only to ask if he physically caused her disappearance by murder, kidnapping, etc., and not just caused her to leave because she was upset over their conversation Monday morning in bed. She explained to him that she was only going to ask him about Shanann on the test. She told him that it wasn't hard to assume that Shanann and the girls were just likely somewhere together. He asked, "That's gonna loop the kids with it though, right?" She explained to him the polygraph test she was going to administer was only going to ask him questions about Shanann.

Next, the agent told Christopher she was going to ask him on the polygraph test if he was lying about the last time he saw Shanann. He replied, "No." She asked him to describe the last time he saw Shanann and he said the last time he saw her she was in bed after he talked to her. Christopher said Shanann was lying in bed and had just told him she was going to take the girls to a friend's house and she would be back later. He said Shanann didn't take her make-up off before she went to bed that morning. He said the last time he saw his children was on the baby monitor as it was cycling back and forth.

She told him she had to talk about the worst-case scenario and told him if he murdered Shanann, the image he described would not have been the last time he saw her. Christopher said, "I know . . . I agree with that." She told him if he murdered Shanann in the house, she was obviously removed at some point, so her lying in the bed would not have been the last time he saw her. Christopher said he agreed.

Lastly, she told Christopher she wanted to ask him on the polygraph if he knows where Shanann is now. He replied by saying "I do not." I told him he was cooperating with the missing person investigation and the question centered around him actually knowing the location of Shanann but now telling the police.

There was a known acquaintance test to assess Christopher's suitability for testing and to establish baseline physiology. Christopher was able to follow instructions and showed suitable responses.

The following relevant questions were defined and reviewed in detail and asked of Christopher over three (3) chart repetitions:

1. Did you physically cause Shanann's disappearance? Answer—*No*
2. Are you lying about the last time you saw Shanann? Answer—*No*
3. So, do you know where Shanann is now? Answer—*No*

I assessed Christopher's psycho-physiological responses to the above relevant questions.

It was their professional opinion Christopher was not being truthful during the testing.

Global analysis of the physiological data revealed it was of sufficient interpretable quality to complete a standardized numerical analysis of the test results.

Analysis of the polygraph tests using the Empirical Scoring System resulted in statistically significant numerical scores that support a conclusion of "deception indicated" when Christopher was answering the above-listed questions.

While the agent was out of the room scoring the polygraph charts, Christopher remained in the interview room and watched videos on his cellphone of his girls giggling and playing. When the agents returned to the room to speak with him about his deception, they also had a printed photograph of Bella and Celeste placed on the table in front of Christopher. They informed him it was clear he was not honest during the testing and he did not pass the polygraph test. Chris replied by saying, "Okay." The agent told him they now needed him to talk about what actually happened. He stated, "I didn't . . . I didn't lie on that polygraph, I promise. The agent replied to him, "It's time," and asked him to stop and take a deep breath.

CHAPTER 18

First Confession

There are typos and grammatical errors, but these are word for word interviews.

The FBI told him they appreciated him coming to take the polygraph test even though he knew he wasn't going to pass it. They told him he stayed because he needed to get everything off his chest. They asked him to start again and tell them everything that happened. He replied to them, everything he told them was true. They told him the most important thing was to find out what had happened to Shanann, Bella, and Celeste. Christopher replied "Okay." He was told holding the lie inside of him would do nothing to help him, and he responded, "I know this . . . like I'm not like, trying like . . . to cover things up." He said he wanted his wife and children to come back home. The agent told him he knew his wife and children weren't coming back home. He continued by saying he "hoped" his wife and children would come back home, "and I don't know they are not coming back home." The agent told him they were confused and they had a lot of leads over the past day. He continued to say he didn't know where his wife and children were located. He said, "if I could have my wife and babies right now, I would . . . I want them back . . . I want everybody back . . . that is the God's honest truth."

The agent said he couldn't understand why there were two Chrises. Christopher then said, "I cheated on her . . . I'm not proud of it . . . she accused me of it . . . I denied it . . . and I feel horrible for it . . . like, she was pregnant I didn't hurt her, I cheated on her, I hurt her emotionally." He admitted he did not go to the Rockies game. He said the five weeks he spent alone, he spent it with "her." He explained he fell out of love with Shanann because he fell in love with "her." The agent asked what her name was but he said he did not want to get her involved in what was going on and didn't want to ruin her life. He said she was a wonderful person who knew he was married and knew he was having issues in his marriage. He told her he was going to separate from Shanann, but he didn't know what that was going to look like. He said she took his breath away and he never thought in a million years something like that could happen. He said he never felt that way with anyone in his life as he felt about her. The agent told him they didn't think his girlfriend had hurt anyone and could they leave it and just get back to talking about his wife and daughters. Christopher agreed, and the agent asked him where his wife and daughters were located and he said he didn't know. He said the affair was the only thing he was holding back. The agent reminded him he was not questioned about infidelity on the polygraph. The agent then informed Christopher they already knew all about his girlfriend "Nikki."

The agents told Christopher they were very worried about his wife and daughters and he replied he was also concerned. The agent told him this should have been the happiest time in his marriage, and that he believed Shanann was probably a very controlling person who didn't listen to him and could do whatever she wanted. He said he wanted to give Christopher the opportunity to help them find Shanann and the girls. He replied he wanted to do whatever he could to help the police find his wife and babies. Christopher said he didn't know where his wife and kids were located.

The agent reminded him his father flew across the country and was waiting in the lobby. He told Christopher that he was lying to his father and everyone he talked to. The agent pleaded with him to help them find his babies. Christopher replied he wanted to find them.

The agent asked if they could go back and talk about "that night." Chris agreed and the agent told him they have his Alexa (which he claimed was trained to record distress) and the police also had the contents of his and Nikki's and Shanann's text messages. The agent asked him again to tell him about that evening. Christopher reiterated he got up at 4:00 a.m. and woke up Shanann at 4:15 a.m. to talk about the house and the separation. The agent asked him if they talked about Nikki, and he replied Shanann accused him of having someone else. He said he denied having an affair. She asked him why he had a bill for $68.00 at dinner the other night, and asked him if there were two of them at dinner. He admitted the charge came from his dinner with Nikki. He said he couldn't bring himself to admit the affair because Shanann was already crying really hard. He said he told her he just really wanted to separate. The agent asked Christopher about selling the house, and he said Shanann had initiated it the week prior because they both knew neither one of them could afford to live there on their own. Christopher said Shanann contacted the real-estate agent "Ann." On Monday August 13, he texted Ann to give her instructions as to what she could do.

The agent then asked Christopher to tell him about the pregnancy. He said Shanann was about 80/20 when they discussed the pros and cons of having a third child. He said once Shanann got pregnant, she told everyone it was his idea. She told people Christopher wanted to have a son. Shanann told her friends after she got pregnant that she was 70/30 against the pregnancy. He said he was confused about what she would say of such a thing. The agent asked him if he realized some of what he was saying didn't make sense. He said, "I know." The agent said he didn't understand how a woman and two kids could just vanish off the face of the earth. Christopher said, "I promise you . . . I have nothing on my hands that—I did nothing to those kids or her . . . to make then vanish."

He told the agents it was on a video that he left in his truck. He said, "I didn't like, load anything into my truck besides my tools, my container, my book bag, my water jug, my lunchbox." The agent asked him what happened next and he said he drove out of his driveway. The agent asked him, "What happened to your wife and kids before you drove out of the driveway?" Christopher replied, "I didn't do anything with them . . . they were still in the house." The agent asked him where his wife and kids went and he said he didn't know. The agent told him his wife wasn't the type to vanish and Christopher agreed. The agent said Shanann had plans that day and during the week and she did not leave because she wanted to. Christopher said "Kay," then said he didn't do anything to Shanann or the girls.

The agent asked if it was an accident and he said, "I didn't do anything." The agent asked him again if there was an accident. He said there was no accident and if there were, he wasn't in the house when it occurred. He said he didn't cause an accident and didn't do anything to his wife and kids.

The agent then asked if there was a misunderstanding and he said the only misunderstanding there was that he didn't tell Shanann about the affair. He said he could not bring himself to tell her about the affair.

The agent asked him how the separation was going to work and he said he was going to get his own place. He said he anticipated having a 50/50 split with the kids. He said he planned on taking it slow with Nikki to see if anything developed.

The agent told Christopher he had a hard time believing that he had an emotional conversation with Shanann where they both were crying but he had yet to shed one tear over the two days they had been interviewing him. He said he loved his girls and it didn't mean anything that he hadn't shed tears (at that point, he seemed to force a sniffle). He said not crying didn't mean he didn't love his kids or his wife. The agent told him it just didn't make sense. He said, "I'm hoping they're still around some—I'm hoping they're still around somewhere . . . alive." The agent told him he no longer has his girls around to take care of and the loss of them should cause him pain. He said he did feel pain. The agent told him she wanted to see the guy who felt bad about what he did and wanted to get it off his chest so the police could find his little girls—his girls were not out in the middle of the field somewhere. He said, "I love those girls to death." He said, "I'm showing you the Christopher that cares about his girls and wife." He said his lack of tears didn't mean he lacked love for them.

The agent told Chris it was weird and didn't make sense. He replied he understood and could see their point.

The agent said she understood how some people could be pushed to do something they regret. He replied, "I know." The agent said they could keep talking to him once his girls were found. She said they would continue to talk to him no matter what he told them. She asked him if Shanann did something to the girls and he said, "No—I don't know—I have no clue." She asked Christopher if Shanann did something to the girls that he felt like he had to do something to Shanann and then felt like he had to cover for her. Christopher sighed and said, "No—no they were at the house when I left . . . they were there."

She told him the only way she could have left was in his truck. Christopher said, "There's no way cause like, I didn't just throw them in, in my truck." She reminded him his truck had GPS installed. She asked him if he knew the GPS should ping every 10 seconds and he said yes. She told him they were going to find out exactly where he went. He said, "uh-huh, I know."

The agent said to Christopher, "Are we not asking you the right questions?" He replied, "You're asking all the questions." They asked him what they were doing wrong and he said they weren't doing anything wrong. They asked him if Shanann did something and he said, "I don't think she did anything to those kids . . . we both loved them with all our heart. There's no way." She told him it could have been an accident because he knew something happened inside his house. She asked him if something happened to his baby girls and he felt like he had to take matters into his own hands and deal with it. The agent asked if he had to clean something up for mistakes. She asked Christopher what he was thinking and he replied, "she couldn't have."

The agent asked him which of the girls had breathing problems. He replied both of his girls had inhalers, but Celeste had the endoscopy and surgeries. She asked if he thought Celeste had trouble breathing and Shanann freaked out and decided she didn't want to live without her baby girl. He said he didn't think so.

Next, she talked to Christopher about a cold case homicide from Aurora where a male beat a family to death with a ball-peen hammer. She told him that the only survivor of the attack was a three-year-old girl. She told him the girl grew up with no family and she admitted she wished she had died with her family. She said, "Christopher, I have seen parents panic and decide their children can't live without each other." She told him, "I have also worked on a case where a mother smothered her two children because she didn't want her husband to take her children away from her. That mother felt she was doing right by her children and was saving them future pain." Christopher asked, "Why, how was she saving them pain?" The agent explained, "Because the mother didn't want them to have to live without her."

She told Christopher this is a weight that is going to be with him forever if we don't resolve it. She said we are making you a lifeline and you need to take it.

The agent then pointed to the photograph of Bella and Celeste and asked if they look like the photograph. Christopher pointed to Celeste and said she wore that same dress on August 8 or 9 because he recalled having to unbutton two buttons on the back in order to get her pajamas on that evening. The agent asked him if he made sure the girls were warm when they left the house. He seemed confused by that question and said his girls were always warm and their beds were always warm. She asked him if they were taking care of the girls at the very end. Christopher replied, "The girls were always taken care of, they never missed a meal." She said he took the girls out of the house with their blankets and animals because he cared. He said, "I mean, I'm always caring for these kids . . . there's nothing in this wor—they're my life." She told him she believes either him or Shanann made a mistake. She said, "I'm getting worried, maybe you did something to all three of them." He replied, "I did not do anything to these girls."

The agent asked him what Shanann did to the girls and he immediately asked if he could talk to his dad. The agent recommended his dad to be brought into the room. She said, "Will you tell your dad what happened?" He told her he had been in there five to six hours and asked if he could just talk to his dad. She recommended his dad come into the room since there was a lot of activity in the lobby area of the Police Department. She asked him what he would tell him, and he said he would tell him he loved him and he needed him by his side. She said it seems you want to get everything off your chest and asked him if he can explain further what happened between Shanann and the girls. Christopher said he talked to Shanann about the separation, the house, and Shanann asked about the affair. He said she had mascara running down her face and it was very emotional. She asked him if he promised to tell his dad everything, and he agreed. She asked if it would be easier if he told his dad and his dad could tell them. He replied, "I don't know." She said she believed he was the kind of guy that needed to take responsibility. The other agent in the room said he was worried his dad would distract him and Christopher asked if he meant it would distract him from talking to them. He said, "I just need to talk to my dad."

At that point, the two agents met with Ronnie Watts in the lobby. Ronnie was wearing a polo shirt that said "Papa Ronnie" embroidered on the chest. They explained to Ronnie that Christopher wanted to talk to him about what happened. They told him that everything that was said in the interview would be audio and video recorded. Ronnie said it was fine and he understood. Ronnie was escorted to the room and they told Ronnie and Christopher they had as much time as they needed. Christopher pointed to the digital recorder on the table and asked if we were going to leave it there, and they told him yes. The door was shut for privacy but still had the key in the lock.

Ronnie asked Christopher if he was going to tell him what was going on. He told his dad he failed the polygraph. "He said they are not going to let me go." Ronnie asked if there was a reason they would not let him go. Christopher said the police knew he had an affair. Ronnie asked if he was going to tell him what happened. Christopher told him when he and Shanann had a conversation that morning, it was emotional as they talked about the separation. Christopher said he went downstairs and then told his dad, "I don't want to protect her . . . I don't want to protect her, but I don't know what else to say." Ronnie asked him what happened and Christopher replied, "She hurt them." He said, "And then I freaked out and hurt her." His dad asked him if that is when Shanann took the girls and left. He said, "She—they were—"

Ronnie said, "Talk to me and tell me what happened." Christopher whispered, "She . . . she smothered them . . . they were smothered." Ronnie immediately said, "They what!!"

He answered, "She strangled them . . . they were smothered." Ronnie answered, "She smothered them? Or choking em?"

Christopher replied by saying, "Like, I didn't . . . I didn't hear anything. When I was downstairs, I came back up and they were gone. I don't know, like, me ta-ta-ta-talkin' to her about that . . . ta-talkin' to her about the separation and everything . . . about, like . . . I don't know, like, what else to say. Like, 'cause I freaked out and I did the same thing to fuckin' her. Those were my kids."

Ronnie asked if Shanann freaked out over the separation as he was leaving for work. Christopher said Shanann laid back down when he went downstairs, but he heard a "little commotion" upstairs and didn't think much about it. When he went back upstairs, he saw Shanann on top of Celeste. Ronnie said, "Was she choking Celeste and if Shanann killed Celeste?" He said, "They—they were blue."

Ronnie asked, "Both of them?" and Christopher said yes. Ronnie asked if Shanann choked both of them to death and he said, "I freaked out and did the same fucking thing to her." Ronnie said, "Oh my God." Christopher said he didn't call the police about what happened. Ronnie said, "So then, what'd you do . . . haul the bodies off or something?" Christopher said he didn't know what else to do and freaked out.

Ronnie reiterated that Shanann choked both Bella and Celeste to death and he "lost it" and choked Shanann, then Christopher said, "Mm-hm . . . that's just . . . it's rage." He told his dad he was sorry and Ronnie said, "I know you are sorry." Christopher said he knew Shanann knew in her heart about his affair but she was waiting for him to admit it. He said he believed Shanann just "lost it" because she knew he was cheating and he denied it. Ronnie said, "Is that the point where she lost it?" And he said that it was the point when Shanann started crying.

Christopher asked his dad what was going to happen.

Ronnie asked if Shanann was upset over the separation or the affair. He said he believed she thought he was having an affair. Christopher kept denying the affair to Shanann. He said he had talked to her prior about separating, but Shanann hoped they could go to counseling. Christopher said he didn't want to go to counseling. He kept denying the affair to Shanann.

Christopher told his dad, "This will be the last time I will see the light of day."

Ronnie questioned why Shanann would have to "hurt the babies." He continued to apologize to Christopher and told him he would love him no matter what. Ronnie asked Christopher if the FBI agents knew about what happened and he said he wanted to be the one to tell him (Ronnie) first. Ronnie said, "Well, we need to get a good lawyer and find out what the hell they can do."

At that point, the FBI agents re-entered the interview room and Ronnie said, "Come on in." The agent asked if Christopher was doing okay and Ronnie answered, "No, he is not." The agent sat down next to Christopher and said, "Help us work through everything with you." The agent asked him to tell them everything he shared with his dad. He said after he and Shanann had their conversation Monday morning, Shanann accused him of the affair and he denied it. He said Shanann knew in her heart that he was having an affair. He said she also knew about the dinner on Saturday night and that it was too expensive for just him. He said he went downstairs and started packing up some things and heard "a couple of things upstairs." He said he didn't think anything about the noise. He said he continued packing and went back upstairs to talk to Shanann before he left for work. He said that he saw in the baby monitor that Bella's covers were pulled off and she was just lying on the bed; he figured she was just hot. He said the baby monitor cycled over to Celeste's bedroom and "Shanann was in there with her . . . on top of her." He said he "freaked out" and ran into Celeste's bedroom and got on top of Shanann. He said Celeste was blue and "those were my babies . . . those were my kids."

The agent asked him then what happened and he said, "I did the same thing to her." He said he was in Celeste's room when he did the same thing to her. He then said he put her back in their bed. He said he didn't know what to do and he was shaking. He said, "Both of my kids were blue and they were gone. And then in just like, I'm not that person, like, she hurt my kids . . . fuck I had to do the same thing to her." The agent asked him what happened after Shanann was in her bed and he said, "I pulled the sheets back over her and covered her up because I couldn't see . . . I couldn't look at her . . . I felt horrible for what I did . . . then I look at my kids and I see what she did."

The agent asked Christopher where Shanann and the girls were located now and told him they needed to find his babies. She told him they could help him get them out of the cold. Christopher said, "They're . . . they're gone . . . there's no getting them back."

She asked him where they were and he said they were at the first location he went to work that day, which was Cervi-319. She asked him where they were located at Cervi-319 and he said, "Right there, off the site." She asked him how he picked the location and he said it was the first site he was to go to that morning. She asked him where they could find the girls at that site and he said, "I don't know what to do . . . I didn't know what to fucking do . . . like, none of, none of this makes sense . . . why would she hurt my fucking girls." She then asked him if his girls were in something or under the ground.

He just sat there and did not answer so she asked him if he would take them out there. Christopher said there was no way he wanted to go out there. He said he would go if we wanted him to but he didn't want to go out there. They had a map of the site, and the agent asked him if he could point to where his girls were located, and then we could get them out of the cold. Christopher said he was sorry and then began to cry. He then asked the agents not to think anything less of him. The agent asked him if all three girls were out at Cervi-319 and he said yes. The agent asked Christopher what Shanann was doing to Celeste and he said she was on top of her with her hands around Celeste's neck. She asked him if he actually saw it and he said yes, he saw it on the baby monitor. He said that is when he ran into Celeste's bedroom and threw Shanann off of Celeste. He said that she was already blue and not moving. He said he went into a blind rage and did the same thing to Shanann. The agent asked Christopher if he ever went into Bella's room and he said after he put Shanann back in their bed, he saw Bella on the baby monitor and he "just knew" by the way she was "sprawled out." She asked him if that's when he packed up their blankets and animals and he said "yes." She asked him how he got the girls out to the Cervi-319 and he said he took them out there in his truck. He said he put Shanann and the girls right behind his driver's seat. She asked Christopher what he was thinking and he said he was thinking that his girls are gone and he put his hands around Shanann's neck and "did the same thing to her." She asked him if Shanann fought back and he said "not much" because he had a lot of rage. The agent asked him how he knew Shanann was dead and he said because she wasn't moving.

Ronnie asked the FBI agent to look at Shanann's Facebook page. He explained that two days ago, Shanann posted a photograph of a five-foot-tall baby doll that was lying on the couch. He said the doll was completely covered with a sheet. Ronnie said, "I'm thinking this might have been planned . . . I don't know." He said the caption read, "what do you say about this?" He said the sheet covered the doll's head and the only thing sticking out was its feet. Shanann commented that Bella had put the sheet on the doll. He then said a child wouldn't do such a thing. The agent asked Christopher if he recalled the incident. He said Shanann made fun of it and thought it was funny. The agent asked him if Bella did it and he said he couldn't recall. Ronnie said he was around Bella and she would only cover her dolls up to their stomach. He said he never saw Bella cover a doll's head like it was a body.

Christopher looked at the agents and said he was sorry for lying to them. The agent looked at him and said, "You're a good man," and Christopher immediately replied, "I'm not a good man." The agent told him he stayed even though he knew it was going to be difficult. Christopher said, "I've been here for six hours and eleven minutes so far."

Ronnie said he could understand rage coming out if you saw your kids dead. Christopher told his dad he didn't understand what it felt like to see your girls blue in the face. The agent told Christopher his dad was going to love him no matter what. He looked at his dad and asked him how he could love someone who just killed his wife. Christopher said, "Nothing will ever be the same again."

The agent asked if Shanann was on top of Celeste when he got into the room. He said, "Yes." Ronnie asked him if Shanann's hands were around Celeste's throat and Christopher said he didn't know what to do. The agent asked him if he tried to save Celeste and he said, "It was too late, she was already blue in the face and she was not moving." He said, "Her head was just laying over limp like that."

The agent told Chris it was very important to know where he put the girls at the oil well site and he said, "I didn't know what else to do . . . I didn't know what else to do . . . I was so scared . . . it's like my wife just did this and I just did that . . . what do I do . . . anything that I would do from there was just going to be, just a fuckin, just insensitive and a horrible thing." The agent told him he was in a tough spot. The agent asked Christopher if he would show them where the girls were located. He asked, "What's gonna happen?" The agent told him they were going to help get the girls out of there. She asked him if he preferred one of his co-workers to go out there, and he said, "Oh my God no, *no*!" The agent told him everyone thinks of him as a good man, but they will say, "What the fuck did you do Chris . . . why didn't you just tell the cops, to begin with?"

He said he could not have his co-workers show them out to the oil well site because they were just going to form their own opinions about him "once they figure everything out." The agent told him they were still his babies and he didn't want someone else to find them out there. He agreed to show them where they were located at the site.

The agents told him they needed to step out of the room to get some things ready. Ronnie said he would stay in the room with Christopher.

While the agents were out of the room, Ronnie told Christopher he was sorry. He replied, "I didn't know what the fuck to do . . . this is just fuckin' horrible." He said, "The problem is I don't even know if they (police) believe me or not." Ronnie said, "I know you'd never do nothing to hurt no children . . . never . . . that was your life right there . . . those little girls."

Christopher said his mom always said Shanann was an unstable person, but he never believed in a million years "that could happen." Ronnie said he was asked if he believed Shanann could ever do anything to hurt Bella and Celeste and he told them, "No, herself? Maybe." Ronnie said he did not have a clue Shanann could do such a thing. Christopher asked his dad, "Why did this happen to me? Why did this happen to those little girls?" Ronnie told him he was sorry.

Ronnie told Christopher he would get a lawyer and see what they could do. He asked him if Shanann killed both of the girls while they were sleeping. He answered, "Yep." Christopher said, "I emotionally drove her to do something stupid."

Ronnie said it wasn't his fault and not to blame himself for it. He said, "It's all I can do right now." Ronnie said they would probably call it a "crime of passion." He replied, "I don't know, like, just because I hid it . . . I hid it . . . that's the thing . . . that's the thing that broke the camels back right there . . . I didn't just call the police right after it happened." Christopher asked Ronnie if he told his mother yet and Ronnie said no. He told Ronnie that Shanann had a temper—one minute she would be okay and the next minute, she would not be okay. Ronnie asked him what Shanann said that morning when he told her everything. He said Shanann asked him why and why he wanted to give up. He said Shanann told him, "Fuck you, and fuck you, and fuck you."

Ronnie continued to question Christopher why Shanann would have taken everything out on the girls. Christopher said, "I've ruined everyone's life including our family and friends."

He asked Ronnie if he should call his foreman and let him know he will be coming out to the oil well site. Ronnie asked him if they could just describe where Shanann and the girls are at instead of going out there and he replied "no."

Ronnie asked about the "babies" and Christopher said, "That—that's what I feel horrible about . . . they're in a freakin' oil tank . . . I didn't know what else to do." Christopher said, "Please God, forgive me for everything." Ronnie said "babies, babies, babies." Christopher replied by saying "they're gone." Christopher said Shanann took everything out on the girls because of him. Christopher told Ronnie he didn't know how unstable Shanann was. Ronnie replied that his wife Cindy believed she was unstable, a narcissist, and bipolar.

CHAPTER 19

Locating Shanann and the Girls

The agents came back into the room and Ronnie told them he needs to use the restroom and contact his daughter. Ronnie asked the agent about finding a lawyer who wasn't a public defender. The agent and Ronnie agreed they would discuss that later. The agent walked him to the lobby and returned to the interview room. The agent returned to the room with a colored photograph that had been taken by a drone that day. The drone had flown over Cervi-319 and the image showed a tank battery and a field surrounding the site. There was a white image that was actually a sheet at the bottom of the photograph. The agent asked Christopher to show him where the girls are. He asked the agent how old the picture was and the agent told him it was taken that day. He looked at the photograph and pointed to the patch of dirt in the field below where the batteries were located. Christopher said Shanann was buried in the "same, at that location." He pointed to the tanks and said Bella and Celeste were in the tanks. The agent gave him a pen and asked him to mark where everyone was located. He put an S where Shanann was and a B and C on each oil tank to indicate where Bella and Celeste were located. They were in separate tanks. The agent had Christopher sign the bottom of the photograph and it was labeled with the time and date.

The agents asked if the girls were in the tank and Christopher said, "Yes." He then asked him if someone that didn't know what they were doing could open the tanks. Christopher nodded yes. The agent asked him what was in the tanks and he replied oil and water.

He asked Christopher about the sheet, and he said the sheet was what Shanann had been wrapped in. The agent asked what the girls were wrapped in and he said the girls were just in their pajamas. The agent asked if the girls were wrapped in their blankets and Christopher nodded "no."

The agent asked where the girls' blankets and animals were and he said they probably blew away in the wind. Christopher said the blankets and stuffed animals were left by the sheet which was near Shanann's grave. He explained he dug Shanann's grave with a shovel he had in the back of his work truck. He said he always had a shovel with him at work. The agent asked how Shanann was dressed and he said she was wearing a black or gray t-shirt and blue underwear.

The agent asked Christopher how much time went by from when he put her back in bed deceased until he put her back in the truck. He said it only took minutes.

The agent asked if he was sure the girls' blankets and stuffed animals were not going to be in the tanks, and he said no they were not. Christopher reiterated the blankets and stuffed animals were left by the sheet by the grave. The agent asked him what the girls were wearing and he said nightgowns. He said Celeste was wearing a pink nightgown with birds on it, and Bella's nightgown, a unicorn or "believe" on it.

The agent asked him how someone could get the girls out of the tank and he said the girls were inside twenty-foot tanks, which had hatches on the top. The agent asked how far down the girls were in the tank and he replied it depended on the fluid level in the tank.

The agent asked Christopher if there was any chance his baby monitor recorded anything and Christopher said no. He then asked what he thought made Shanann "snap." He said it was Shanann knowing he had an affair even though he didn't admit anything. He said Shanann needed him to admit it and he refused. He said he was numb but he felt strangling was over fast. The agent asked if there was any way her neck could have been broken and he said no, he didn't think so. He described strangling her with both of his hands. The agent asked if Shanann was strangling Celeste with one hand or two. Christopher said he came up from the back so he wasn't sure. He explained he knew Shanann was on top of her because the monitor is black and white because it was dark.

The agent asked him why he thinks Shanann would hurt the girls and he said they both loved those girls more than anyone knew. He said people in his family have always told him they believed Shanann was unstable. He said his friends also told him they thought she was unstable. He said however he didn't want to paint a bad picture of her. The agent said it didn't look good. He asked if there would be something on the girls other than the cause of death being Shanann's hands. The agent told him it was hard to believe Shanann did it and Christopher said, "I know." The agent asked if it were possible that he (Christopher) killed one of the girls and Shanann did the other daughter. He asked him if there was a possibility, they were going to find his handprints on the girls' necks. He said, "Oh Lord, no." The agent told him they would be able to compare the diameter of the finger marks on the girl's necks, and he said he understood.

The agent asked Christopher what he was thinking about, and he said, "He let his family down. He said he let down his dad, his mom, sister, niece, nephew, friends, co-workers, everyone." The agent asked him about the point when he witnessed Shanann on top of Cece and he pulled her off. Did he think about calling an ambulance? He said no because "she was blue and limp." He said he had never seen anything like it in his life. Christopher said Celeste was "Laid over, she wasn't moving and all and wasn't gasping for breaths." He said she was "totally just blue." The agent told him she had been doing her job for a long time and most parents cannot fathom their child is dead even if their kid is stiff and blue. He said parents always want to call to see if someone can revive their child. She asked him to tell her what was going on in his head. And he said, "The rage I felt for what she was . . . what she did . . . it just took over." She asked him if he agreed it sounded weird and he said, "I understand . . . I see where you're coming from."

She told him she would hate Shanann to get a bad rap if she didn't have anything to do with it. He said, "I know." She said it wouldn't be fair. He replied, "I know." She asked him if he wanted to tell the truth about what happened and he said it was the truth. He said, "I did not hurt these girls." She asked him the question again and he said, “Yes, because I did not hurt these girls.” She told him she didn’t think he meant to hurt his girls and he said, “I didn’t hurt them.” She told him he didn’t save them either and he said, “I know that.” He said none of it made sense. The agent asked him if he was sure Shanann didn’t catch him in Celeste’s room and he said, “No God, no.”

The agent told him it looked like he found a new life and the only way to get the new life is to get rid of the old life. The other agent said he believed Christopher killed the girls before Shanann came home. He said “no” and his voice started trailing off as he said, “this is the truth.”

He said he was not a monster and he did not kill his babies. He said what is going to happen when the cause of death comes back to him. Christopher said it wouldn’t come back to him because he is 100% sure it wouldn’t come back to him. The agent said, “Who would it come back to then? And he replied, “It will come back to Shanann, she was on top of Celeste.” He said Bella “was sprawled out laying on the bed.” He said his fingertips would not be on Celeste’s neck and the fingertips would belong to Shanann.

He said he did not witness it but she also killed Bella. The agent asked why he would take the bodies out of the house and bury them. He said he did not know what to do. He said he was afraid of what everything was going to look like. He said, “My two babies were dead and I just did that to my wife.” He said it was a nightmare.

The agent said it looked like Shanann was a pretty good mom. He said, “I was a pretty good dad as well. You don’t know a person until you don’t know a person.” The agent said, “I would hate for someone who didn’t know Shanann, Bella, or Celeste who couldn’t defend themselves to have someone lie about them.” She asked him why he didn’t put Shanann in the tanks and he said he didn’t know what to do. He estimated she was buried approximately about two feet down in the ground. He said it took him about 20-30 minutes to dig the grave.

The agent asked how often the tanks are checked and he said about once a week. The agent asked if he wanted someone else to find the girls and he said he didn’t know what else to do. He said he was going to Cervi-219 that morning anyway and didn't know what else to do.

The agent asked him what he meant in a former interview when he said that something happened to his wife and daughters, which was "an act of pure evil." He said he was referring to the evil he witnessed when Shanann was on top of Celeste. He said he also felt evil for what he did to Shanann.

The agent asked him again what he witnessed in Celeste's room. He said Shanann was wearing the same clothes she was wearing when he buried her. The agent asked him if Shanann ever went to bed when she got home and he replied all of that is true.

The agent told him that he believes Shanann may have been up purchasing hair products at 2:30 a.m. on her cell phone and her credit card was denied. He said he wasn't aware of the purchase if it occurred. The agent asked if Shanann got angry with Christopher because there wasn't any money and he said he wasn't aware of the purchase.

The agent asked Christopher if it was possible Shanann could have a black eye and he said no. He said he did not punch or slap Shanann. He then asked him if Shanann would have a stab mark on her body, and he said no. The agent asked if the Coroner would find out that Shanann was poisoned, and he said no.

The agent asked what he and Nikki had talked about before his wife got home and he said they always talk and they were just talking about their day. He said she also knew about the disappearance by what she saw on the news.

He also said Nikki didn't know his wife was pregnant but she does now. He said he was afraid to tell her because he feels if she had known, she wouldn't have gone on a date with him. She knew he was married with kids. He then asked the agent if they were going to talk to her. They said yes. The agent asked him if Nikki was going to tell them she knew he was going to kill his wife and he said no.

He said Nikki just knew they were going to hang out more once he had his own place. Christopher said, "She genuinely liked me." He begged the agents not to put Nikki's name in the news because she had been through enough in her life.

The agent asked if he was sorry for what he did, and he said, "I wish I hadn't lost control and gotten on top of her . . . and then I did that referring to dumping them at the oil well site.). Christopher apologized to both agents for lying. The agent told Christopher he believed he was there for a reason. He said, "There's a reason why I didn't—that I came in because, I mean there's a reason I didn't come in with a lawyer either . . . so I just, like, and this is gonna happen so."

The agent told Christopher that he was struggling with the fact that as many people that would say he was a good person, there was an equal amount that would say that about Shanann. Christopher said, "I know." The agent said again, "I am struggling with it." He replied again, "I know." The agent asked him how he would prove he didn't murder the girls. He said we could compare the hand marks on the girl's necks. The agent asked if he was sure the girls would have had hand marks on their necks and they weren't smothered. He said, "They shouldn't have been smothered no . . . and Bella, I don't know, but Celeste, she was on top of her and her head was to the side." The agent asked if he saw that Shanann might have used a pillow on Celeste, and he said, "No"

The agent asked Christopher why there were sheets inside his kitchen trash. He said he used the fitted sheet to wrap Shanann in to take her to the site and he had the flat sheet and pillowcases that were leftover and didn't know what to do with them so he threw them away.

The agent asked him why he didn't try to hide the sheet out at the oil well site and he said he was so scared and didn't know what to do. The agent asked him if anyone came up on him and he said no, he knew his co-workers were on their way out to the oil well site. The agent told Christopher they took the electronics from his house and could he provide him with the passwords.

The agent wrote the passwords down. The agent asked if he had any questions for them, and he said he needed to use the bathroom. The agent asked Christopher if he had any weapons on him and he said no. The agent did a pat-down search on him and then escorted him to the restroom. Then, he returned him to the room.

The two agents also returned to the room and asked Christopher if he was sure Bella and Celeste were both in the tanks. He said yes, he put them into the tanks by the hatch on the top. He said he had to walk up the stairs then open the hatch. The agent asked if it was hard to get them into the tanks and he said, "No". The agent asked if he had to push the girls into the tank and he said, "Not really."

The agent asked if Shanann was buried because she was too big to fit into the tank. He replied, "Yes." He then asked if the girls were in separate tanks, he replied again, "Yes." The agent told him the detectives on the scene could hardly put their arms through the tank opening. Christopher drew an imaginary circle on the table to show the approximate diameter of the hatch. He then said he didn't know how much fluid was in the tanks. The agent asked if he could hear them drop, and Christopher replied, "Bella's tank sounded emptier than Celeste's tank." The agent asked if he felt Bella hit the bottom, and he said he heard a splash.

The agent asked him if he is sure he didn't put the girls in the tanks when they were alive and he said "No, God no, no, no, no, God no, God no." Christopher said there was no way the girls were alive when he dropped them in the tanks. The agent asked him if the Coroner was going to find any resuscitation marks on the girls. Christopher asked, "Like from CPR or something?" He said, "No." The agent asked if he knew CPR and he said he took a class one time at work, which was two years ago. He said the class used adult dummies and he wouldn't even know how much pressure to apply to a child. He confirmed that the girls were "gone" so he didn't try any resuscitation. The agent asked him if he ended up checking on Bella and he said yes. He said Bella was "blue in the face and not moving. I didn't hear anything such as a pulse or a beat of any kind."

They allowed Ronnie to come into the room and tell Christopher goodbye as an officer was going to drive him to a hotel for the night. Ronnie told Christopher the police took his Lexus. Ronnie said the other detectives he had talked to said Christopher changed his story a few times.

Ronnie asked Christopher if the baby monitor was upstairs or downstairs. Chris said it was upstairs, and Ronnie said he thought he said it was in the kitchen.

Ronnie told him he loved him no matter what. Ronnie said he was interviewed and told the detectives there was no way he would ever hurt his children. Ronnie told him it was a problem that he didn't call the police. Christopher agreed.

Ronnie said they would just have to prove it some other way. Ronnie said it was too bad the baby monitor didn't record. He hugged Christopher and left the department.

One of the agents came back into the room and asked Christopher to clarify the size of the hatch. He asked him to compare the size to his paper plate. He estimated the hatch was twice the size of his paper plate. The agent asked him if he had to squeeze the girls into the hatch. Christopher said, "It wasn't right." He said he put the girls into the hatch feet first. He described the girls with their arms stretched above their heads.

The agent asked him why he put them in separate tanks. He answered that he wasn't thinking at that point and time and was scared out of his mind and didn't know what to do. Christopher said he walked up the stairs and put one of the girls in the tank and then returned with the second daughter and put her in the second tank.

The agent asked him if he had to cut the girls up or anything and he said no. Christopher assured the agent he'd put the girls in the tank batteries.

CHAPTER 20

Recovering the Bodies

Bringing Home Shanann, Bella, and Celeste

Bringing the three girls home—that was the objectives of the agents that day. Many people helped in finding and recovering the bodies of Shanann, Bella, and Celeste. The endeavor was not an easy task, but the men and women that undertook this had no idea they would need emotional help themselves when they were done. No one there that day had ever had to do something as unthinkable as this.

To look around the setting is Colorado's vast open land. The Cervi-219 was actually a ranch that had been rented by Anadarko. The fields were thick with sunflowers and wild prairie grass that waved in the breeze—a scene too beautiful to have been part of something so evil and dark. This would not be the final resting place for Shanann, Nico, Bella, and Celeste. If you listened closely, there were almost whispers of something hidden beneath.

On August 15, 2018, at 2:00 p.m., two CBI agents met with other police agents and some people from Anadarko at the Love's truck stop in Hudson, Colorado. They had been requested by the Frederick Police Department to assist in searching the area around the oil well site located at the Cervi-219 in the county of Weld in the state of Colorado. They were searching with a small Unmanned Ariel System (sUAS) for anything that might be related to the disappearance of Shanann Watts and her two daughters, Bella and Celeste Watts.

They were led to the site by the worker from Anadarko. One of the agents confirmed from Anadarko that they had permission to search the area. They advised the agents this is where Christopher had come to this site for work the morning Shanann, Bella, and Celeste went missing confirmed by the GPS in his work truck.

When they arrived at the site, the Anadarko employee explained the layout of the site. The site was surrounded by a barbwire fence and the main site was within that fence. On the south side of the site was the well, to the northeast of the well was a separator, and to the northwest of the separator was a small tank that was open on top with a net over it that held water and two larger tanks that were direct to the west of the water tank that held oil and water. He explained the water in the smaller tank was removed from the larger tanks as the oil and water separated, leafing primarily oil in the larger tanks.

The two agents set up Matrice 1 (sUAS), and they completed the UAV Mission Checklist. The agent piloted the sUAS and started by taking overall photos of the area and the oil well site. He then began a systematic search inside the fenced area and started by flying over the south side of the site. Within a few minutes, he discovered what appeared to be some type of white cloth/fabric in the field to the south of the site. The agent hovered over the white fabric and requested the other agent to walk out to where the fabric was to see if he could determine what it was. An eerie feeling fell around them. Somehow, they knew something was not right.

As the agent walked south towards the material, he came across an area where the ground had visibly been disturbed as if somebody had been digging there. He reported his findings to the other agent. At that time, he was told to go back to their vehicle as he had been able to get close enough to the material to identify it as a bedsheet. The agent realized it matched the bedsheet they had seen in the kitchen garbage can at Christopher Watts' house that morning during a search. The agent then reported that he had discovered where the ground was disturbed.

The agent then took the sUAS and photographed the well site from the south, incorporating the sheet and the disturbed ground into his photographs. He also took photographs of the disturbed ground and located the head of a rake in the dirt. He later located the handle of the rake to the east of where the ground was disturbed. There wasn't much left for the imagination. They knew now what they were going to find, yet it would all be worse than they could have imagined.

The agents both then went out to the field to verify that the item was a sheet. They approached the sheet by circling around the fence line to the south from the west and approached the sheet from the south. They were able to confirm it was a sheet and also located two black garbage bags with red drawstrings in the field near the sheet. After identifying the sheet, they came back to their vehicles the same way they went in.

Later, the two agents went with a third agent out into the field by circling around the fence line to the south from the west, and approached the sheet from the south again. One of the agents confirmed the pattern on the sheet matched the pattern from the Watts' residence and that it was a fitted sheet which was the type of sheet missing from the Watts' residence.

While they were waiting for further direction, another agent came up and advised them that Christopher had confessed to killing Shanann, Celeste, and Bella. The agent said he disposed of the bodies somewhere near the oil site where they were.

Later, an agent brought over and showed the others one of the pictures he had taken with sUAS, showing the disturbed ground and well site in it. They were told Christopher had marked on the picture where he had disposed of the bodies. The disturbed ground had initials written on it, and each storage tank had initials written on them. He said Shanann was buried where the ground was disturbed. Bella's and Celeste's bodies were each inside one of the tanks.

One of the agents redeployed the sUAS and photographed the oil storage tanks where Celeste's and Bella's bodies were presumed to be.

CBI's crime scene unit arrived on the scene and requested that they take more photos of the oil storage tanks, and a video of the entire scene. The agent redeployed the sUAS and photographed the oil storage tanks from various angles, and then recorded a video showing the site from a 360-degree view as well as close-ups of the major areas of interest. That concluded the use of the sUAS at the well site.

The police identified the freshly moved dirt and went about extracting Shanann's body from the clandestine grave. During the extraction, the agents bagged Shanann's hands and also placed a clean sheet at the bottom of the cadaver bag in an attempt to preserve any evidence that may have been present but not visible at that time. They removed her body from the scene around midnight. Shanann's body was so decomposed they could not identify her by the pictures they had, but because of Christopher telling authorities where he buried her, they felt sure it was her.

After the grid search was completed, an agent was assisted with additional digging around Shanann's gravesite using shovels in an attempt to locate Bella and Celeste's blankets and stuffed animals. No blankets or stuffed animals were located. A short time later, Weld County Deputy and Forensic Pathologist arrived on the scene to assist with the recovery effort.

The CBI contacted an agent from the Colorado State Hazardous Material Section with an ongoing investigation.

On August 16, 2018, at 5:00 a.m., an agent from the CBI sent a text message to agents with the Colorado State Patrol Hazardous Material Section (CS Hazmat), advising them to contact him in reference to a CBI request. At 5:04 a.m., the Trooper texted back and advised that he would be en route to Roggen, Colorado.

At 5:30 a.m., the CBI agent had a phone conversation with the trooper of the Hazmat team to assist in recovering the deceased victims from crude oil tanks in southeast Weld County. This stemmed from a case that Frederick Police were investigating where three members of a family were missing in their jurisdiction. Investigators had reason to believe that two of the missing persons were deceased and dumped in two 400-barrel crude oil tanks on an Anadarko Petroleum drill site. They were asked to meet CBI agents at 7:30 on the north side of the Roggen Exit on I-76.

CBI agents arrived and they followed them to a remote Anadarko crude tank battery site north of Roggen. Representatives from Frederick Police, Anadarko Petroleum, DT Welding, and Northern Plains Trucking were already on the scene at the tank battery. There were two 400-barrel crude oil tanks at this location.

Anadarko employee met with everyone on the scene to talk about the plan to off-load both crude oil tanks and on-site safety.

At 8:54 a.m., the Trooper contacted the Morgan County dispatch center to ask for a member of the Wiggins Fire Department to contact him. At 9:02 a.m., the Trooper was contacted by someone from the Wiggins Fire Department. The Trooper explained the recovery effort and requested a brush truck and a tender to respond to the scene. At 9:36 a.m., a person from the Fire Department called and stated he had a brush truck and a tender headed to Roggen to the staging area.

They were advised to flag any items that did not belong on the ground in the area. They walked to the east, then along the east fence to the north. CSP personnel did not see anything that appeared new or out of the ordinary to the environment.

Northern Plains Trucking had tanker trucks on the scene and was methodically pumping crude oil out of the tank to the east first. The crude oil was first being drained into a metal pool. A hose with a screening device at the end of it pumped the crude oil out of the metal pool and into the tanker truck. CBI agents were watching the metal pool for any items that may be evidence in this case. An Anadarko employee used a four-gas monitor to constantly monitor the air around the metal pool to stop the work if the air became toxic or flammable.

While the first crude tank was being off-loaded, one of the troopers along with two of the CBI agents put rope handles on two containment pools. They anticipated the bodies to be covered in crude oil and were going to use the pools to put each body in once recovery would take place.

The first tank was emptied enough to start opening the rear manway on the tank. The DT workers took most of the 64 bolts off the tank door and continued to pump off what crude oil was seeping from the bottom door. An agent went up to the top of the tank and looked in the thief hatch. He could see what looked like a body, face down on the south side of the tank. The CBI agent took photos through the opening using the Weld County Coroner's office camera. He also photographed and measured the opening to be approximately 8" in diameter utilizing a metal measure tape.

The trooper and the FBI agent donned the proper personal protective equipment and finished removing the rear door to the first tank. They had DT Welding employees move to an area not in view of the recovery. They used a squeegee to remove as much crude sludge from the manway entrance that they could. They put two hydrocarbon booms in the entrance to the manway to help hold back the crude sludge so room could be made. They had a piece of plywood to use when entry could be made. They then had a brief meeting to discuss the process of removing the body.

The agents then donned the structural fire-fighting gear and readied their SCBA. They donned gas masks and waited at the manway. The CBI agent made entry to the tank and a trooper was not far behind him. There was a body face down on the bottom of the tank. It appeared to be a body of a small female child.

They waited for the east tank battery to be off-loaded into tanker trucks, which took approximately six hours due to the oil being methodically drained into a metal pan and then pumped into the tanker trucks through a filter. After almost all of the crude oil was removed from the tank, the rear manway cover of the tank was removed. Members of the CSP Hazmat entered the east tank and recovered a deceased female child later identified as Celeste Watts. Celeste was covered in oil and was wearing a pink nightgown and it could be seen she was also wearing a pull-up. Once outside the tank, there was a doctor who patted her stomach area down with oil absorbent pads. Celeste appeared to have skin slippage and was wrapped in a white sheet and then laid inside of an open body bag. After Celeste had been recovered, the CBI agent left the scene. The trooper tried to take a hold of her right upper arm and turn her over. He took a hold of her right arm as the agent lifted her by the left arm and they moved toward the manway.

The trooper grasped the left wrist and shoulder area as the agent did the same thing on the right side. As the victim passed through the manway, her left hand was de-gloved. The trooper and the agent continued to support her body as she was placed into a containment pool. The agent retrieved the removed skin that was from the left hand and gave it to one of the gloved Fredrick police officers. The agent and the trooper then moved up the dirt berm and put it on a table. They both walked around in approximately 4" of crude sludge and looked for anything else in the tank that may be evidence. They did not see anything in the sludge. They exited the tank at 3:44 p.m. and walked to the field behind the tanks to be decontaminated. Someone from the Weld County Coroner's Office was on the scene and took control of the recovered body.

Wiggins Fire Personnel sprayed them down and tried to remove as much crude oil as possible from our PPE. They went off air at 3:46 p.m. They then walked back over to their trucks, changed out of the PPE, and back into lighter clothing to recover.

The CBI agent continued to monitor the victim using a four-gas monitor as the Weld County Coroner and Pathologist attempted to remove the crude oil utilizing several crude oil absorbent pads. The first victim was then placed into a body bag and taken to the Weld County Coroner's vehicle.

The second tank to the west had less crude oil in it and was pumped off quicker than the first tank. The trooper went to the top of that tank and looked in the thief hatch. He said he could see another body that appeared to be facing up on the south side of that tank. The trooper took additional photographs using the Weld County Coroner's camera. He also photographed and measured the open to be approximately 8" in diameter utilizing a metal measuring tape. DT Welding employees also removed most of the bolts from the manway door on the second tank. While the Trooper and an agent from CBI were donning the same PPE, the other agents finished removing the manway door on the second tank. The Wiggins Fire Department Personnel again charged a hose line and moved closer to the second tank by placing a piece of plywood and two hydrocarbon booms by the opening. The trooper monitored the entranceway with a four-gas monitor. The levels were measuring about the same as the first tank.

The Trooper and the agent went on air at 7:53 p.m. and made entry into the tank at 7:54 p.m. The agent went in first with the Trooper close behind. The agent walked over and could see a small child's body face up. I grabbed her right arm near the wrist area and moved her toward the manway. At this point, the Trooper was able to secure her left arm and left leg. He and the agent then passed the body through the manway. The Trooper grasped the left wrist and shoulder area as the agent did the same on the right side. As the victim was passed through the manway, the Trooper and the agent continued to support her body as she was placed into a containment pool. During this extraction, there was some skin slippage where they had to touch the victim's body. There was also some skin on the plywood where her back made contact. The trooper and agent walked around the inside of the tank. They exited the tank and walked over to the field south of the tanks. The body was turned over to the Weld County Coroner.

The trooper continued to monitor the second victim using a four-gas monitor as the Weld County Coroner and Pathologist attempted to remove the crude oil utilizing several oil absorbent pads. The second victim was then placed into a body bag and taken to the Weld County Coroner's vehicle.

Both bodies were decomposing and covered with crude oil.

Wiggins Fire again decontaminated the two with hose spray and firefighting foam. They went off air at 7:56 p.m. The trooper and agent then went back to their response trucks and removed their PPE. They cleaned up their equipment and began putting everything away. The Trooper and the agent changed back into their patrol uniform.

The on-scene Hazmat Team continued cleaning up and putting equipment away. All of the contaminated equipment was gathered and placed within a large tarp. The Anadarko employee said he would make an arrangement with a clean-up contractor to take care of the contaminated items.

They cleaned the scene at approximately 8:45 p.m.

It was said later that many of the people who worked on the rescue team to recover the three bodies needed therapy afterward.

CHAPTER 21

The Autopsies

The following is not the full autopsies. They are the observations of the autopsies.

On Friday, August 17, 2018, at approximately 10:00 a.m., two CBI agents along with several others gathered for the autopsy of Shanann, Bella, and Celeste Watts. The autopsy was done at the McKee Medical Center, which is located in Loveland Colorado.

Prior to the performance of the autopsies, an email was read aloud which included a request by the public defender's DNA expert to have the necks of the victims swabbed, removal/scrapings of the fingernails, and x-rays.

The first autopsy performed was on Shanann Watts. Shanann had x-rays taken prior to the autopsy and they were informed that she had prior neck surgery. Shanann was wearing a purple/gray t-shirt, black bra, and blue thong underwear, which were removed and collected as evidence. Shanann appeared to have a large amount of skin slippage and her amniotic sack protruding from her vaginal area. The doctor examined the amniotic sack and removed Shanann's fetus. The fetus was collected as evidence and CBI Laboratory Manager arrived during the autopsy to transport the fetus directly to the CBI's Forensic Laboratory.

During the autopsy, the doctor pointed out several important findings. He advised Shanann's hyoid bone was not broken although he pointed out there was bruising to the soft tissue on the right side of the hyoid bone. The doctor also noted bruising to muscles and tissue in Shanann's neck. He advised he did not note any other trauma to Shanann's body and found no evidence of disease. The doctor advised Shanann's preliminary cause of death was asphyxiation due to manual strangulation.

The second autopsy performed was on four-year-old Bella. Bella was dressed in a pink nightgown covered in butterflies and a pair of underwear, which were removed and collected as evidence. Bella also had a large amount of skin slippage. Bella was x-rayed and there was concern she may have had a broken jaw. The x-rays were sent to a Pediatric Radiologist at Children's Hospital who advised it appeared to be gas in the area of the jaw and not an actual fracture. It also appeared Bella had some scrapes to her buttocks and the tops of both shoulders. The doctor pointed out several important findings. He advised Bella's frenulum (skin connecting the top lip to the gum) was torn, which created a large hole. The inside of Bella's gums' inner lip also appeared bruised and it appeared she had bit into her tongue. The doctor indicated Bella's death was violent as it appeared she struggled to get away. The doctor's preliminary cause of death for Bella was asphyxiation due to manual smothering. He did not note any bruising or injury to Bella's neck.

The final autopsy performed was on three-year-old Celeste. Celeste was dressed in a pink nightgown, Minnie Mouse underwear, and a pull-up. The nightgown and underwear were collected as evidence. Celeste had a large amount of skin slippage. Celeste did not have any obvious signs of injury or bruising to her neck area. There was no injury to Celeste's mouth or face, to include petechiae. The doctor advised Celeste's preliminary cause of death was asphyxiation due to manual smothering

Simultaneously, investigators learned that the GPS on Christopher's work truck showed he had driven to an oil battery, known as CERVI-319, in Roggan, Colorado on the morning of August 13.

The definition of sane is a being of sound mind; not mad or mentally ill; able to think/reason clearly, lucid, clear-headed, rational, coherent, balanced, well balanced, stable, and normal. Christopher does not fit the description of a sane person with what he did. So, is he insane? The definition of insanity is being in a state of mind which prevents normal perception, behavior, or social interaction; deranged demented, out of one's mind, unhinged, unbalanced, unstable, and disturbed. Was Christopher's behavior more of this definition? Could he be right about having an evil presence around him? The definition of possessed is a being completely controlled by an evil spirit (of a demon or spirit, especially an evil one), having complete power over (someone), and being manifested through their speech or actions.

CHAPTER 22

Evidence

As the authorities were putting together a case, they did several searches of Christopher and Shanann's house. The following is the account of one of the Frederick Police Department officers who helped with one of the searches. By the time this search was done, they had searched the house three times, all with Christopher's consent. They included the Frederick Police Department, canine search, and the CBIs. For this search, Christopher had given full consent for them to collect any and all evidence that the police could use to locate his missing family. Christopher told the detectives the home could be processed with forensic methods to obtain evidence relating to his family's disappearance.

The detective was told to photograph the residence, utilize Bluestar latent bloodstain reagent on areas alerted on by the canines, and then assist with the collection of any evidence located in the residence. It had been agreed that CBI would not collect the evidence. The Frederick Police Department would collect and package all evidence located in the search.

According to the Frederick Police, Christopher had been living and accessing the home prior to and since the disappearance of his family on Monday.

Scene Observation

The neighborhood and home are located within a newer residential area consisting of large single-family homes. 2825 Saratoga Trail is a two-story, single-family residence located on the south side of the street with the front doors facing north toward Saratoga Trail. The home has five bedrooms and four bathrooms with an office space, an unfinished basement, and a three-car garage.

Upon entering the front door, there is a living room and dining room. To the left is a staircase that leads to the upstairs bedrooms, laundry, and loft area. Near the staircase that leads upstairs is a hallway that runs to the east side of the house. The hallway provides access to the basement stairs, a bathroom, utility room/garage entrance, and an office. On the south side of the residence are a full kitchen, eating area, and an additional family room. A door on the south side of the kitchen opens to the backyard of the home.

The upstairs portion of the home consists of three bedrooms, a playroom, a laundry room, and a central living/television room. The home is in "like new" condition with no visible signs of damage and was clean and organized.

A walk through the home showed no signs of forced entry at all basement and first-floor windows; no doors appeared to have been forced or damaged.

Scene Processing

Photos were taken of the scene.

Bluestar latent blood reagent was applied to all bathroom fixtures (tub/shower, sink, toilet), which resulted in no signs of chemiluminescence. Bluestar was also applied at the locations where the searching canines had alerted (Mudroom by the garage, and at the top of the basement stairs in the hallway to the mudroom). No signs of chemiluminescence were observed in these areas as well (Prior to testing, positive and negative presumptive tests were done with expected results.).

While assisting with the search of the home, the police officer observed in the kitchen trash bed sheets and pillowcases. The sheets and pillowcases were greyish in color with numerous small light blue/ light green/lavender colored squares on the sheets. The bedding was buried beneath other items of trash; further examination showed the sheet to be a "flat sheet" and three matching pillowcases.

Stains were observed on the sheets and pillowcases. Some of the stains on the sheer according to the Coroner report that it was makeup.

The items that were collected at the Cervi-219 oil site for evidence are:

2 black plastic bags
Gray and white sheet—The sheet had red stains on it, covered in dirt, and placed in a dry room locker.
Rake head
Rake handle
Suspected hair from the east tank

The evidence collected from Shanann are:

Blue thong-style underwear mostly see-through; covered in dirt.
Shirt—White on top purple on the bottom; appeared to have a heart logo in the middle of the shirt. The shirt was covered in dirt. It was placed in the same dry locker as the bra and underwear.
Black bra—The bra was covered in dirt. It was placed in the same dry locker as the shirt and underwear. It was placed on a shelf.
Oral swabs from Celeste Watts; control swabs from Celeste Watts, oral swabs from Bella Watts, left palmar swabs from Bella Watts; right palmar swabs from Bella Watts; control swabs from Bella Watts; right palmar swabs from Shanann Watts; left palmar swabs from Shanann Watts; control swabs from Shanann Watts; driver side seat cover from work truck; trace lift from the center console; trace lift from the back seat.

The items that were not taken by CBI were transported back to the Frederick Department and checked back into evidence.

On August 15, 2018, at approximately 8:59 p.m., the Police Department requested an officer to secure the doors, hatch, hood, and fuel door of Shanann's white Lexus SUV. Her car was a vehicle of interest in this active investigation. They were then asked to have the vehicle impounded and towed by the towing company they used. They wanted it stored in their secured inside vehicle storage unit.

Once the towing company arrived, they had to unseal the front driver's door so the vehicle could be loaded onto the flatbed tow truck. The police officer followed the tow truck to the secured storage lot. The vehicle was brought inside the storage and sealed with yellow evidence tape. The officer was then notified that the truck Christopher drives was another vehicle connected to this investigation and also was being brought in. The officer remained at the storage facility until everything was closed up and locked.

CHAPTER 23

Reflections from Christopher

> "In order to learn the most important lessons in life, one must each day surmount a fear."
>
> —Ralph Waldo Emerson

The following are the reflections Christopher shared with me through informal conversations:

How does a person sum up his life in a few paragraphs? I'm only 34 years old, and just like my family, my life stopped at this age. I took my own life; I lost my family, my house, my job, my friends, everything that meant anything to me.

I know now Shanann and I were not meant for each other. I'm afraid if I tell you my thoughts you might feel I'm blaming Shanann for what happened, but I'm not at all. We were just two completely different people; each with our own views and personalities. Mostly, opposites attract and do well. That wasn't the case with us. When I really think about it, I wasn't true to myself when I first met her. Shanann was so beautiful, I remember; I just couldn't relax and be myself around her. She was confident and a real presence; I am quiet and I like the background.

I tried, probably too hard, and always wanted to impress her except on our first date. We were meeting at a theatre and I had no idea what kind; I was thinking of a movie theatre so I just dressed in sandals, shorts, and a t-shirt. I felt like an idiot when I showed up and she was dressed to the nines looking so beautiful and here I was, dressed for a night of relaxation. I felt so bad and figured she wouldn't give me a second date, but it turned out to be a great evening, and it gave us something we could always remember and laugh about.

We dated for over a year, and then, we got engaged. I was so proud to buy her one of the biggest diamonds I could afford. I had spent six months' wages on her ring, and she loved it. I arranged for both of our families to come down to the beach the weekend I proposed to her. We were so in love and so happy. She loved me, and I loved her; her family loved me.

At one point, her mother told her she better hang on to me. We spent the next few months preparing for the wedding. Shanann had everything planned perfectly for the perfect day.

Our wedding day was the happiest day of my life. When I think of good memories, I definitely think of that day. We had a beautiful wedding and no bride could have been more gorgeous than Shanann.

Life settled into a routine and some days were mundane, like anyone else's life. We had the girls and they were blessings to our lives. Everything revolved around them and we were giving them the best life possible. When I think back on what I had, I still cannot believe I lost my whole family—a family I had wanted my whole life. It's the most horrible thing I could ever do, and I'm still saying it was not my mind or my hands that did this to them but the hands and mind being controlled by something evil. I hope people will believe me.

Many things made my life a lot less than perfect, at least I thought. Although if you were to ask me now, I might have a different story about that. Shanann had created a life for us that looked on the outside to be perfect. It almost was, except for me. I needed to rise to the occasion and be a man and to help my wife see she could not control everything and everyone around her. If she couldn't come to terms with that, then we split. I was not able to confront the situation though as I could not go to Shanann and tell her my feelings.

I did not need or want such a big house. I was raised in a small ranch home and we were perfectly happy but not house poor. Life was much easier for my parents than it was for me when I was raising my family although relevant, I guess, to the time and paychecks.

The big house was totally Shanann's idea. I knew we could not afford it, but as usual, I wanted to make Shanann happy and would not tell her no. We had the house built when we first moved to Colorado.

We lived with one of Shanann's friend's in her house in the basement for about a year. After we moved out of our friend's house, the friend and Shanann most likely had a falling out because they stopped speaking. I never knew what happened between them but I felt really bad about it because they had been very nice to allow us to stay there for such a long time.

Our house payments were $2800.00 a month with $500.00 of that payment being insurance; that was not including the Home Association Fees. We were house broke and that was another stressor for me. I also felt another stressor was when I got paid, I could watch our bank balance go straight down. Shanann spent a lot of our money. I felt completely trapped because how would I ever be able to afford my own apartment when we never had an extra dollar? I really didn't like living like that. We also had a lot of bills from the girls' medical bills and Shanann's neck surgery, and there were a lot of debts on our charge cards also. It had always been important to me to be on time with paying my bills and have a few extra dollars in case of a rainy day, but we just never got there.

We had the house built for us exactly how we wanted it. My only contribution to the house was the outside stonework and the color of the exterior of the house. I was not allowed to have any voice inside of the home, and the house was in my name only.

One of the reasons Shanann wanted a big house is because she liked throwing big parties, and she wanted to make it look like we had everything. The parties Shanann would throw were very extravagant. How things looked to other people meant everything to Shanann.

My health has always been very important to me. I love to work out; in fact, when I get a chance to exercise in prison, I do. Shanann resented my working out; she said it took time from us. So, because of that, I started getting up at 4:00 a.m. to work out. I used to weigh 245, but I lost down to around 170. Shanann used to get dressed in running clothes and then asked me to take pictures of her, so it could look like she ran with me. I remember how we would laugh about it. Some evenings, I would run after I put the girls down at night, but Shanann did not like for me to do that either. I told Nikki this was one of the reasons I wanted to separate. We obviously were headed in separate directions or at least that is one of the things I told Nikki. Now when I say that, I can see how shallow it sounds.

I told everyone we had been talking about separating for the last few months, but honestly, we were not. Shanann was blindsided by all of what was happening when I was building walls between us. I felt like if I built walls, I wouldn't have to explain anything to Shanann. I did sleep in the basement some time but only at the very end after we got back from North Carolina. We went to San Diego on June 22 and came home on June 26. Shanann and the girls left that afternoon, and my life then quickly spiraled out of control.

I feel a big reason I wanted to separate was that Shanann was so bossy. She did not show me any respect, and she was teaching our girls to act the same. I realize now we should have gotten counseling. Shanann wanted to, but by then, I felt our marriage was too far gone. I also was tired of how controlling she was, and I was especially tired of her keeping me and the girls from my family. There wasn't a good reason for me to be kept from them.

In the morning, that's probably the main thing I was so angry with Shanann about—being told she would keep the girls from me. When Shanann would get so upset with my family, it worked on me. The drama from it was constant, and I regret saying some horrible things to my parents; they never fought back. They lived so far away and were honestly willing to help whenever we needed anything.

I regret I never tried to remain close to them, mostly because I was trying to do what would make Shanann happy at the time, but I didn't want to be told I could not see them either. It always seemed when she would have problems with my mom and sister, she would then want me to step in, call them, and go off on them for how they had treated her. I felt thrown in the middle all the time, and I just wanted all of us to get along. Shanann was not really bossy in front of other people because she really was all about appearances so when we were around friends and family, she wouldn't act like that as much. However, around my family, she would order me around.

I did not notice it as much because it was my usual, but my mom used to ask me why I allowed her to treat me that way. When someone is having an affair, it becomes second nature to blame the spouse for all sorts of things while trying to justify why you are cheating, so I don't want this to sound like I had an excuse.

Shanann and my communication had been broken for the last five to six years, but it had steadily gotten worse. I blame myself for that because I did nothing to fix it or help it. It got to the point we didn't have anything of substance to say to each other. I tried very gently to talk to her many times, but it fell on deaf ears; she gave no validity to how I felt.

To keep the peace, I would sometimes hang out with her by the bed and keep her company until she fell asleep. Most of the time when I did though, she would just continue to flip through her iPad and talk on the phone. When I tried talking to her, she would ignore me. She would stop and say, "Oh, were you talking to me? Because I wasn't listening to you."

I had been thinking about killing my family. I didn't want to, but I knew I was going to do it. I did not realize I would feel anger because I didn't know what that felt like. I just knew there was something in me that felt like it was controlling me. There was a feeling of something dark around me. It had seemed like that for a couple of weeks. I am not blaming Nikki; she is a victim also. However, I started feeling that way around the time I was seeing her. I call it a demon, and I don't mean that in a religious sense. A demon is the only thing I know to call it. My conscious mind could see what it was going to make me do before I did it. I knew that when I started to see how something was going to go, it would definitely go that way.

I knew if she had to tell my parents they couldn't see the kids, it would be really rough on them, especially my dad. It was hard on my mom if she couldn't see me, and of course, she wanted to see the girls, too. I was afraid of what it might do to them.

My dad has had his struggles before, and I didn't want to be what caused him more problems, but now I realize I have caused him the greatest heartache of all. My dad misses Shanann and the girls so much; both of us do. My dad is my hero and Shanann knew I felt that way. I was always the person who would just go with the flow; I didn't rock the boat, but not that day.

It made me angry to think about the ultimatum I was given by Shanann. I was tired of not feeling like I could be myself around her, that she tried to think for me, and that I couldn't make decisions on my own.

That is one of the things I loved about Nikki—I could be myself. I didn't have to pretend or try to be a certain way, so she didn't get mad. I could just be me. In actuality, Shanann had told me she wanted a man that would stand up for himself and not be pushed around. I don't know why I couldn't be that man for her, except she was the only one telling me that. I think it may have been the criticism. It wasn't her fault any more than it was my fault who we are. Our communication started breaking down a couple of years after we were married; it just wasn't easy for me to talk to her. I felt beneath her. She seemed more accomplished than I am and smarter somehow.

In the years I was growing up, I really didn't have to think about these sorts of things. My parents never gave me a hard time just being myself. I was actually somewhat different from some of the other kids, more socially withdrawn. The choices I made that morning of August 13 will and should haunt me for the rest of my life. I hear my baby's voice every day as she tried to stop me from killing her.

After I was in prison and after I was moved to Wisconsin, I received a letter from a woman I did not know; and she said she did not know me. She had heard something briefly on the television about the case but said she really did not pay much attention to it, so she was not at all familiar with the story. She wrote to me about a dream she had a couple of nights before. In her dream, she was walking past a room and saw a baby bed in the room and could hear a small child crying. She walked into the room and noticed something was dripping out from under the baby's bed. It was dripping onto the floor. She walked over to the bed, looked, and saw a little girl covered in liquid. It was all over the child. So, she picked up the little girl who said, "I am having so much fun up here." The woman realized the small child was covered in gas. She woke up and was very disturbed by the dream. She remembered something about gasoline from the news. She did not remember my name or anything else pertaining to the case so she googled it and found the story. When she saw pictures of my family, she told me she realized that the little girl in her dream was Bella. She said she was writing me to let me know they are in heaven and I did not need to keep beating myself up over what happened. I wrote her back, but I never heard from her again. I appreciated her writing to me about the dream, but I already know without any doubt that Bella is in heaven. As far as beating myself up, that will happen for as long as I live.

My life for all intents and purposes was over, and then I received a letter that lit a fire in me. I was told God could still use me and that I can help others. Maybe I could reach those who are planning on doing something as horrendous as I did and offer them a way of hope. I could help save lives that way and serve for the rest of my life.

CHAPTER 24

The Arrests, Plea, and Sentencing

Lastly, an agent asked Christopher if a Frederick police officer could come in and photograph him without his shirt on to make sure he didn't have any marks or injuries on him. Christopher agreed and the officer photographed his face, head, arms, chest, back, hands, and legs. The officer told the FBI agent the photographs would be placed into their digital evidence storage system. Following the interview, Christopher was taken into custody. There was a belly belt put on him attached to the handcuffs. He was escorted to the Frederick Police Department SUV. They drove to the Weld County Jail. On the way there, the officer said he did not talk to Christopher, and Christopher was silent the entire time. At 3:00 a.m., he was released to the Weld County Jail Facility.

Between the time Christopher was arrested and sentenced, there were things that happened at his house that makes a person take a pause.

There is an opposite to good; it is evil. Evil can present itself in different forms. Strange things connected to the story, such as one evening not long after the murders. The police were called. The neighbors were seeing a woman walking around in the garage. There are police cam videos of four policemen arriving at the Watts house. Clearly shown, the garage lights were on. As they opened the front door, they were met with eerie darkness coming from the house. They went inside and yelled several times for whoever was in the house to make themselves known. There was no answer. They went to the garage and with guns drawn, opened the door to the garage and yelled again. When they opened the garage door, however, the lights were off. They searched every inch of the house but no one was there. There was no way out of the garage without coming into the house and without opening the big garage door. But then, they would have had no way to shut it. It was obvious on the police cam video that they felt something too. They kept shining their lights into the darkness over and over. Who turned the lights on? Who turned them off?

Still another evening, at 9:05 p.m., the police were called to the house regarding an unknown person seen going up to the house. Upon arrival, the police advised the neighbor from next door that had a video to point toward the Watts' house. The video showed a large black vehicle pulling up to the address (2825 Saratoga Trail) and then an unknown female stepped out of the vehicle and walked up to the door of the house. The police said the woman could not be seen leaving the residence, and the garage lights came on when they had been off. As the police entered the house, they gave loud announcements they were entering, but no one was there. They searched the house again and found no one. They turned off all lights that were on in the house and locked the doors as they left.

On September 21, 2018, the police received yet another message from some unknown person who said "her deceased daughter's back door is open at her house. This is the home of Shanann Watts."

The police walked the perimeter of the home. All doors and windows were secure, and there was no sign of forced entry to the home. Again at 8:50 p.m., another call came in to respond to the residence. There were lights on that had not been on earlier. Several police officers responded; they searched the residence again. There were lights on, but they did not see that anything was bothered. They turned off the lights and left, making sure all doors were locked. What or who is playing with this house? Is it something supernatural? Research shows that often, demons will play with lights and electronic things.

When the agents knew Christopher was lying and he had flunked the polygraph test, things moved swiftly. First, they had to find out where the bodies were. It was an unreal task for them to have to empty crude oil batteries in order to get little girls out.

His mother in her quest to find out what had really happened met many dead ends. The judicial system was very difficult for them to deal with. After the authorities arrested Christopher, his family was not allowed to see him or talk to him until the day before the sentencing. Christopher's attorneys flew Ronnie, Cindy, and Jamie to Colorado to see him before he was sentenced. They were told he had pled guilty to killing his entire family. His family feels his attorneys did not make him plead guilty, but they strongly advised him to all in an effort, they told him, to save his life.

This did not sit well with Christopher or his family but for different reasons. He says he had a hard time with it but did not want the death penalty. His family, not having been told any details, felt like he should not have pled guilty if Shanann had killed the girls. He told his family he was pleading guilty to all of the murders for a reason. However, he gave them no details, so they went into the sentencing having no idea about the circumstances surrounding them.

The state of Colorado automatically gives a life sentence to someone who murders another individual. The DA said he wanted to seek the death penalty and would have, except Shanann's mother begged him not to. If he had sought the death penalty, he probably would have gotten it. How could circumstances have been any more favorable for it? This may show how Sandi Rzucek loved her son-in-law more than he realizes. She is to be commended for that. This is very difficult. If it all had not come down the way it did or if they had not arrested him as soon as they did, Christopher says he had decided to plead guilty anyway. He said he had to get past the anger and the memory loss first. In Christopher's own words, however, the morning of the murders did not happen because he just broke into a rage. He may have been angry for sure, but this anger had been building for weeks. Some of it for years. He started to plan these killings. Once started, he was not able to stop it; he became obsessed with it.

Christopher said had they not gotten the evidence to arrest him, he already planned on confessing to the murders. He just couldn't remember everything about the murders to tell them, he says. It was hard for him because at that time, he did not feel remorse but he had to pretend like he did. He does not like for people to hate him, he says. He even apologized to the agents during the interrogations that he had lied to them. Yet, he continued to lie.

His attorneys kept telling him and told his family they were just trying to save his life.

After he was arrested and told his attorneys what he could remember, they were willing to tell whatever he wanted them to tell about the murders. He said they had some very angry, very stressful times going over the case, and what his options were. He said he felt heartless, angry, and defiant up until October 1 when it all broke for him.

Below is the written plea that was presented on his behalf:

Written Waiver and Guilty Plea

1) I am the defendant in this case.
2) I have had enough time to talk to my lawyers about this case, and he/she has discussed the evidence against me. I have fully explained my side to him/her.
3) I believe the District Attorney has enough evidence to convict me at trial.
4) I am satisfied that my plea of guilty is in my best interest.
5) I understand that I have the right to exercise any or all of the following rights, even against my lawyer's advice.
    a) The right to remain silent about this case.
    b) The right to have my lawyer represent me and be present with me during any conferences or questioning by anyone about this case at all court hearings and at trial;
    c) The right to plead *not guilty* and have a jury trial; and,
    d) The right to appeal my case to the highest court if I am convicted at trial.
6) I understand that the right to a jury trial includes:
    a) The right to help select a jury,
    b) The right to confront witnesses who testify against me, and to have my lawyer cross-examine them about their testimony;

c) The right to be presumed innocent unless and until the District Attorney proves my guilt beyond a reasonable doubt;
d) The right to have my lawyer call witnesses to testify for me if I want and if necessary, to have the judge order witnesses to come to court.

7) I have read and understood the elements of the charge or charges that I am pleading guilty to, as shown on the attached sheet(s).
8) I have read and understood the possible penalties that I could be sentenced to, which are shown on the attached sheet(s).
9) My plea is freely, intelligently, and voluntarily given. I know that I am giving up all the rights described above. I understand these rights. I am giving up these rights and pleading guilty of my own free will. No one has pressured me or tried to make me plead guilty against my will. I have not decided to plead guilty because of anything I have been told except for the agreements shown on the attached sheet(s).
10) I understand that the record may be further supplemented by police reports, affidavits, or other documentation attached or provided at the time of sentencing.
11) I understand if I am not a citizen of the United States, this guilty plea may cause collateral consequences, including, but not limited to deportation, exclusion from admission in the United States, or denial of naturalization.
12) I understand that following the sentencing in this matter, I have, in certain circumstances, the right to appellate review of my conviction and sentence. A Notice of Appeal must be filed within 7 weeks (or 49 days) of the sentence. I also understand that if I am determined indigent by the court that I have the right to assistance of appointed counsel upon the review of my conviction and the right to obtain a record on appeal without payment on costs. Additionally, I understand that I may have the right to seek a post-conviction reduction of my sentence in the trial court

within 18 weeks (or 126 days) of the imposition of sentence pursuant to Crim.P.35(b).

13) I have read this form and understand it. My lawyer has answered all my questions to my satisfaction.
Defendant Christopher Watt
November 15, 2018

14) I represent that I have reviewed this advisement with the defendant. I believe he/she understands his/her rights, the charge or charges to which he/she is pleading guilty, and the possible penalties. I also believe that the defendant's plea is freely, intelligently, and voluntarily given.
Attorney for the defendant
November 15, 2018

15) On behalf of the office of the District Attorney:
District Attorney
November 6, 2018

Agreement

Defendant will plead guilty to all counts set forth in the complaint and information:

- Count 1, Murder in the First Degree—After Deliberation (Shanann Watts), a class one felony;
- Count 2, Murder in the First Degree—After Deliberation (Bella Watts), a class one felony;
- Count 3, Murder in the First Degree—After Deliberation (Celeste Watts), a class one felony;
- Count 4, Murder in the First Degree—Child under 12 (Bella Watts), a class one felony;
- Count 5 Murder in the First Degree—Child under 12 (Celeste Watts), a class one felony;
- Count 6 Unlawful Termination of Pregnancy in the First Degree (Nico), a class two felony;
- Count 7 Tampering with a Deceased Human Body, a class 3 felony;

- Count 8 Tampering with a Deceased Human Body, a class 3 felony;
- Count 9 Tampering with a Deceased Human Body, a class 3 felony.

All sentencing options on all counts are open to the court. However, in exchange for the defendant's guilty pleas, the office of the District Attorney agrees that it will not seek the death penalty. Whether sentencing on separate counts run consecutive or concurrently is open to the court, with the exception that, at a minimum, the parties stipulate that sentencing on counts 1 through 3 and count 6 shall run consecutively as each charge references a separate victim. Defendant will not be permitted to waive a factual basis for any charge.

The parties further stipulate that the defendant will pay restitution as determined by the court, including but not limited to the expenses for funeral and burial expenses for Shanann Watts, Bella Watts, Celeste Watts, and Nico Watts. Furthermore, the defendant agrees to pay restitution covering the actual costs of specific future treatment pursuant to C.R.S.

Finally, the parties stipulate that the people may withdraw from this agreement if the defendant commits a new felony offense while awaiting sentencing.

Christopher Lee Watts

Elements

Count 1: Murder in the First Degree (F1):

1. On or about the 13th day of August 2018, in the County of Weld, State of Colorado,
2. *Christopher Lee Watts* unlawfully, feloniously, after deliberation, and
3. with the intent
4. caused the death of a person other than himself;
5. caused the death of Shanann Watts.

6. *After deliberation* means not only intentionally but also the decision to commit the act has been made after the exercise of reflection and judgment concerning the act. An act committed after deliberation is never one that has been committed in a hasty or impulsive manner.
7. *With intent*—A person acts intentionally or with intent when his conscious objective is to cause the specific result proscribed by the statute defining the offense. It is immaterial whether or not the result is proscribed by the statute defining the offense. It is immaterial whether or not the result actually occurred.
8. *Person*—A human being who had been born and was alive at the time of the homicide act.

Count 2: Murder in the First Degree (F1):

1. On or about the 13th day of August 2018, in the County of Weld, State of Colorado,
2. *Christopher Lee Watts,* unlawfully, feloniously, after deliberation, and
3. with the intent
4. caused the death of a person other than himself;
5. caused the death of Bella Watts.
6. *After deliberation* means not only intentionally but also the decision to commit the act has been made after the exercise of reflection and judgment concerning the act. An act committed after deliberation is never one that has been committed in a hasty or impulsive manner.
7. *With intent*—A person acts intentionally or with intent when his conscious objective is to cause the specific result is proscribed by the statute defining the offense. It is immaterial whether or not the result proscribed by the statute defining the offense. It is immaterial whether or not the result actually occurred.
8. *Person*—A human being who had been born and was alive at the time of the homicide act.

Count 3: Murder in the First Degree (F1):

1. On or about the 13th day of August 2018, in the County of Weld, State of Colorado,
2. *Christopher Lee Watts* unlawfully, feloniously, after deliberation, and
3. with the intent
4. caused the death of a person other than himself;
5. caused the death of Celeste Watts.
6. *After deliberation* means not only intentionally but also the decision to commit the act has been made after the exercise of reflection and judgment concerning the act. An act committed after deliberation is never one which has been committed in a hasty or impulsive manner.
7. *With intent*—A person acts intentionally or with intent when his conscious objective is to cause the specific result is proscribed by the statute defining the offense. It is immaterial whether or not the result proscribed by the statute defining the offense. It is immaterial whether or not the result actually occurred.
8. *Person*—A human being who had been born and was alive at the time of the homicide act.

Count 4: Murder in the First Degree (F1):

1. Between and including the 12th day of August 2018 and the 13th day of August 2018, in the County of Weld, State of Colorado,
2. *Christopher Lee Watts* unlawfully, feloniously, and knowingly
3. caused the death of Bella Watts,
4. a child who had not yet attained twelve years of age and,
5. the defendant was in a position of trust with respect to the victim.
6. *Knowingly*—A person acts knowingly with respect to conduct or to a circumstance described by a statute defining an offense when he is aware that his conduct is of such nature

or that such circumstance exists. A person acts knowingly with respect to a result of his conduct when he is aware that his conduct is practically certain to cause the result.

7. *Position of trust*—one in a position of trust includes any person who is a parent or acting in the place of a parent and charged with any of the parent's rights, duties, or responsibilities concerning a child, or a person including foster care, family care, or institutional care, either independently or through another, no matter how brief at the time of the unlawful act.

Count 5: Murder in the First Degree (F1):

1. Between and including the 12th day of August 2018 and the 13th day of August 2018, in the County of Weld, State of Colorado,
2. *Christopher Lee Watts*, unlawfully, feloniously, and knowingly
3. caused the death of Celeste Watts,
4. a child who had not yet attained twelve years of age and,
5. the defendant was in a position of trust with respect to the victim.
6. *Knowingly*—A person acts knowingly with respect to conduct or to a circumstance described by a statute defining an offense when he is aware that his conduct is of such nature or that such circumstance exists. A person acts knowingly with respect to a result of his conduct when he is aware that his conduct is practically certain to cause the result,
7. *Position of trust*—One in a position of trust includes any person who is a parent or acting in the place of a parent and charged with any of the parent's rights, duties, or responsibilities concerning a child, or a person including foster care, family care, or institutional care, either independently or through another, no matter how brief at the time of the unlawful act.

Count 6: Unlawful Termination of Pregnancy in the First Degree (F2):

1. On or about the 13th day of August 2018, in the County of Weld, State of Colorado,
2. *Christopher Lee Watts,* with the intent to terminate unlawfully the pregnancy of a woman, namely Shanann Watts,
3. feloniously and unlawfully
4. terminated the pregnancy of the woman,
5. Further, the woman died as a result of the unlawful termination of the pregnancy.
6. *With intent*—A person acts intentionally or with intent when his conscious objective is to cause the specific result proscribed by the statute defining the offense. It is immaterial whether or not the result actually occurred.
7. *Pregnancy* means the presence of an implanted human embryo or fetus within the uterus of a woman.
8. *Unlawful termination of pregnancy* means the termination of a pregnancy by any means other than birth or a medical procedure, instrument, agent, or drug for which the consent of the pregnant woman or a person authorized by law to act on her behalf has been obtained, or for which the pregnant woman's consent is implied by law.

Count 7: Tampering with a Deceased Human Body (F3):

1. On or about the 13th day of August 2018, in the County of Weld, State of Colorado,
2. *Christopher Lee Watts,* believing that an official proceeding was pending, in progress, or about to be instituted, and acting without legal right or authority,
3. unlawfully and feloniously
4. willfully destroyed, mutilated, concealed, removed, or altered a human body, part of a human body, or human remains
5. with intent to impair its or their appearance or availability in the official proceedings.

6. *Official proceedings* mean a proceeding heard before any legislative, judicial, administrative, other government agency, or official authorized to hear evidence under oath, including any magistrate, hearing examiner, commissioner, notary, or other person taking testimony or depositions in any such proceedings.
7. *With intent*—A person acts intentionally or with intent when his conscious objective is to cause the specific result proscribed by the statute defining the offense. It is immaterial whether or not the result actually occurred.

Count 8: Tampering with a Deceased Human Body (F3):

1. On or about the 13th day of August 2018, in the County of Weld, State of Colorado,
2. *Christopher Lee Watts*, believing that an official proceeding was pending, in progress, or about to be instituted, and acting without legal right or authority,
3. unlawfully and feloniously
4. willfully destroyed, mutilated, concealed, removed, or altered a human body, part of a human body, or human remains
5. with intent to impair its or their appearance or availability in the official proceedings.
6. *Official proceedings* mean a proceeding heard before any legislative, judicial, administrative, other government agency, or official authorized to hear evidence under oath, including any magistrate, hearing examiner, commissioner, notary, or other person taking testimony or depositions in any such proceedings.
7. *With intent*—A person acts intentionally or with intent when his conscious objective is to cause the specific result proscribed by the statute defining the offense. It is immaterial whether or not the result actually occurred.

Count 9: Tampering with a Deceased Human Body (F3):

1. On or about the 13th day of August 2018, in the County of Weld, State of Colorado,
2. *Christopher Lee Watts*, believing that an official proceeding was pending, in progress, or about to be instituted, and acting without legal right or authority,
3. unlawfully and feloniously
4. willfully destroyed, mutilated, concealed, removed, or altered a human body, part of a human body, or human remains
5. with intent to impair its or their appearance or availability in the official proceedings.
6. *Official proceedings* mean a proceeding heard before any legislative, judicial, administrative, other government agency, or official authorized to hear evidence under oath, including any magistrate, hearing examiner, commissioner, notary, or other person taking testimony or depositions in any such proceedings.
7. *With intent*—A person acts intentionally or with intent when his conscious objective is to cause the specific result proscribed by the statute defining the offense. It is immaterial whether or not the result actually occurred.

The Sentencing

Christopher hadn't thought very far ahead when he offered the plea deal to the DA. He says his head was all mixed up, that he was living in a fog, and he couldn't make sense of what was going on. When his attorneys came up with asking for a plea, Christopher was angry about that. He did not like that. They told him they were trying to save his life. Had he not done a plea deal, he probably would have gotten the death sentence. Of course, the attorneys would go whichever way he decided. Christopher said when they offered the plea agreement to the DA, the DA was very surprised. He did not see it coming.

Penalties

Count 1: Murder in the First Degree (F1):
Shanann Watts: The minimum sentence is life in prison without parole; the maximum sentence is death. Christopher received life in prison without parole.

Count 2: Murder in the First Degree (F1):
Bella Watts: The minimum sentence is life in prison without parole; the maximum sentence is death. Christopher received life in prison without parole.

Count 3: Murder in the First Degree (F1):
Celeste Watts: The minimum sentence is life in prison without parole; the maximum sentence is death. Christopher received life in prison without the possibility of parole.

Count 4: Murder in the First Degree (F1):
Murder in the First Degree—Child Under 12 (Bella Watts), a class one felony.

Christopher received life in prison without the possibility of parole.

Count 5: Murder in the First Degree (F1)
Murder in the First Degree—Child Under 12 (Celeste Watts), a class one felony.

Christopher received life in prison without the possibility of parole.

Count 6: Unlawful Termination of Pregnancy in the First Degree
A class two felony (Nico).

Christopher received 46 years.

Count 7: Tampering with a Deceased Human Body
A class three felony; Shanann Watts.

Christopher received 12 years.

Count 8: Tampering with a Deceased Human Body
A class three felony; Bella Watts.

Christopher received 12 years.

Count 9: Tampering with a Deceased Human Body
A class three felony; Celeste Watts.

Christopher received 12 years.

The judge's face expressed the grief and horror this case brought him. It looked like he tried to make eye contact with Christopher, but of course, Christopher did not look up at him. He probably could feel the judge's eyes on him. The judge said that out of his seventeen years on the bench, this was the worst and most brutal case he had ever presided over. He gave Christopher the maximum that the law would allow, other than death.

CHAPTER 25

The Family

Right before the sentencing, Ronnie, Cindy, and Jamie were allowed to see Christopher for thirty minutes each with someone in the room with them. When Cindy went in to see Christopher, she asked him if he was sure he wanted to plead guilty. She says they yelled at her and said, "Stop asking him those questions or we will shut this shit down right now." They were confused about all that was taking place because nothing was explained to them. They were having to come to terms with the fact that the most heinous thing was putting the girls in those battery tanks. Christopher had done that. Bearing the pain of that alone felt like more than they could handle. However, because of people who contact Cindy saying there is evidence that Christopher's first confession is his real confession, it confused her and she still felt she doesn't know what to believe.

Shanann had many videos online that can be watched. It's evident she liked upscale quality things. Thrive promotes a lifestyle of materialism and having more, more, more. Shanann was good at selling Thrive; she was making 60–70,000 a year plus a car expense free. The pressure to keep up that sort of goal could have been exhausting. She promoted Thrive would make you feel you never had a day off. She may have been materialistic, but she was very driven even more. Several people said she was a natural salesperson, and she could sell anything. She was on Facebook constantly, showing everything. Christopher, on the other hand, was raised by a family of German descent and did not need anything beyond his necessities. In everything she did, he just wanted her to be happy. He never told her no or argued with anything she wanted to buy or do. However, the kindness and thoughtfulness he had for her were not reciprocated. He knew this, and it started to build inside of him.

Two sweet little girls were hardly old enough to even realize there was anything bad in the world. Their life was mom and dad, each other, and playing all day. They caused no harm; they were totally innocent.

Sweet Bella was only four years old. Shanann had put many videos of her online. She seemed a little timid, and the most like her daddy. Christopher described her as a sweet and very soft-spoken little girl. Her grandmother described her as cautious. Her hair was kept short; Cindy said Shanann's mom would cut it so that it would grow back in a little thicker, but she still had baby fine hair. Cindy says it breaks her heart to think about it because Bella wanted long hair, but it would just not grow long. It's heartbreaking her hair was caught on the hatch door as he pushed her little head through the 8" hole.

There is a posted video of Shanann working with Bella on her vision board. Shanann was trying to instill confidence in Bella. She was helping Bella to grow into a confident little girl, and taught her she was beautiful inside and out and smart—something only a mother can do. Had Bella grown up, she would have probably remembered this the rest of her life. She had approval from her mom, something most girls long for but never achieve. The videos also reveal her younger sister helped her gain the confidence to do things she otherwise would be afraid to do.

She sang a song on a video one day about how her dad was her hero.

If Christopher thinks of it now, how much it must hurt. These videos are no doubt a treasure their families can have forever, but these videos show a little girl frozen in time as a four-year-old. Never will they be able to see their faces as they grew from four-years-old to ten, to fifteen, to twenty. These grandparents have suffered so much. The pain they have faced is indescribable—pain that even time cannot dull. Perhaps soon, the media will leave them all alone and allow them to grieve privately. People do not understand how cruel it is. They have not only had to endure their pain from their loss but the pain the media and people who had some kind of a cruel agenda have made things even more difficult.

It almost seems Bella had some sort of a sixth sense. Even though a child, she must have felt something awful was going to happen. Maybe that is the reason she was so cautious and timid. She didn't know how to express those feelings yet; those were things she knew nothing about.

As Christopher put Bella in his truck that morning, it's hard to imagine how scared that little girl must have been. Her whole world as she knew it was falling out from under her. Yet, she had a thread of trust that her dad was going to make it okay. She had no idea at that moment her dad was going to steal her life. What torture it must have been to watch as her father snuffed out her baby sister's life and then see Christopher walked up those stairs to the crude oil battery and drop her sister through a hole on the top. She saw what he did to CeCe and when he came back for her, she asked in her soft little voice if he was going to do the same thing to her. Christopher said he does not think he answered her. Her last words were "Daddy, no!" as he snuffed her life away. Christopher says he hears her gentle voice every day.

The day that Bella was to start school is the day she lost her life. Shanann and the girls already had the clothes they were to wear for the first day of school pick out. They were excited to start school. They were robbed of a future. In good times, Bella would play with her dad, ride on his shoulders, and get piggyback rides. He spent time reading to her and nurturing her. This very sweet soft-spoken little girl was described by many as much as her dad. She loved her sister and the videos show the two of them were friends. The DA said at the sentencing that the girls were put in different tanks so they could not be together even in death, but they are together now with their little brother and their mommy. The strong faith of these two girls assures them that someday, they will all be together.

Celeste, also known as Cece, was just barely three when she was murdered. She was so full of life and energy. Her grandmother described her as fearless and her smile would light up the room. Life was a party for her; she had no real fears. She always had a big smile on her face. Without a doubt, she was her sister's shadow. She was a daddy's girl who loved to ride on his shoulders and show Bella it wasn't scary that high up; that she could do it too. She loved hugs and kisses and loved to tease. Just a week before she was murdered, she took her first trip to the beach. The videos show her fearlessly jumping in the waves and loving the water and sand on her feet, giggling, squealing, and encouraging Bella to join her. On the way to the oil site that fateful morning, she sat curled up with her best friend, her sister. She clung for comfort from the other who needed comfort. Celeste was really still a baby, so pure and innocent.

Shanann probably dreamed for her little girls to grow up and enjoy every phase of life. She would always love their mother-daughter relationship. Shanann was having Christopher's boy; he would have someone to enjoy as he was growing up—the father/son bond he'd had with his dad. However, that was not enough for him then, but now if you were to ask him, he grieves over that loss. There is so much more to this story that Christopher does not even know.

Very impressive is the way we see the love for Shanann and the girls by the Rzuceks. It is heart-wrenching to watch their grief and to only imagine the daily pain they must be in. It is unimaginable that Frank Rzucek has had to ask people who are harassing and making things worse for them to leave them alone.

They never got to tell their family goodbye as their bodies could not even be shown. The crude oil the girls were in and the extent of decomposition the bodies of Shanann and the girls made it impossible to give them the usual funeral where their bodies could be shown.

CHAPTER 26

Prison Life

> "We are not the same persons this year as last, nor are those we love. It is a happy chance if we, changing, continue to love the changed person."
>
> —W. Somerset Maugham

The night after the sentencing, plans were made to take Christopher to Weld County Jail. Christopher was in the Colorado prison for 7 and 1/2 weeks during which time he was threatened, yelled at by the other inmates and told ways he could kill himself. They would scream almost constantly at him for a while until as he says they either lost interest or since he had no reaction, they realized they couldn't get to him, so they stopped. Had they been able to get to him though, they would have most definitely killed him.

He was on suicide watch, so he was stripped of everything except a paper gown. He had not even a pillow or blanket, only a small pad to lay on a cement floor. He was in a state of extreme trauma from what had happened and nothing still made sense to him. Because of that and because he could still feel a dark spirit inside of him, he says he was not able to remember very much about what happened. Christopher prayed and asked God to please remove him from this prison so he didn't have to live in constant fear.

Around the first part of December, the guards got Christopher late one night to put him in a van and handcuffed him to an inside pole in the van. He realized he was being moved to another prison.

There was a Colorado prison he had heard so much about; he prayed that was not where they were taking him. He had been told it was one of the most feared prisons in Colorado. He knew if they took him there, he would not survive. Sure enough, they pulled into the very prison he was so afraid of. He had resolved with God though that if this is what he wanted for him, he had no right to ask for anything else. He knew there was a huge price to pay for what he had done.

After a few minutes, he realized they had just stopped at this prison so they could all use the facilities there. After about twenty minutes, they had resumed their trip. They drove all night and most of the next day into the evening. He had no idea still where they were taking him. It was nighttime when they pulled into Waupun Wisconsin; the trip had been fifteen hours long; this was to be his home possibly for the rest of his life. He knew nothing about Dodge Correctional Institute but definitely would be learning. As they pulled into the town, he could see it was a very small town; nothing like what he had come from. He didn't mind coming to Wisconsin. He was far from his family in either place.

There isn't a prison that's nice to be in. The guards, however, seemed better in Wisconsin than they were in Colorado. He's not treated badly by them.

The food is tolerable but sometimes, Christopher craves things like ice cream or pizza and Shanann's spaghetti sauce. Shanann was a very good cook. How different his life could be right now had he made different choices; he thinks about that every day. He remembers sitting at home on a cold night with Shanann and the girls enjoying a meal and playing with the girls. He can't help but think where did it all go so wrong or why did he think it was so wrong.

He was given a handbook of the prison as soon as he got there, and he is to keep it the entire time he is there. Something in the book that gave him a reality check was the part about *Family Illness and Funeral*. It dawned on him that if he is there for the rest of his life and a family member passes away or becomes seriously ill, he will not be able to visit or go to a funeral. If a chaplain approves, videos of funerals may be sent for viewing. This shook him to his core, and he dreads for those days to come. He realizes he had everything and lost everything; he actually threw everything away.

The unit Christopher is housed in is called a pod. There are about seventeen men in the pod. Most of them are handicapped. They are there together because they are close to the infirmary, and many are in wheelchairs. He's with some inmates that have been in prison ever since they were children. They committed crimes when they were younger, and some went from juvenile incarceration to adult facilities. Most are inmates who do not talk about their crimes, for the most part. Some of them are there for only eight weeks for observation and then moved to an area of the prison that's most suited for them. Christopher does not talk about his crime with anyone in the prison. In fact, he will not talk about his crime with much anyone other than his sister, a friend, and recently, with this author.

There was a murder and kidnapping crime in Wisconsin recently that was committed by Jake Patterson. He received two life sentences for the murders he committed. Christopher had hoped he would cross his path because as a twenty-one-year-old, he has a lot of time to think about and to deal with what he did. Jake ended up in the cell right next to Christopher, so hopefully, he says he will be able to reach him.

Christopher is in his cell for most of the day. He now has a recreational time when on good weather days, he gets to go outside for forty minutes. He plays basketball and says it's nice just to be in the sun and enjoy a breath of fresh air.

They have roll call at 6:45 followed by breakfast. Lunch is served at 11:30, then dinner at 3:30. There are no snacks. They go to the commissary once every two weeks where they can buy extras such as toothpaste, deodorant, and personal items. One of the hardest things to get used to is no privacy. There is no freedom in prison.

For holidays and birthdays, he might be able to purchase a card he can write in and send. He buys those things with commissary money. He says he has already lost the knowledge of what things cost out of prison.

Christopher will never be at a birthday party again, have birthday cake, or enjoy going out to dinner with his wife for her birthday or their anniversary. He misses things such as washing his car, mowing the lawn, or feeling the rain or snow on his skin. He'll never go swimming again or grocery shopping. He'll never go golfing or go to a car race with his dad. Holidays are not recognized at the prison, so he will never again enjoy or look forward to celebrating an upcoming event. He will never have another love.

Christmas of 2018, only four months from the murders, was an extremely lonely time. He did not have a Christmas tree, didn't get to take his girls for sledding, didn't play Santa Claus, and didn't trim the tree with his family. A hard thing for him is realizing Bella would have turned five that month. How much was lost!

Most of his days are spent reading. When he is not reading, he is usually writing letters. He still receives an enormous amount of mail; most he will throw away; some he will answer. He has no desire into getting involved in the love letters he receives. He tries to stay busy so he will not think about time, but it's the nights that are so lonely.

He has not received any mail from his former mistress Nikki and hopes he will not. He says he hopes she was able to find peace and move on with her life. However, he would like for her to know he is sorry she lost her job and had to move.

He spends a lot of time looking out his window and reminiscing about what was. He can't believe what he had wasn't enough for him. He would give anything to have it all back.

On June 22, 2019, Ronnie Watts was able to visit Christopher for the first time since the murders. He had meetings in Chicago, and his boss told him to take that opportunity to go see his son in Wisconsin. Both Christopher and Ronnie were elated at the possibility of the meeting. They spent three hours together in a face-to-face meeting.

When a visitor goes into the prison, they can take up to twenty dollars in quarters with them. The visitation room has vending machines all along the wall. Ronnie bought Christopher a hamburger and heated it in a microwave nearby. He bought a package of Doritos and a Red Mountain Dew (Christopher's favorite). He bought a Kit Kat bar, a Milky Way bar, and a Nestle Crunch bar. Christopher devoured all of them. When their three hours were over, a guard came and told them their time was up. The goodbyes were the hardest part of all. Ronnie said he and Christopher both held it together. As Ronnie walked out of the building where Christopher is housed, however, he broke down and completely lost it. Never would he have thought he would be visiting the son he raised in a prison, especially the fact he was in the prison for killing his whole family.

On June 25, 2019, Lawyers for Frank and Sandi Rzucek called Christopher to discuss the probate with him. Christopher signed absolutely everything over to the Rzuceks. When the conversation with the lawyers was over, according to Christopher, Frank Rzucek came to the phone and said, "Thank you, Chris" to which Christopher replied, "You are welcome, and I love you guys." Frank responded, "Love you." What a wonderful freeing thing that is! For the Rzuceks still to be able to love or forgive him is such a huge thing—beyond anything most of us could picture if it were us. If they have, but maybe it's at least one step toward that. The forgiveness of what he did is not for Christopher; it's for the Rzuceks. Christopher said he went back to his cell and cried and cried; he never thought he would ever hear those words again. It brought to his mind, however, what a senseless thing he did. It's been said that to harbor unforgiveness toward someone is like drinking poison and expecting it to kill the other person.

It's all very sad to see where he has come from and where he is now. Many would say he deserves less than he gets. However, if he was oppressed by a dark spirit, does he deserve another chance? He is not seeking an appeal right now, but should he? I will leave that answer up to you as the reader.

Ronnie and Cindy recently received the wallet he had on him at the time he was arrested. He had $13.00 in it. Is this a coincidence?

CHAPTER 27

Christopher's True and Final Confession and His Testimony

"All acts performed in the world begin in the imagination."

He felt so alone. There was really no one left in his life, and he had done that to himself. He kept asking himself over and over again—why would he do such a thing? What was in him that he allowed this to take his life from him by taking his family's lives? He knew had there been any doubt it was a dark spirit he was dealing with, he for sure found out on August 15 that it had to be something dark because he came face to face with it. Since he had never believed in that sort of thing before, he realized no one else was going to believe it either. Did he dare step out in faith and tell his story? He made the decision to just not say anything. He thought of asking for a Catholic priest. He had read somewhere before about exorcisms through the Catholic church. The night the dark spirit left him, he believed there were two of them. He talked to them, saw them, and knew what had confronted him. They appeared to him, he says, in the form of his maternal grandparents.

Some things in this bank may seem repetitive because of the order in which Christopher told during the research. The following are some of the main letters he wrote. I did not post all of the letters but some of the main letters. There are things in the letters that can shock people. With apologies, this is the way Christopher wanted to tell his true confession and his truth. Those who know him know he is not confrontational or outgoing to be able to tell everyone, but this book is his way of "putting all the missing pieces of the puzzle together" and a way for him to get it all out. He says there is nothing left to tell after this. He prays this will start to bring healing, especially to his family and Shanann's. He asks everyone whom he has touched with this tragedy to please forgive him. He says forgiveness is all he can ask for but knows it is a big request.

The first letter starts with the letter he is writing to the Rzuceks. He did not send them this letter but is using this platform to talk to them. He hopes they can take this letter to heart.

These letters from Christopher Watts contain the things that Christopher did not share with the FBI or even his family. This is the platform in which Christopher was the most comfortable to tell all; the only way he would tell all. Included here is also his testimony that was promised to be told for him, in his words exactly. I would tell it on his behalf, but I wanted to tell it with his words exactly. His testimony is riveting, and he tells it to you, the readers. The letters may contain grammar errors and typos, but I have given you the content word for word from Christopher. There are a couple of letters that he sent me something to insert into the letters he had already written.

> Dear Frank, Sandi, and Frankie:
>
> I'm sorry for the pain and utter anguish that I've caused your family. This is a travesty that I never thought could or would occur. Shanann, Bella, Celeste, and Nico are four beautiful souls that will live on forever in Heaven and in our hearts. I know you must hate me for what I've done and honestly, I would be surprised if you didn't. This is a moment in my life that I will never be able to undo and it rips me apart every single day. I see their beautiful faces, their beautiful smiles everywhere I look. When I read to them at night, I can feel them snuggled up next to me like we were at home. I want you to know that I still consider you my Father-in-law, my Mother-in-law and

my Brother-in-law, and that I love you all yesterday, today and forever. I pray that one day you can have forgiveness for me, but most of all I pray you can have compassion on my family. They are hurting so bad from all of this and I know they would love to reconcile if that is something you would allow to happen. I pray every day that both families can meet at the grave-site, hold hands, pray and talk about great times. Share about birthdays, and visits and funny FaceTime conversations. I know this prayer hasn't been answered yet, but I know God is working this request of mine in your hearts. Forgiveness is the start of healing and I pray you can start that process with my family.

Love, Chris

Dear Cheryln, April 4, 2019

Hello again! I hope you are doing well! Yes, I am still on Protective Confinement and I'm supposed to hear back from the Security Director tomorrow to see how much longer. I've never had any trouble with anyone here, but the Institution is just being cautious. The Security Director doesn't want anyone to see all the media coverage and then come after me. I'm in my cell over 23 hours a day, but I know God is here with me. He has given me a lot of extra time alone with Him over the past month. Also, He has opened my eyes to a few things I was holding onto in my heart that I didn't acknowledge to myself.

In answer to your question, no I've never had a psychological exam. If I were to see a doctor during my case, then anything I said could've been subpoena by the court or DA. And the Asperger's symptoms do make a lot of sense and I can match up a bunch of instances in my life that correspond with it too. It would've been much easier to diagnose me with it when I was 11 years old instead of 33 years old. Next time I talk to the psychological department, I will ask what it takes to get an evaluation.

The media is horrible with what they put out there sometimes. Is my diet really that exciting? The sale of my house was pushed back to July before the investigators came to see me, I have a civil case against me (wrongful death lawsuit), and in the matter of the Probate Court, the attorneys thought the house could be sold at a profit and the money would go to the wrongful death suit and help Shanann's family. After evaluating with the realtor, she told Shanann's parents that the house wouldn't sell for more than what was owed. So, then Chase Bank pushed the auction to July 17. It had nothing to do with the investigators, just another example of the truth vs "media truths."

I received notification that you are on my visitor list now. I look forward to meeting you for the first-time face to face. From what I am told the only items you can bring into the visiting room are quarters, $20.00 worth, for the vending machines. I will be allowed to get a radio and TV soon, but CD's I believe are contraband because they can be made into a weapon.

I like your question, what does it mean to die out to Christ daily? To me, that means to look at His character and model yourself as He was when He walked the earth. "Jesus is the stone which the builders rejected, but that same stone has become the chief cornerstone. Whosoever shall fall upon that stone shall be broken; but whosoever on it shall fall it shall grind him to powder (Luke 20:17-18 paraphrased)." To die to Christ daily is to fall upon the stone daily. What breaks when your fall is your allegiance to self, lust, and pride. I look at things I do daily and always ask, "Should I think about that?" or "Should I be reading something like this?" We are not all perfect, but we can all make a diligent effort to be better every day.

I know a lot of people, especially inmates, will be able to relate to my testimony and be able to see the trust, the hope, the peace, and the love in Christ. I hope people on the outside can be able to relate and be able to look at their own lives, and receive the Lord into their hearts. I believe if roles were reversed and I had read a book about this happening to someone, I would have come to the Lord! It would have hit home and show me what was important in life.

My grandmother is in a nursing home. She is 93 and has dementia. I know it's hard for my dad somedays to go see her even though she doesn't recognize him. He had me on speaker phone the other day and she could hear my voice. I said hi to her, and my dad said she smiled really big! That made my day!

I hope you are doing well and I look forward to hearing from you soon.

God Bless,
Chris

The following letter he wrote tells of coming face-to-face with the dark spirits he says were pursuing him. In this letter, Christopher refers to wearing a "turtle suit." Turtle Suite: An anti-suicide smock, Bam Bam suit, or suicide gown is a tear resistant, single-piece outer garment that is generally used to prevent a hospitalized, incarcerated, or otherwise detained individual from forming a noose with the garment to commit suicide.

Dear Cheryln,

Hello again! I hope you're doing well! I think that Wisconsin weather can compare to Colorado's weather as it can vary so much from one day to another. I think Spring hit for a week then summer for a day and now it's been a mixture of fall/winter the last few days. I would say I'd rather be cold than hot, especially in this little shoebox I'm in! Ok, let me start right into the Weld County Jail experience.

I arrive at the Weld County Jail the night of August 15. I get booked, finger printed, and my picture taken and then escorted by a deputy and two technical officers to the unit I'm staying in. One of the officers as he's slamming my door shut says "Good Luck." I'm standing there alone in the darkness. The only light was that of a dim night light used for guards to check on you. I'm standing there wondering; is this my normal for the rest of my life? I lay down in the bunk in my turtle suite (as I'm in their suicide watch pod) and just stare off into the darkness. Nothing is adding up and it feels like none of this can be real. To my astonishment I look in the front corner of my cell and see two dark figures standing there. I thought "OK, this is my eyes playing tricks on me," so I closed them and opened my eyes again and, yet, they are still there. As I focus more intently, I can see one is male and one is female. The male is in a black suit and the female is in a black dress with a Victorian style hat, both their wardrobes looked vintage. Their faces were ash colored and almost familiar, until the familiar feeling turned into a sure thing. This was my grandfather and grandmother on my Mom's side, their faces being unmistakable now, I almost want to move closer to them when their eyes opened in unison. They motioned me toward them, but I was frozen and knew I didn't want to go toward them. Their eyes were as red as blood, crimson. This eerie feeling came over me as I had four eyes staring back at me as if piercing my soul in a bad way. The only problem was, I felt like I was in a trance and had to keep eye contact, somehow, they would not let my eyes move off of them. I felt like I needed to go over to them, as the one motioned his hand for me to come near, but all of a sudden something broke the trance. I looked away and looked back and the corner of my cell was empty. The pair was gone. I obviously couldn't sleep much after this event, thinking this type of visit would only get worse if I let my guard down. I knew without any doubt this was part of what was inside of me. It completely freaked me out! I realized I did have a demon inside of me. Now what was I going to do? I stayed on this unit for a week until I was moved to restrictive housing unit or "the Hole." The suicide unit was quiet but I soon learned the hole was not the same. As soon as I entered the unit, the screams and shouts pierced my soul. Out of the twenty cells, I'm sure 90% of them were screaming at me, and the barraging remarks raged from "I'm going to rip your face off" to "Kill Yourself" to "I'm going to fuck your wife in the afterlife." All of these comments felt like daggers hitting my heart. This went on for weeks and I finally drew the conclusion that this must be what Hell feels like. The screams, the pounding on the walls had to stop at some point, right? They eventually did either by them losing interest or the fact I wasn't responding to anything they said. It was like restless animals at the zoo. If your head isn't messed up going into the hole, it will be coming out.

During this time is when I started reading the Bible. I didn't know if I should even pick the Bible up because I thought I was too far gone because of what I had done. I was lost, broken, and I even listened to the other inmates informing me the different ways I could kill myself while in my cell. Their words were "if you don't do it yourself, we will do it for you, we'd be glad to." With these thoughts flowing through my head, I didn't think God could forgive me for what I'd done. But, I picked up the Bible and started reading because there had to be a message in this book that could help me persevere.

I finished the Bible in about two weeks. Some days were harder to concentrate than others due to the noise in the pod and the horrible letters that were flooding in. Not all of the letters were terrible. There were a few that had encouraging messages and even pointed out scriptures in the Bible for me to commit to memory. These Bible verses showed the mercy and loving kindness of God. After about five weeks in the "Hole," I was moved into the RS pod to give me a little extra movement. My attorney team would come to visit me 3—4 times a week and I can't thank them enough. They were my only human contact; they treated me not like a client but like a friend. They didn't treat me with hostility, but with compassion and would be there in a moment's notice if I was struggling with something. On November 5, my attorney team flew my mom, dad and sister out to talk to me via video monitor because the next day, I was going to plead guilty to all charges against me. I got to spend thirty minutes with each member of my family individually. These were some hard heart felt moments, and I cherish the time I was able to spend with them at that moment. How does a person look their mother in the eyes who is hurting more than can be imagined and tell them you are guilty of killing their precious granddaughters, but of no explanation as to the reasons why. My family, although unable to speak without tears, were stronger people than I ever realized and loved me no matter what horrible things I had done. I will hold close to me those moments forever.

After the visit was over, I was swiftly moved to another pod. I'm guessing the visit was being watched by other officials in the jail and they felt it was prudent to move me to a more secure location if I was taking a plea deal the next day. This next pod was called "close watch" and it was just me and a deputy (hence the name close watch). This was a dry cell and padded and kind of felt like a shoe box as was 5.5 ft wide. I stayed in this cell from November 6 to November 26, and the fact that it was just me and another deputy gave me an opportunity to talk to them. Some could care less than to have a conversation with me, but others did. When I was reading my Bible, they would ask me what part I was reading and that would spark up a conversation about the Word. I was amazed how much I had retained from reading the Bible and it felt good to talk with someone that is a believer just like me. One deputy was telling me about some miracles that had happened in his life; in particular when his son's great grandfather was leaving a single rose in sporadic places just to let his son know he was there with him. I'm not doing the story justice but *wow!* It was spectacular! When I returned from my sentencing hearing on November 19. I was very emotional as you can imagine. The deputy could tell I was having a hard time holding it together and asked if he could pray with me. I was shocked by this but was completely honored at the same time. Picture it; a deputy in his uniform and an inmate in his oranges. Two entities that are usually at enmity with one another, praying through a cell door! Remarkable! After he was done praying, I took over and read Psalm 33:13–22 (which I wanted to read during my sentencing hearing but I thought it better I didn't) and said a little prayer for my wife and kids and everyone affected by this tragedy. I was in tears; he was in tears. It was a very moving moment.

In the end, I can look back at every pod I was housed in and relate it to a stage in my life: 1) Realization—realizing who I am and that I am nothing without God in my life. 2) Sanctification—God was filling my soul with his Word to make me ready to spread His grace and mercy 3) Salvation—I gave myself, my life and my soul completely to the Lord. 4) Consummation—God has taken absolute control and He is keeping me on the straight path that leads to life everlasting.

The Weld County jail was a rollercoaster; full of ups and downs and twist and turns, but it is also the spot of my Salvation. When Jesus said I have come "to preach deliverance to the captives" (Luke 4:18) that rings true if you're physically captive and/or spiritually captive. I went through a lot of dark times in that jail, but Jesus showed me a light at the end of the tunnel. And "that is the true light that lights every man that comes into the World (John 1:9)."

My mom asked me if you could use the letters I wrote to Bella, Celeste, Nico, and Shanann back in December, and I think that will be a good idea. The HLN wanted to use them as part of the documentary to show part of my character, but I believe God didn't want them used there. He wants the book to be the platform they are used on, so I will give you the green light to go ahead and use them.

You wanted me to give you some detail into the life of me, Shanann, and the girls so here we go. It seemed like the perfect life, I had a beautiful wife, two beautiful daughters, a good job, a home . . . everything felt like it fits. My life and Shanann's life revolved around Bella and Celeste. We would do anything to make sure they were healthy and happy. We worked as a team the best we could, even when it was evident the girls only wanted me or only wanted her. I loved picking them up from school! When I walked into Celeste's classroom our eyes would meet, a huge smile would shine from her face and she would sprint over to me, almost tackling me in the process. Bella would usually be on the playground, so I would usually have to go into the playset to corral her. Once in the car, Bella would find their car ride snacks and disburse one to Celeste and then I would buckle them up. The car ride home would consist of a lot singing to "Moana," "Frozen," or "Trolls" soundtracks. I loved hearing them sing, and they loved telling me to stop singing! I guess I didn't sing that good. Once home, they would run to Shanann and then eat their dinner. Now shower time! They usually got me so wet from the bathtub that the shower was a welcome change. They loved washing their hair like big girls. Afterward, Shanann would come up and help lotion them up and get their pajamas on. Then it was off for a snack, a cartoon, brush their teeth, inhalers/meds and time for bed. Usually, Bella wanted Shanann and Celeste wanted me. Celeste picked about every book in her room some nights and had so many questions. I loved it! She was such the little character! Bella would be waiting for me to sing her a little song (You are my sunshine) and get one extra kiss from me. Once in bed, Shanann worked on her phone the rest of the night while we watched our shows on TV. There wasn't a whole lot of conversation going on and that's my fault, too, for not speaking up. The weekend usually consisted of getting the girls outside as much as we could as they were very active. I would take them to the backyard to play on their playset, play some tee ball, or pull them around the neighborhood in their wagon. At night on the weekend, we would usually take them to the splash pad because they absolutely loved water! When we would go to the pool, it would be a chore to get them to go home! The smiles on their faces were worth every second though! As I write this, I can see I didn't put much effort in my marriage other than being the best Dad I could be, and performing my husbandly duties (cleaning, etc.). I did as much as I could to keep Shanann from being distracted from her work that I forgot to focus on her. We did everything as a family: pumpkin patch at Halloween plus all of us wearing costumes, I even wore the costume to the girls Halloween party at their school. Christmas was always fun cause I dressed up like Santa and the girls would absolutely love it! Their birthday parties would be a little over the top, but we would do anything for Bella and Celeste. Shanann and I did go out from time to time, usually for birthday and anniversaries. My favorite memories of her are the early ones, like: the beach photos we took while on the trip where I proposed to her in 2011. Her smile was captivating and we were having a blast. Another would be obviously the wedding. I'll never forget her walking down the aisle, looking flawless, and seeing her look into my eyes when she walked up to me and saying "Breathe." She literally took my breath away. That love never died yet the focus of that love went toward the kids.

I can say with a certainty that I always loved Shanann and always will, but there was always that lingering fear that I would do something wrong. The verse 1 John 4:18 comes to mind "There is no fear in love, but perfect love casts out fear . . ." because how can you fear what you love? Or how can you love what you fear? The two feelings are at enmity with one another, polar opposites if you will. I seemed to always walk on egg shells around Shanann. There was uneasiness and careful/ fearful planning with every step I took. That is not what love should feel like, but I never communicated that to her. When I was with Bella and Celeste, being a Dad, there was no fear, just overwhelming love. It would have been just how my personality is structured to be nervous/ submissive around Shanann, but that's still not how love should be. Finishing off the rest of the verse "because fear has torment. He that fears is not made perfect in love" resonates with me because fear is nothing but torment for the soul. That's what the fear eventually did to me; it broke me down spiritually, emotionally, and mentally. Was I aware of it? I don't think so. It's like the frog that was put in a pot full of water, and slowly, the water turned to a boil and the frog boiled to death. I didn't see what was happening until it was too late and that mistake cost me the chance to grow old with my family for the rest of my physical life! Love is a resounding warmth that envelops your entire being. We should all strive for that because fear should never conquer love. Love is from God! When we are made in His image it was in the image of love and that quality is what will overcome the world!

I think I will end this letter here! I hope you are doing well and your entire family too! Take care and God Bless!

Chris

Dear Cheryln,

Hello Again! I hope this letter finds you doing well!

Thank you for the two songs you sent, "Who You Say I Am" and "Be Still." I'm sure the song will take on a new meaning once I can hear them with music although the lyrics are good all by itself.

You ask if there's anything I haven't talked about in regards to Nikki, honestly, I'm not sure what I've said and what I haven't, but this is what I know. She had a small group of friends that she didn't tell me about. They were dark and did some dark things. She didn't tell me a lot about them until the end. She had been involved in an abusive relationship a few years before, and after that, she removed most of her social media (not sure if she was hiding from someone). She took medications (never told me what for though). She came over to my house two times July 4 and July 14. I didn't have to work in July 4, so I stayed at Nikki's house in July 3. That morning, I missed tons of phone calls from Shanann. I went outside to call her and when I called her back, she was obviously furious! I went back inside and told Nikki I was going home. She was in the shower, and I told her I was going home and I had decided to stay home the rest of the day, which made Nikki upset (I think this was the first time she realized in her head that she wasn't #1 in my life.). Later, though, Nikki came over anyway and we went over a protein eating plan for me. She didn't look around the house much on that visit. On July 14, we were heading back from the Shelby Museum and stopped by my house before we went to get something to eat. While in the house, she was playing with Deeter and he led her upstairs and she saw a lot of pictures of Bella, Celeste, and Shanann (I was downstairs at the time). She came back downstairs with this frozen dazed and confused look on her face (probably now realizing for the first time in her head the family life I lived and the family that would be broken to pieces). I walked over and took her to the couch and we laid on the couch and she said "You have all this, more than most people, and we are doing this? Why are we doing this? Are you willing to give all of this up? Is your relationship with your wife that bad? I told her "Shanann and I were drifting apart and we didn't talk anymore (I'm not sure if I believed that fully, but I can see the deficiencies in our relationship today)." Then I also said "Shanann and I were actively trying to have a baby before her and I met." Nikki immediately freaked out! She yelled and said our relationship (mine and Shanann's) couldn't have been that bad if Shannan and I were trying to conceive. She was so angry and stormed out to her truck. She sat out there for about thirty minutes texting me while I was inside my house. I somehow calmed her down (Nikki repeatedly reminded me I was the only guy she had ever met that tried to fix problems, smooth out issues and talk about things. Ironically, I never did that with Shanann. Maybe I thought she wouldn't listen! Thinking about that made me somewhat sick to my stomach). After all of that, Nikki still invited me over to her house like nothing had happened between us. She said "I got mad because I thought I could give you a son, and when you told me you and your wife were trying, that made me upset." She said "that would be a first for you that we could have together." After all of that, we went to the drag races in Bandimare in July 21, then we went camping in the mountains in July 28 and 29. When I was at the airport leaving for North Carolina, she sent me a text "use this time to fix the issues with your wife and enjoy time with your family." The first night I was there, we were at Shanann's parents house. I texted Nikki and told her I would not be able to call her, only text with her. Nikki responded: "Why not, are you with her?" I thought she wanted me to spend time with my family. It all of a sudden became about her. I realize now if I had allowed that to be a turning point for me, it could have changed everything. I couldn't see that then and being able to see that clearly now, makes me hurt inside. I was not able to make that choice then; I really wasn't; whatever had a hold of my mind did not allow me to go to making those kinds of rational decisions. Obviously, Nikki was insisting that I make more time with her no matter what. The first night I was there was the first night

I gave Shanann the Oxycodone. I thought it would cause her to have a miscarriage. I had looked up on the internet and read about it and 80 mg of Oxycodone should have caused her to lose the baby. The next 8 days, I ignored Shanann every night. I did this so I could disappear and talk to Nikki for hours. It was obvious during these conversations she didn't want me to spend time with my family or try to make things better with Shanann because she had nothing good at all to say about my family life. This twisted my head. I knew I should be giving them attention but was unable to. I felt like a programed robot. Things started to not make sense to me.

When I returned to Colorado, I saw Nikki after work (I went to her place in my work truck), any hope of repairing my marriage pretty much was over when Nikki gave me a key to her place. I saw this as a pretty big step because, what woman gives another man a key to her house without wanting to take a big step in the relationship? I had told her that Shanann and I were going to get a separation and that the marriage was going to end, but that she was still actively trying to fix our marriage. I think this was the day I realized I had to do something because I couldn't have my family and her at the same time. The last time I saw Nikki was August 11 when we went out to eat. That's when Shanann was in Arizona and I had gotten a babysitter that night which is something I never did before while Shanann was away. I told her I was going to a game with some guys because I had won the lottery at work. Nikki and I talked about our future plans, and she told me about apartments she had found for me. She said she was looking at apartments that were big enough for me and the kids. She said after I had my own apartment, we could move at a slower pace and treat our relationship as a normal relationship. This told me her main objective was to get me away from my family specifically Shanann. She said she felt we had been taking things really fast since we were together pretty much every night possible in June and July. She had started telling her friends about me and I could tell she was making plans for our future together. I don't know why because I had a beautiful wife and beautiful kids at home. There was nothing she could offer me that I wasn't able to get from home, except I could be myself around her. That is not a reason to get rid of my family. Shanann did not do anything for me to get rid of her.

I don't know if all of this is common knowledge or not, but that's regarding Nikki from me. Everything else is probably in discovery. I hope this sheds some light on that relationship. I pray that she has peace now and she can find peace in the Lord. Everyone involved in the tragedy has had their lives turned upside down, and I pray they will seek the Lord with all their heart to get back on the right path.

OK enough of Nikki relationship! Let's get to forgiveness night October 1, 2018. I know that was the night because the Kansas City Chiefs were playing Sunday Night Football on that night. I remember watching that game that night, it's weird what our minds can remember about certain nights and give us some clues.

The pod I'm in is called "RS" and attached to the cell, there's a room with a table, TV, and phone. I've only been in this cell for two days so all this is very new to me. I'm sitting at the table reading a book when the news comes on around 9:30 pm, then I hear my name. I look up and see myself sitting in a courtroom in an orange jumpsuit, never thinking in my entire life I would ever see that image. Then, I see a picture of my family on the screen. That is the first time I've seen a picture of my family since August 15. All the newspaper articles were cut out of the newspapers so I wouldn't see them.

Lockdown was at 10 pm and I went in my cell and laid on my bunk in the dark with the picture of my family frozen in my head. I see Bella, I see Celeste, I see Shanann. I see their bright shining faces, their radiant cheeks, their beautiful smiles. Now more memories flood my brain: memories of the pool when both girls would jump into my arms and I would fly them around, memories of snowstorms when I would pull the girls around in a sled, memories of the wedding when I see Shanann walking down the aisle and seeing her standing right in front of me looking absolutely stunning. Memories of Celeste tackling me every time I picked her up from school (the smile she gave me every time when she saw me was priceless). Memories of Bella's first-time seeing fireworks, memories of being a family. These images came at me like tidal waves, flooding my mind with the love that I once had and piercing my soul knowing that they were gone, and I'm the one that took them away. I longed to hold my family in my arms again, to read one more bedtime story, to give another goodnight kiss, to hold my son for the first time, to sing one more song in the car, to be a dad, to be a husband . . . one more time.

I rolled over in my bunk onto my knees and cried out to the Lord, "Please take this pain away, take the guilt. How did I let this happen? How did I let it get this far? I cried out this pain is too great for me to bear, I can't handle it, I can't bear it alone! I'm sorry for the pain I've caused, please take this guilt, this shame that I feel and help me follow you. Heal my heart, cleanse my soul and help me follow you. *Please forgive me!* You're my Lord and Savior, and I want to do *your* will." At that moment, I felt a hand touch the top of my head; it didn't startle me, it didn't scare me, what it did was overwhelm me with so much emotion I had never ever felt before. I couldn't stop crying. I looked over in the corner of my cell and I promise you I saw my grandmother again! She opened her eyes and they were crimson red, and she motioned for me to come over to her. I cried until I though my chest was going to come out. I physically could feel the pain. I knew the demon had come out of me and I had been forgiven. That hand that touched me was God's hand and

He made the demon flee. He healed me that night with His divine Spirit. That night changed my life and set me on a course that I will never forget. Yes, I would love to be a free man, but no I don't deserve to be. I want to pay my price for what I did to all those who loved me.

These verses from the Bible Lamentations best describes that night: "I called upon your name O Lord, out of the low dungeon. You have heard my voice: hide not your ear at my breathing at my cry. You drew near in the day that I called upon you: You said, 'Fear Not' O Lord, you have pleaded the causes of my soul, you have redeemed my life (Lamentations 3:55-5, ERV)."

My hand is starting to get tired, haha!

I pray that God will use me and what I've gone through to help countless people all over the world with the words that we shall write.

I know I've shared a lot of information in this letter and I believe you can use some for my testimony as well. The more questions you ask the more the gears in my brain start turning.

I hope this letter finds you in good spirits and doing well. Take care and God Bless! I'll talk to you soon!

Chris

Dear Cheryln June 17, 2019

Hey! I hope this letter finds you in great spirits and growing in God's grace every day. I'm sorry your mountain trip was so soggy, but I know it had to be great to be out in God's creation experiencing His energy, power, and blessings. That's where Jesus did most, if not all, of His sermons to the multitudes, He could draw from the Father when he was teaching the Gospel.

Thank you for sharing John 15! I think we all have a calling on our lives, some are different than others, but all work for the glory of God. "And we know that all things work together for good to them that love God, to them who are the called to His purpose (Romans 8:28, ERV)." God doesn't need to use us but He wants to use us for the growing of the Kingdom and disciples here on earth. The calling He has on my life is not fully known yet, but slowly it is coming into the light.

In regards to the fruit that we bear, that deals directly to whether we are listening to the mind of the Spirit or the carnal mind. The carnal mind is enmity against God, but the spirit mind is one with God. Going against God is what separates us from Him and gets us cut off the branch. Being without the Vine we go out and venture on our own. That leads to self-sufficiency and pride, which leads to vanity and self-exaltation, all things or traits the carnal mind loves. We go down this road too much and this will eventually lead to a lfe consumed in depression and hopelessness. However, living in the mind of the Spirit helps us yield so much fruit that His reservoir of joy inside of us spills out to everyone around us. The good fruit we bear the more we manifest a life of Christ in our everyday actions. We can leave the darkness that consumed us and reach further to the light that calls us. That's my hope for everyone that is stuck in the carnal mindset!

As far as Shanann's friend that was at the house that day, I have nothing against her. She spent a lot of time with Shanann in Arizona and knew that Shanann was upset at me and probably told her about the marital problems.

When she didn't hear from Shanann the next day she knew something was up, as she knew Shanann always had her phone. Her actions at my house were that of a concerned friend who believe I had done something, or caused my wife's depression over the weekend. She caused the police to come back a few minutes after they left to search the house and she set up the news crews to come the day after. She was always nice to me when she came over so, like I said she was just a concerned friend. The YouTube presence I know nothing about. Shanann's friend was a reserved person that Shanann encouraged her to put herself out there more selling Thrive. She wasn't as shy as me, but she wasn't as outgoing as Shanann when it came to direct sales. Shanann was her leader, and she looked up to Shanann. I want to tell her I'm sorry for what I put you through, and thank you for being a faithful friend to Shanann. I hope you find peace and contentment in your life going forward.

I never knew anything about the Child Protective Services claims. This report about Shanann only being allowed around the kids 90 minutes a day, was something that was never made aware to me. If it were true I would think I would have been notified. I will admit I was in the dark when it came to a lot of issue, but I just can't see that being veiled from my vision. I guess there is a CPS claim out there, from what my parents tell me. [This claim is not true] And a court date, but I was not in the loop on this if there is any validity. When I worked on the weekends, Shanann was with the kids by herself. She took the kids to school early during the week because she liked to keep a schedule and get the day going early. She used the time alone to work the Thrive business and I would go pick up the girls when I got home from work. There are so many things that don't make sense that people are grasping at that have no presentence in my eyes, but I have been very shielded from the logistics of my marriage. I just can't see this being true.

My daily schedule here starts at 6:15 a.m. Standing count (basically to make sure everyone is still alive and counted for). We eat breakfast at or around 6:45-7:00 a.m. Depending on the day we either have showers next or cell clean-up. Most of my time between 8:00-11:00 are spent reading and praying.

I spend a lot of my morning praying. It usually takes well over an hour because I feel led to pray for everyone

I have met in here. I know their struggles and I feel they might not have anyone praying for them on the outside. I also pray for all my friends, family, Shanann's family, people who have touched my life, people who have wrote me (the bad letters as well) and my wife and kids. I also thank the Lord for all His blessings and for moving me to a safe place and for everything He is doing in my life. The relationship I have with the Lord is exponential to what it was before. Lunch is at 11:15 a.m. and then 12:30 p.m. standing count. The time between 12:20 and 4:00 p.m. I spend reading praying or writing letters. Dinner is at 4:00 p.m. and then recreation is at 4:30 p.m. five days a week. Another Standing Count is at 5:30 p.m. with dayroom time from 6:00-7:30 p.m. Dayroom time is when we can all use the phone, watch TV, play cards/other games and talk to each other. The rest of the night I spend reading or writing letters until I fall asleep sometimes around 11:00 p.m. As you can see, I read and write a lot! My faith in the Lord and his ability He gives me to spread His Word, consumes most of my day, and I love it. The Lords presence lets me rest in peace, knowing that His grace and love sustains me.

You were saying the K-9 dogs went crazy in one spot of the basement and I can't think of a physical reason why. I went downstairs that morning (to the basement) to get some trash bags, but that's it. I know dogs can see/feel things humans can't so, maybe they felt the evil spirits that are in the house. That's the only reason I can come up with why the dogs picked up anything in the basement.

Yes, I only gave Shanann the oxycodone the first night I was at my in-laws. I was obviously not in the right state of mind, but the idea was for her to lose our baby so it would be easier for me to be with Nikki. It's hard even writing that and I feel like such a monster, but I know those 2 ½ months were not the person I am today or was before. I'm so glad the Lord delivered me from whatever evil was tormenting me and my family. I just wish they were still here.

I never saw my marriage as a struggle until I met Nikki. That temptation brought out my negative perceptions I had about my marriage and shut away all the good as well. "I have found who my soul loves" (Song of Solomon 3:4). Does that mean we have a special person out there who is made for our soul? Romantically? Friendship? I can't say Shanann was my soulmate because we were so different, but we fit and I love her. There was fearfulness, there was nervousness, on my part that led to shutting down. I never thought it was healthy to argue and I just wanted peace in every aspect. I was never an argumentative person, and that kind of peace-keeping kept me walking on egg shells to make me sure to not mess up or do something wrong. She was always so stressed about money that I felt the slightest thing would set her off. That's why I did everything around the house I could inside the house, outside the house, and with the girls. That just created more of a communication barrier that was almost insurmountable. We hardly spoke about anything with substance, and I guess you could say we had fallen into a rut, but didn't acknowledge it. The fact that I would shut down during an argument is a product of my personality. I knew anything I would say would be of no importance, wouldn't contribute constructively, and would only make her angry even more so than she already was. Even if I did come back with something, in the argument then I knew it would get cut down by whatever she would say next, so I didn't bother. I just stood there avoiding eye contact and nodding like I always would. We didn't argue a lot but this is how it transpired each time. I guess you could say in the end we were more involved in a routine than a successful relationship because our days were so choreographed. Sure, every relationship needs a plan but ours were to-the-tea. We just needed to sit down and express ourselves in a non-judgmental environment to convey our feelings. We, unfortunately never got to do that. She may have not been my soulmate but she's my baby girl, my boo, my wife and my friend. I love her with all my heart.

Going back to the Song of Solomon 3:4 and the question of, if we have soulmates? I love Shanann, my girls, my son, my family and my friends. They will always be a part of my soul. "Never the less I have somewhat against you, because you have left your first love (Revelation 2:4) ERV." The one who our souls love is the Lord (our eternal soul-mate) and that will never change.

The last ten months have definitely been an up and down roller coaster of emotions, a crushing experience if you will. But those are the kinds of experiences God has put in our path to overcome. Not of ourselves to overcome but, in our faith in the Lord to overcome them. When we encounter tribulations, we often ask why? Then we start to worry how to remedy the issue without looking to God. Worrying is counter- productive and keeps you from experiencing God's blessings. Worrying is a by-product of fear. Fear is a choice, but love is everlasting. That love is from God and God is our strength. That strength is what carries us through by faith. "For by grace you are saved by through faith; and that not of yourselves it is the gift of God (Ephesians 2:8) ERV."

Blessings to you and your family,
Chris

CHAPTER 28

Letters to His Family

Below are letters that Christopher wrote to his mom and dad (Cindy and Ronnie) for their birthdays.

To Cindy, his mother

April 7, 2019

Happy Birthday Mom! 64! I wish I could be there with everyone to celebrate, or even just FaceTime to feel like I'm there. I want you to know that whenever you want me there, I am there in spirit.

I know being incarcerated is not where you wanted me to be, or even thought I would end up here, but God knows how to reach people. Sometimes a little nudge will work, but others it takes a dramatic life shift to open their eyes to the truth. We are all predestinated in the image of Jesus Christ and ask have a purpose and this tragedy has brought me on a path to help others. We are all given talents and abilities that differs from others, and those gifts, he will utilize with me where I am.

No matter what anyone says, I want you to know you are an amazing Mom, past, present and future. All kind of people will form opinions because of this tragedy, but what they say doesn't matter. Their words should be like the wind; it come then it passes away. They can't see the love you showed me and the sacrifice you made from when I was a baby (10 lbs, Yikes!) all the way forward.

This tragedy has left a huge hole in my heart as I know it has yours. Isaiah 66:9, "The Lord will not allow suffering without bringing something new to be born". We talk every day and our relationship is stronger than ever. We talk about faith and honestly that's the closest you get to one's soul. So, I thank God every day! Happy Birthday, I love you Mom! I've enclosed a picture of a Scripture I have as well! (Psalm 46:1)

Love and God Bless
Chris

"With my soul have I desired You in the night; yes, with my spirit within me will I see You early" ...Isaiah 26:9

"The Lord is near to all them that call upon Him, to all that call upon Him in truth." Psalm 145:18

To Ronnie, his dad

April 7, 2019

Happy Birthday Dad! 63! Two more years and you can retire right? I'm sure all the higher ups don't want to even think about that, or they might not even allow it. That place wouldn't know their right hand from their left without you. Mom keeps saying you're working too much and the dark circles are getting darker around your eyes; the only cure for that is...more GOLF!

I know that being incarcerated isn't what you thought my future would hold, but just know that I'm doing OK. I mean, don't get me wrong, I still have my bad days, but I have my Lord and Savior in here showing me the way: as well as your support on the outside. Whenever you're at a race, ball game or at a golf course, and you wish I was there, just known that I am in spirit. And not just me either, we have a lot of guardian angels that are with us every day. We can't see them, but trust me, they are always watching and listening.

Just like Bella said I am her hero; you are mine as well! I know that I fell short of the example you set, but know I never forgot how I was raised. I won't be defined by that one moment in time. I'm still a Dad! I'm still a son! No matter what! Now, I can add servant of God to that mix! He has shown me hope, peace, love and forgiveness, and that's how I live every day.

I'm going to enclose a picture of the verse Deuteronomy 31:6 since I don't have a card to send. I hope you have a great birthday! Love you Dad!

Love and God Bless
Chris

"The Lord is gracious, and full of compassion; slow to anger, and of great mercy. The Lord is good to all: and His tender mercies are all over His works." Psalm 145:8-9

On December 4th 2018 Christopher writes a letter to his Family asking them to read the letters he is sending to his girls and Shanann.

Dear Family,

As the Bible says "The Lord will come grab you like a thief in the night". That's what happened, He took me on a 15-hour trip to Waupun, Wisconsin. When I get phone privilege's I will call. They use Securus here too. The number to call to set up the account is 1-800----- My DOC # is----. I'm sure it's the same account you already have set up, but just in case. The commissary is called Canteen and it's probably the same way as it was in Colorado. Probably through the Wisconsin DOC website. I can receive pictures here. Nothing bigger than 5x7. If you have one you can all send me (Mom, Dad, Jamie, Robert, Jamie, Dilyn and Dalton) that would be cool. And one of Shanann, Bella and Cece altogether. Bella's birthday is Dec. 17th if you could go by the gravesite for me. I'm going to write something for you to say to them from me, if you could that would be great. I'm not sure what's going on in the outside world or the sports world so I hope I can call soon. I love you all so much! Thanks for being there for me! I will write what I want you to say for Shanann, Bella, Cece and Nico at the site on another piece of paper.

Love you All,
Chris

On December 17, 2018 Christopher writes to Shanann, Bella, Celeste, and Nico

Shanann, Bella, Cece, Nico,

Where do I begin? I love all of you to the moon and back or as Bella would say, "I love you all day!" You guys will always be my shining stars, my light in the darkness, and my guardian angels. I'm so sorry for the pain and terror I caused all of you. It rips my heart to pieces knowing what happened. Being a husband and father, you all true blessings from God. I was blind from seeing those gifts he bestowed on me. I hope when you look down on me you don't see the person that hurt you, but the person that loves you. I pray that you say "There is my husband" and "There is my Daddy." I love you all so much and remember you will always be my sun shines. I miss you guys so much! Every time I close my eyes I see you Bella jumping on that trampoline in Myrtle Beach and swimming like a big girl with your floatie, I see you Celeste running back and forth from the ocean feeling the sand on your feet for the first time and seeing the waves crash down, I see you Bella playing with your friends and breaking out of your shell. You even go me good with a few water balloons! I see you Celeste sprinting into every situation showing how spunky and tenacious you are. I see an ultrasound of the 3rd miracle God was putting in my life, not knowing if it was a boy or a girl yet. I see you Shanann in the kitchen with a "Oops We Did It Again" T-shirt to announce the 3rd bundle of joy was on the way. I see you Bella with those amazing curls that remind me of my hair when I was a kid! I see you Celeste tackling me every time you see me. You truly are Daddy's Girl! I know this because you would only let me tuck you in at night. Oh, how I miss getting both ready for bed. You two always got me soaking wet from the shower, but you always had a blast. Then it was snack time and story time. And you both loved story time. Celeste you loved your Lion Book and Bella loved her Frozen Short Story Book. You especially liked the Olof story. You always kept asking for one more story and I would cave in and do it. I still read to you now, I hope you both hear me! Nico you would've been about a month away from being born and I know your sisters would've been fighting over who held you first! I know they're doing that right now as we speak. I love you little man!

Shanann you were so good to me our entire relationship. I know we had our struggles and disagreements but you truly did love me. You would do anything for me. You painstakingly tried to show me that toward the end, but whatever wall I put up resisted every attempt. I wish I could've opened my eyes and saw the love you were pouring out at me.

I went to church yesterday! Sitting there, seeing Jesus and the Cross, hearing Holy Night being sung and knowing that I didn't have you four with me broke me into tears. I knew you were spiritually with me there. As soon as I looked up a couple rays of sunlight hit the cross and I knew you were there. What will I do without you and the kids for the rest of my life.? How am I supposed to go on? You were my everything, and I took that all away. I don't know why my love for you all wasn't stronger than the evil force. There will be more birthdays, graduation, Christmas, Easter (Holidays you made so special), weddings, funerals, as life goes on and those days will be torture not having you here with me. We didn't get to see our girls and little boy grow up. It's my fault, I was given the responsibilities to take care of you all, watch over you, make sure no one or nothing hurt you, and I'm the one that hurt you myself. I cry out to God sometimes *why, why*, did this happen? I would rather have chosen death than to have hurt you all.

With Christmas a week away, I have something to confess. Your Daddy was Santa Claus! And I am going to miss every second, I got to put on that suit. The smiles and excitement on your faces were priceless! In closing, I wish I could be tucking you girls in tonight. Celeste with the best kisses, Bella with the best hugs. I wish I could give you a kiss goodnight Shanann and feel Nico kick around in your belly. You all mean the world to me and the love I have for you can't be measured, it's like the sand of the sea. I love you all! Always and forever.

Now I have to get serious with you all. I am sorry. I wish I could take your place and you all be back here with your family, and I would if I could go in your place. My heart is broken in four pieces. A piece for each of you. Please forgive me for what I did to you. There truly isn't a word that can describe how sorry I am. To be living in this cell without all of you in my life is the most horrible thing that could be imagined. Never would this be something I would want to have happened. You were my life! You are my life! I just need you to know, that wasn't me that morning that did such a horrible thing. Something not of this earth came over me, and I succumbed to it and allowed it to take over my head, my actions, my life, your life. I'm not blaming it on anyone else, but had I not gotten mixed up with the wrong kind of people and allowed a dark spirit to enter my life I know something like this could never have happened. I beg you a million times to forgive me for what I've done! Soon I will be in Heaven with you and we will rejoin our family and be together for eternity. I love you so much!

Happy Birthday and Merry Christmas Bella! Merry Christmas Cece! (Roar Lion's Voice) Merry Christmas Nico! Happy Birthday and Merry Christmas Shanann!

Keep living for God faithfully and waiting patiently for his plan. For he is Savior faithful and good. Keep trusting in Him even when we experience heartache. God Bless Everyone. Amen

Mom, Dad and Jamie December 30, 2018

I enclosed two letters from December 17th and December 25th that I wrote to Shanann, Bella, Celeste and Nico. I also have enclosed the visiting requests forms with the rules and regulations too. Thank you, guys, for the letters, phone calls and song lyrics. I know having only 15 minutes a call is hard, but it truly helps just to hear everyone's voice.

It's devasting to think about what our families and friends have lost this year. And I know things will get worse before they get better, but I always try to think about a Bible Verse that will pick me back up. Jeremiah 29:11 seems to always be a go to for me. It reads, "For I know the thoughts that I have toward you, says the Lord, thoughts of peace and not of evil, to give you hope for the future."

God Bless All of You,
Chris

On Christmas Day, Christopher had written these letters to Shanann, and the kids.

Shanann, Bella, Cece, Nico, December 25, 2018

As I sit in this lonely cell, I look out my window and I see snowflakes lightly falling to the ground. Immediately I see how excited you, Bella and Cece get when the soft powder is on the ground. I imagine seeing both of you girls rush to get your cold gear on so I could pull you both around in your sleds. I remember pulling you both around in the front yard, back yard and on the sidewalks. It was a blast!

I remember us all being in Elf outfits last year. Everyone was so excited. Your Mommy and me loved every second of it. From the Frozen juke box to the Frozen jeep, the fun never ended.

The hole I have in my heart knowing I can't be with you four today is unrepairable. You don't know how much I want to hold all four of you in my arms right now. Spiritually I know God is with me, Jesus is with me, and all four of you are with me here in this cell. And as I look out this window, I see the snow falling again, I am reminded of all the blessings God blesses me with.

Merry Christmas Shanann, Merry Christmas Bella, Merry Christmas Cece. I love you Shanann, I love you Bella, I love you Cece, I love you Nico, always and Forever!

Letter from Christopher to Bella for her Birthday.

Happy Birthday! I miss you so much!! I remember last year at the Aquarium for your birthday. You had a blast. Even though you're not physically here I can feel your amazing spirit around me. When I read you a story or sing you a song in my cell, I know you can hear me I feel it in my heart!

Daddy loves you, Always and Forever!!

Celeste,

I miss you so so much my little rocket ship!! I remember every picture of you, you have the biggest smile. It goes from ear to ear and lights up the entire room! I miss picking you up from school and you sprint toward me once you see me. I still read you your lion book to you every night. I know you hear it and it makes you smile.

Daddy loves you always and forever!!

Nico,

I wish I could have met you little man. You were gonna be a great little ball player, but I know you are being an awesome little brother to those two big sisters you have. Daddy loves you little man,

Always and Forever!!

Shanann,

Every time I close my eyes, I see us on our wedding day. Those big eye lashes, your red lips, you looked flawless. The love was undeniable. Oh, how I wish we could have that moment in time back. Just hit the rewind five months ago, but unfortunately life will not let us. You're an amazing mother and an amazing wife and I know you hear me when I pray. The signs are everywhere. As long as I live there will not be a day or night that goes by without me praying to you and the kiddos. I love you with all my heart.

Always and Forever! xoxoxo

Numbers 6:24–26

May the Lord bless you and take good care of you. May the Lord smile on you and be gracious to you. May the Lord look on you with favor and give you peace.

Chris

To Ronnie for Father's Day

Dear Dad, June 11, 2019

Happy Fathers Day!

I know today is tougher than most days because it is the day, we get together to celebrate our father and I won't be present there, but please know I am always there in spirit. I'm there every day not just today.

Thank you for everything you did for me when I was growing up, you're doing now, and everything you will do in the future. Thank you for being the best dad anyone could ask for. I could always count on seeing that "gray flattop" up in the stands when I was playing school ball. Even if I weren't playing you were there in case, I got some playing time. All the days playing catch in the back yard, even though I would throw it way too hard sometimes you were still out there. I always remember that hook shot you got me with when we played *horse* over on the blacktop. I still to this day cannot get the hook shot down. But, hey, I do have a good jump shot from all those days practicing.

Let's not forget all the race track visits either! Somewhere between 50-100 races we went to if you count cup, Busch, and NHRA. You'll always remember that day I got curious and walked over to the track while you were getting food. I think your hair went from gray to white! I will never forget the first time I felt the Top Fuel Dragsters go down the strip, that was epic!

I wish we would have played golf more than once it was still fun hitting the links with you. That sport is definitely harder than it looks. Stay out of the sand, and definitely stay out of the water!

I say all this to bring back some memories we share and to remind you how great a dad you are. I know I'm in a place where no one thought I would be, but please know you always showed me what a caliber of a man should be and what a dad can be. You're my hero and that will never change! Happy Father's Day!!!

Love, Chris

"The just man walks in his integrity; his children are blessed after him."—Proverbs 20:7

"Hear, you children, the instruction of a father, and attend to know understanding."—Proverbs 4:1

"The glory of young men is their strength, and the beauty of old men is the gray head."—Proverbs 20:29

This is the last letter Christopher wrote to me before the book went to print. He wanted this to be the forward, but after consideration, I decided to put it with the other letters instead.

Dear Cheryln July 5, 2019

Hello Again! I hope you're doing well and in great spirits. I didn't see any fireworks last night, but I could hear a number of them being set off around the neighborhood that surrounds the prison. It brought back some good memories of my family from past July 4 celebrations. Twice we were at a cookout and sitting in the front yard of our friend's house when his sprinklers went off during the fireworks! Priceless! I remember in 2015 recording Bella's astonished look watching the fireworks in Denver. Shanann was nine months' pregnant at the time and absolutely glowing. I remember in 2017 the girls were playing with sparklers for the first time. That was a little nerve racking, but they had a blast! Good memories. I will always hang onto during this time of year.

When we spoke on the phone last night you said "I need the prologue ASAP," so I figured I better get on that. I've been in prayer most of the morning laying on my bunk and the Lord has granted me some wisdom in what to say. Here it goes:

Forward

Hope. Wait. Trust. Three little words with some mighty heavy significance. "Now faith is the substance of things hoped for, the evidence of things not seen (Hebrews 11:1)." Do you have hope in things you've seen or things you want that you've seen? Why? Everything that you see is temporary, so why hope in it? If you have hope in this world or in yourself, you've given yourself over to pride. Hope in the world traps your feet in a net, while those who have their hope in Christ safely walk on by "But they that wait upon the Lord shall renew their strength they shall mount up with wings as eagles, they shall run and not be weary; and they shall walk, and not faint (Isaiah 40:31)." It's hard to wait for anything, especially since we're all impatient creatures in an on-demand world. We let waiting bring on stress and anxiety because everything we want, we wanted yesterday. That should be an indication to us all, that we are waiting on the wrong objective . . . usually riches. *"Trust"* in the Lord with all your heart, and lean not unto your own understanding (Proverbs 3:5)." Trust brings a whole new avenue to your heart. If you don't have trust in someone or something, you totally disregard it. But if you do, it can bring a calmness to your life that is almost Heavenly.

So, what do I hope for? What do I wait on? What do I trust in? Christ! I had a beautiful life I experienced beautiful love, but I let temptation steal it away. Darkness can restrain you from making the decisions you should. Darkness can rob you of everything you love. Darkness can blind you from everything you hold dear. Darkness can destroy your soul, but the light can restore it. That light is peace in your heart. That light is the smile and laughs you go home to everyday. That light is the love of God in His Son, a love that stretches from the east to the west.

God didn't create us to be robots. He gave us freewill to see what path we would follow and what decisions we would make. Those of you who knew me before this tragedy would say "Nope! No Way! Not in a million years would he go down that path." Those of you who know of me because of this tragedy have formed your opinions; mostly negative, and I don't blame you. I just want you to realize darkness can enter into our lives in any form (another person, or activity, a feeling, a thought) and jettison us down a path we think is right, being blinded by evil, but only leading to turmoil.

The world tries to negotiate for peace, but the peace you're looking for only comes from the Prince of Peace. Striving for a safe, predictable life won't bring you the peace in your heart until you receive Christ there. Life is a tempestuous wind that never seems to back down but when you have the peace of God, you can be at peace during the storm. "For, lo, the winter is past, the rain is over and gone (Song of Solomon 2:11)."

Acknowledgements

Thank you to my Mom, Dad, and sister! No matter what, you've all been by my side and your love for me never stopped. Through the good days and the bad, you're all right there to support me in every way. Love you all so much! Thank you, Anna, for all your support. You reached out to me and my family from the very beginning. You followed where God was leading you and we have become great friends. Your letters, phone calls, and visits always bring a smile to my face. Your courage and faith have made a huge impact on my life. God bless you and your family!

Thank you, Janelle, for all your support. You took the chance reaching out to a stranger in another country in December and our friendship has grown extensively since. You've basically become sort of a human diary for one and you've helped me become stronger as a person. Follow the Lord's path for you and I'll be calling you Dr. Janelle in a few years. God Bless you and your family.

Thank you, Cheryln, for all your support. You were very persistent in contacting me, even though I didn't respond. You didn't give up. You listened to the Lord and kept writing to me until I listened to what the Lord was telling me. "Write to her! She wants to help!" A few months later and we are great Friends and helping each other grow in our faith. God bless you, and your family.

Thank you to everyone who has supported me and written to me. You've all made a mark on my life that will last a lifetime. I am indebted to you all! God bless!

Thank you to my Lord and Savior for saving my life! Without your help, I would either be dead or surrounded by darkness searching for a way out. "I waited patiently for the Lord, and He inclined to me, and heard my cry. He brought me up also out of a horrible pit, out of the miry clay and set my feet upon a rock, and established my going (Psalm 40:1–2)" You have taken darkness and turned it into your marvelous light "that shines more and more to the perfect day (Proverbs 4:18)." I will praise your name forevermore!

Ok, I think that's all I got for now! I pray the Lord keeps guiding us, protecting us, and correcting us so we stay on His path. I will leave you with a few verses that the Lord brought to my attention. Take care and God Bless!

In Christ,
Chris

Epilogue

Writing this book has been a surreal journey for me. It was certainly a mixed bag of emotions. Meeting Christopher caused a lot of different feelings and emotions. One moment I liked him and felt bad for his situation and the next moment, I hated him for what he did. I know for certain I will never be the same. My heart has just been pierced by all of it. I cannot begin to imagine the pain the Rzuceks face every day. That in itself makes me so angry with him. One thing it has certainly taught me is we do not know how people feel until we walk in their shoes; an old cliché, I know. I also learned how hurtful and how senseless it is to judge others, and to judge does not make us a better person.

I know there has been much speculation about Nikki and if she had any part in Christopher murdering his family. Why did her phone ping in Frederick the morning of the murders? There is no reason that makes sense of why she was there except for Christopher. We may never know for sure.

Even though I was certain I was called to write this book, there were times I wanted to give up. Dealing with a hurting family who is still in some sort of denial is very painful. Their pain is real and I cannot begin to imagine. The family would like to have told me how to write the book, but I went with my moral responsibility. The confusing thing I came against was how they wanted me to present Christopher as not guilty. They want the blame and the brunt of this to lie with Shanann.

There are people out there that have attached themselves to the family, and I'm sorry to say, have not had a positive effect on their lives. There are people who continually try to tell them Christopher did not commit the crimes and others who have tried to bring themselves into the spotlight. What Christopher did is horrific to the highest level. No matter how much people think they like Christopher, he killed his pregnant wife and two small daughters. There has to be something very wrong that he has the ability to do something like this. We cannot lose sight of the four lives lost in this tragedy.

Christopher is not your average or normal criminal. I had never had the experience to talk to an inmate before, but something amazing to me is the group of "fans" he has. He is a very organized person, and he even has his calls organized. There are many people he calls and writes to. It seems to keep him in this state of feeling that he is "okay," that he should be looked at differently because he has asked for forgiveness.

Something interesting is Christopher feels he could have been "demon-possessed" a few weeks before the murders during and until October 1, 2018. I must admit this is something very new for me; however, I don't necessarily doubt it. I just don't know much about it. Christopher says he is convinced of it, and if it were true, does that have any bearing on what happened? My advice to him is to seek help from professionals concerning this.

If you consider how different he was before the morning of the murders and leading up to them, there is admittedly a huge difference. How can we explain what happened to him? It's very much a mystery to everyone who knows him.

It is bothersome that it has been reported in magazine articles that he lives in his own personal "hell" every day. This is not true. Weirdly, Christopher is content.

I learned through talking to him and reading his letters that he cares very much what people think of him, even to the extent he can't help but be very concerned about doing things for people so they will like him. If someone like Christopher is capable of murder, and we know he was, we all need to wonder who lives amongst us. He appeared to everyone around him to be a nice and normal guy.

So, the question remains, "*Why* did Christopher do this; why did he murder his entire family?"

The answer I'm afraid is easy: He did it to clear his life and start over with Nikki. He would have done anything to be with her.

"Try again. Fail again. Fail better"—Samuel Beckett

The End

The Final Chapter and Updates

In my first book *Letters From Christopher,* I was reading different true crime books and I wrote down things I found good and interesting. I went back through those things and deleted them or used the idea to form my own thought. There were 7–9 sentences from another book that was overlooked and left in the book. I ask my readers to please forgive me for that. It was not done maliciously or with any malice. I am very sorry for it and wish I could go back. I do thank you as my readers for giving me a second chance. And I do apologize to the other author. I have seen it posted that almost the entire book was plagiarized. This is totally untrue. I made a mistake, and I'm sure I'm not the first person to make a mistake.

I wanted to put updates throughout this book but didn't want them to be hard to find, so I decided to put them all in one chapter. I am listing these things randomly, there is no real order for how I wrote them. This chapter is the final words I will write about this case. I had no idea when starting this project that as the author, I would face so much as I wrote this story.

I am totally amazed at the hate social media can spew. Some people say things without forethought, not caring how their words may pierce the very soul of the person they are talking about. They might be hoping that the harder they criticize, the more people will like it, and sometimes, that's true. Yet to what end are they spewing that hate? I'm sure all of them would not want that done using their name. Then there are some of the YouTubers—not all of them by all means, but enough of them. These people have such a lack of judgment and basic morals. They get paid to hate; therefore, no holds bar! Just hope you don't cross their path because they will try to devour you in one quick swoop, ripping you apart with their devilish schemes and next set of lies all the while acting as if they are honest and trustworthy but actually receiving money for destroying someone's character. People are too caught up in it and enjoying the gossip so much to even notice they are being totally and completely lied to. In writing my book, I have had the misfortune of crossing paths with these people. Good, bad, and ugly as they are, I have even been stolen from by one of them. Funny how that very person could sit and talk about the mistakes I made with the first book, knowing full well what they did. After a while, I became smart enough to not cry and hide in the corner but turn it all over to my attorneys and allow them to handle it in the best way possible. So, I did. Maybe not the quickest way but the surest way. However, let me state, for every hater and untruthful person, there have been at least ten who are kind, sweet, of great character, and encouraging! So, thank you all for your wonderful thoughts and love.

I will try to answer the many questions that have come to me during the writing of this book. I will speak truthfully and frankly. I am not trying to hurt anyone; I'm just trying to answer the many questions that are still unanswered. I do not have all the answers myself. I can only trust that the answers Christopher gave me are true. I myself believe he gave me the truth and I'm sure some of you will not agree. I do not believe the conspiracy theories, and I am hoping Christopher will not go as far as to seek an appeal to only use one of these theories. That would be such a travesty to Shanann and the children. I would think much more of Christopher to just stick with what really happened.

Below, you will find my answers.

Did Shanann kill the girl? Absolutely, positively *no*. She did not kill her children. I guarantee you for I have sat in front of Christopher and looked into his eyes as he spoke about the crimes. He murdered his entire family with his own hands.

Were the girls alive when Shanann got home? Yes, I totally believe they were alive until early the next morning. I believe around 4–5 a.m.

Did he kill Shanann while she was in bed? Yes, I believe she was lying next to him just like he told me in the letter. I do believe evidence points to that. However, I feel she was asleep or drugged at the time he killed her. That's the reason he had stripped the bed. She had soiled the fitted sheet we've seen in the evidence.

Did Christopher commit the crime alone? Yes, I believe he was alone that morning. Under no circumstances do I believe Nikki was in the house that morning and knew he was going to kill his family or help him kill his family. We may not like her because his relationship with her is probably the biggest reason Christopher killed his family, but that is not a reason to hate her so much. I can't imagine honestly what her life has been like trying to get over everything. Many women get mixed up with married men and most men will tell the mistress he is either in the process of a divorce, divorced, or separated. No, she should have walked away when she found out he was married, but she did not help him kill his family.

Did Jim have any involvement? No, I am sure he did not. However, I feel he was Nikki's shield. Christopher said they were good friends, and again, that does not make him a murderer.

I had asked a question what people thought of Christopher's mother and sister having been part of the reason he killed his family. Let me be very clear —*no,* there is no way anyone can accuse them of being the reason he killed his family. I've listened to their pain. Even though the relationship between them and myself ended, I do not believe the blame for the murders can be put on them. He may tell himself that had they gotten along better, he would not have had to kill them, but he had plenty of chance to talk to his family and let them know it was affecting him that they could not get along with Shanann. It was his responsibility. It is wrong for a man to allow his family to beat up his wife. Whether they are right or wrong, his responsibility was to stand with his wife, and it's his responsibility to tell his wife she needs to treat his family with respect. I believe there were things on both sides that were done wrong but none of it was enough to cause him to murder.

Is there a mental problem with Christopher? In talking with me, he said he has never been tested for any mental issue. So, we don't know the answer to that. I do believe him that he was never tested.

Were there rituals and dark things at Nikki's apartment? I honestly believe there were dark things that went on at her house. Christopher said she is dark and dark things happened. I don't know for sure what all of those things are, but I do feel they were enough to affect Christopher hugely.

Do I believe Christopher was demon-possessed? I do believe there are circumstances where people can have dark or demonic spirits enter their souls and cause them to do very awful and dark things. Someone would, in my opinion, have to be prepped or open to that dark spirit or sell their soul to Satan. If you look up some different entertainers, they claimed to have sold their soul to Satan in exchange for fame and fortune.

Were the murders premeditated? Absolutely, positively *yes.* Out of his own mouth, he had planned the murders for several weeks.

Who gave Christopher the oxy? I believe he did find oxy in his basement. Shanann had been prescribed some by her doctor, I believe, when she had surgery.

Who gave Christopher the idea for the murders? This is puzzling to me as he does not seem capable of coming up with this idea on his own. He has been used to being told what to do and how to do it almost his entire life. But who gave him the idea? I really cannot say, and that, to me, is one of the biggest mysteries. I do not believe it was his parents or his sister though. There is a huge difference in not caring for someone and murdering someone. My relationship with the Watts has been severed, but I can tell you I have heard the hurt in their voices, and I've heard them search for answers themselves. Christopher says it was his own idea so since I'm sure he is not going to tell us if it wasn't him, I'm satisfied with his answer. It does no one any good to keep trying to come up with the answers.

Were the girls dead when he put them in the tank? I really don't know for sure.

Did the girls really wake up after he tried to smother them at home? I truly believe they did. When he has given me that account, I do believe that is one of the true things he told me. I do believe the girls were awake in the truck on the way to the oil fields. Please read that letter. I believe it is a very truthful account as to what happened.

Please do not believe the conspiracies that are out there and the ones that put the blame on Shanann.

Did Christopher sexually abuse the girls? I have wondered this myself, but I do not find or see any proof of that.

Some of you readers are people who have spent so much time investigating this case and literally living in it for two years. You know the case forward and backward, and some of you still feel there are unanswered questions. Here is what I advise:

1) Know that Christopher killed Shanann and her baby; he killed Bella and Cece.
2) He killed them by himself with his own hands.
3) Nikki was not involved in the murders.
4) Christopher cannot blame any of this on anyone else other than himself.
5) Let the case go; move on; don't make him a celebrity.
6) His family had nothing to do with the murders.
7) Let's all find another true crime case to get involved in and let Christopher, his family, and Shanann's family move on. In memory of Shanann and the children, let's make them the celebrities.

Below are the letters from Christopher to myself, family, and Shanann's parents:

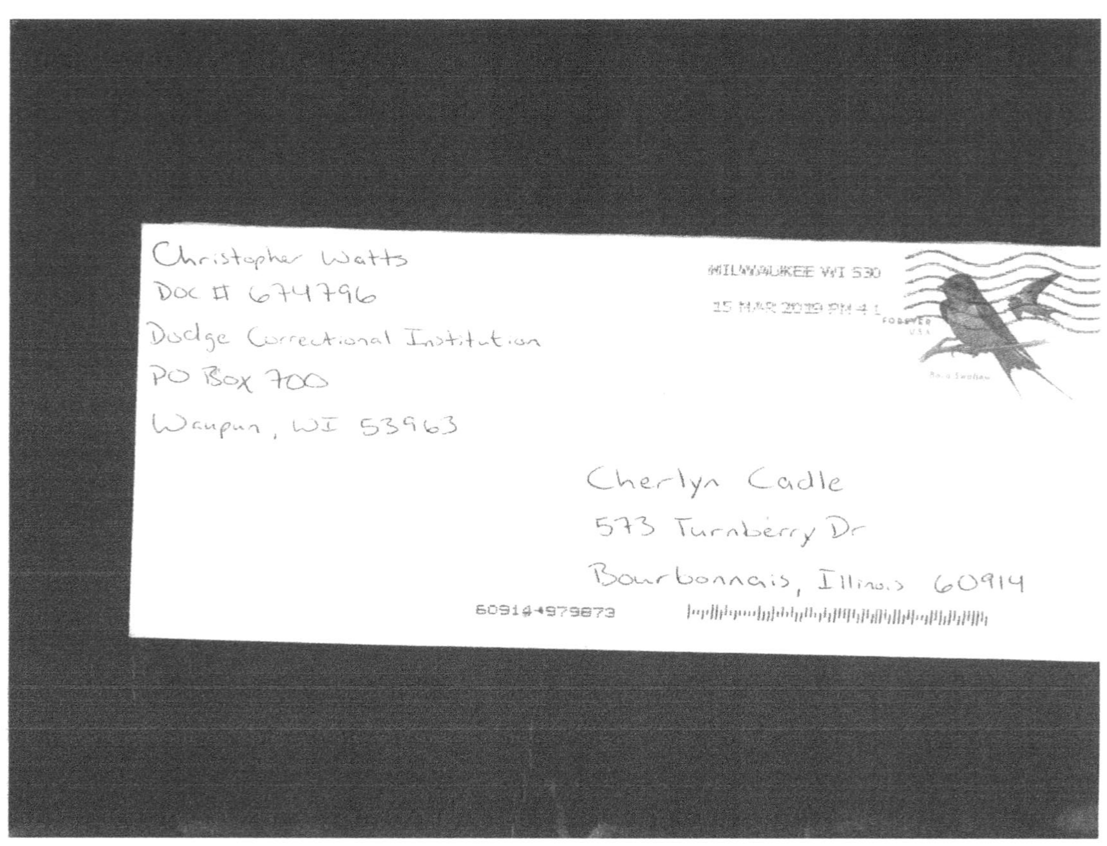
Christopher Watts
DOC # 674796
Dodge Correctional Institution
PO Box 700
Waupun, WI 53963
MILWAUKEE WI 530
15 MAR 2019 PM 4 L
FOREVER USA
Cherlyn Cadle
573 Turnberry Dr
Bourbonnais, Illinois 60914
60914-979873

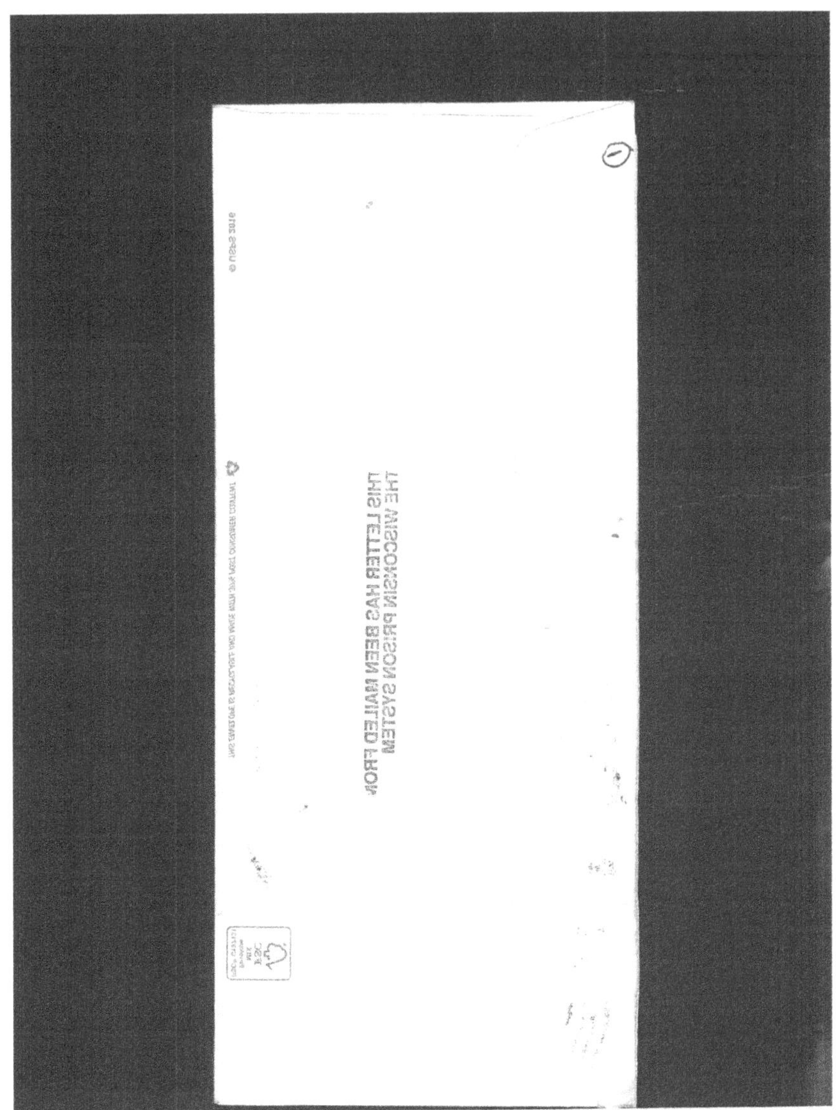
THIS LETTER HAS BEEN MAILED FROM
THE WISCONSIN PRISON SYSTEM

Dear Cheryln, 3·24·19

Hello again! I'm glad you got to talk to my Mom! I was worried you didn't receive my letter when I received your last letter. Thank you for your prayers! I've been in Confinement since March 5th when the last media storm happened so, it has been a little rough, but I know God is here with me and I'm never alone. Maybe there is someone He doesn't want me to run into that's here right now.

I love your quote, "Our fight with Satan is only as ~~[illegible]~~ big as the Victory will be." That's so true! I feel the enemy attacking me all day long in here, it's relentless. The enemy got to me once when he took my family, but I think he knows God is working to bring a lot of souls to the Kingdom through this so, he keeps on the offensive. If we can keep others from the darkness that can creep into their lives, I'm all for it!

It would be awesome to hear your testimony one day! I would never think one testimony is more powerful than another. The same celebration is had in Heaven when any of us receive Jesus Christ into our hearts. Human perception sees that some overcome more heartache and suffering than others, but God sees sin as sin. No sin is greater than the other and He doesn't let any suffering, that is too big for us to handle, come upon us.

Unfortunately, there are judges out there that believe it's their sole purpose to remind you what you've done. This reminds me of John Chapter 8, when the scribes and Pharisees throw a woman caught in adultery in front of Jesus and asking Him to judge her. He asked the multitude "He that is without sin among you, let him first cast a stone at her." One by one they all left the temple until it was just the woman and Jesus alone. Once her accusers had left, Jesus said, "Neither do I condemn you: go, and sin no more." If everyone would just think about their own sins, they wouldn't be so quick to cast the first stone! The world is full of self-righteousness and self-pride, but what we need is self-sacrifice and humility. Those are the qualities of Jesus!

It's amazing to know that God put me on the heart of someone that was halfway across the country at the time. He has a plan for all of us, although it may take a while to realize His plan for us; when it becomes clear, it is crystal clear!

Your example of the 3-pronged attack by Satan is spot on: Worldly things, lust of the eyes and pride of life. We see on TV and social media what we should look like, what we should have and what we need to do to get what we want. Nothing could be further from the truth. Our minds are being polluted all day long. If only we could all see the knowledge, understanding and wisdom that the Bible teaches, I believe the world could be a lot different.

I believe my Mom sent you a Visiting Form so maybe I will see you sooner than I think. I hope this letter finds you in good spirits. Prayers to you and your family!

God Bless

Chris

"I will not leave you comfortless: I will come to you." - John 14:18

P.S. You don't have to put Fon Du Lac County on the address. I think this is Dodge County, but who knows (I'm still learning the geography of this state, HA!) Also, the institution doesn't allow paper to be sent in, although they left 2 pieces of paper and removed the other two, weird!

PPS. Yes, this book could be a real force against the enemy and the media!

(1)

Dear Cheryln, 4.4.19

Hello again! I hope you are doing well! Yes, I am still on Protective Confinement and I'm suppose to hear back from the Security Director tomorrow to see how much longer. I've never had any trouble with anyone here, but the Institution is just being cautious. The Security Director doesn't want anyone to see all the media coverage and then come after me. I'm in my cell over 23hrs a day, but I know God is here with me. He has given me a lot of extra time alone with Him over the past month. Also, He has opened my eyes to a few things I was holding onto in my heart that I didn't acknowledge to myself.

I've never had a psychological exam. If I were to of seen a Doctor during my case, then anything I said could've been subpoena by the court or DA. The Asperger's symptoms do make a lot of sense and I can match up a bunch of instances in my life that correspond with it too. It would've been much easier to diagnose me with it when I was 11yrs old instead of 33yrs old. Next time I talk to the psychological department, I will ask what it takes to get an evaluation.

The media is horrible with what they put out there sometimes. Is my diet really that exciting? The sale of the house was pushed back to

(2)

July before the investigators came to see me. I have a civil case against me (wrongful death lawsuit, prayer or relief) and in the matter of the Probate Court, the attorneys thought the house could be sold at a profit and the money would go to the wrongful death suit and help Shanann's family. After consulting with the realtor, she told her parents that the house wouldn't sell for more than what was owed. So, then Chase Bank pushed the auction to July 17th. It had nothing to do with the investigators, just another example of the truth vs "media truth".

I received notification that you are on my Visitor List now. I would recommend waiting until I'm off confinement. I have a friend in Green Bay that came to visit and they had to shut down the whole facility to move me to another unit. Then I was hand-cuffed to a table and talked to my friend through a video monitor. Even though I was heavily restrained, I thank God everyday for that visit. She stayed for 3hrs and talked to me and she is truly an angel!

From what they tell me, the only items you can bring into the visiting room are quarters, $20 worth, for the vending machines. I will be allowed to get a radio and TV soon, but CD's I believe are contraband because they can be made into a weapon. At some point, the Institution will offer 7in tablets that we can use for downloading music and e-mail. Maybe there will be some praise/worship items available to download.

(3)

I like your question, what does it mean to die out to Christ daily? To me, that means to look at His character and model yourself as He was when He walked the earth. "Jesus is the stone which the builders rejected, but that same stone has become the chief cornerstone. Whosoever shall fall upon that Stone shall be broken; but on whomsoever it shall fall, it will grind him to powder" (Luke 20:17-18 paraphrased). To die for Christ daily is to fall upon this Stone daily. What breaks when you fall is your allegiance to self, lust and pride. I look at things I do daily and always ask, "Should I think about that?" or "Should I be reading something like this?" We are not all perfect, but we can all make a diligent effort to be better everyday.

I like that dream you had! I know a lot of people, especially inmates, will be able to relate to my testimony and be able to see the trust, the hope, the peace and the love in Christ. I hope people on the outside can be able to relate and be able to look at their own lives, and receive the Lord into their hearts. I believe if roles were reversed and if I read a book about this happening to someone, I would come to the Lord! It would hit

Dear Cheryln, 4.23.19

Hello Again! I hope you are doing well! It's been awesome being able to talk with you on the phone, but I know the 15min time limit is a pain. Sometimes I can get right back on the phone, but right now there are other inmates that like to be on the phone as much as I do, so I respect their time as well. How's your Dad doing? I hope you're able to see him. I've been praying on that everyday.

Yes, that petition really blew my mind that people really want to make me suffer like that. Even if they did ever take my pictures, they can't take my memories. An inmate from another institution wrote me about that subject and said, "If they take your pictures, they would need to take the pictures from the other 500-600 people that have their family pictures up in their cell convicted of the same act."

Do I feel like I should be incarcerated? For the act I committed, I most definitely think so. Do I imagine myself ever doing anything like this or be a danger to society? I most definitely think NOT! If I were to ever be released, I know I would go straight to a ministry and start going to jails/prisons and help inmates. If God led me to be ordained, I would go that route as well, possibly

(4)

none and show me what's important in life!

The rapture? Well, that is an interesting topic. Revelation was definitely hard to grasp at first, but I understand a little more each time. We may have to discuss that one in person because I'm running a little low on paper, HAHA! I would love to hear your thoughts on it as well!

I'm definitely praying for your father everyday. I hope his wife doesn't put him somewhere and you can't see him. My grandmother (she's 93) has dementia, and I know some days it's hard for my Dad to go see her when she doesn't recognize him. My Dad put me on speakerphone the other day so she could hear my voice and she started smiling. That made my day!

I hope you are doing well and you are resting in the Lord's peace everyday! Look forward to hearing from you soon!

God Bless
Chris

"For with You is the fountain of life: in Your light shall we see light." -Psalm 36:9

"Humble yourselves in the sight of the Lord, and He shall lift you up." -James 4:10

ever be a Chaplain. Maybe the laws will change one day. My attorney team could see I was different and knew that this was a one time occurrence for me. They even told me that in Europe, the law is I would serve 20yrs or so for homicide, and in California, after 25yrs of imprisonment, on a life sentence, you can be released if you've had good behavior. So, there's hope for everyone to live outside prison walls. I know physically I'm behind these walls, but my spirit is FREE with Christ!

If God keeps putting it on your heart that there is more to the story than what the FBI has, you're correct. I don't like saying stuff like that over the phone because I'm never certain when they screen my calls. I know I already told you about the vision I had before August 13th, when I was laying in bed and all the lights were on in the loft and downstairs and I felt so alone. That's exactly what happened August 14th when I was laying in bed.

I'm not sure if I want this in the book or if God does, but here are the things I left out: 1) August 12th, when I finished putting the girls to bed, I walked away and said "That's the last time I'm going to be tucking my babies in." I knew what was going to happen the day before and I did nothing to stop it. I was numb to the entire world. I had literally taken my kids to a birthday party, played with water balloons, had an amazing time, sung songs all the way home, gave them both a shower, ate dinner, read bedtime stories and sang bedtime songs, and still nothing registered!! When Shanann had to be somewhere, I always enjoyed taking the girls places or playing outside because it was our opportunity to bond, and still, even the night before, I couldn't stop myself from what I knew would occur the next morning. 2) August 13th, morning of, I went to the girls' room first, before Shanann and I had our argument. I went to Bella's room, then CeCe's room and used a pillow from their bed. That's why the cause of death was smothering. After I left CeCe's room, then I climbed back in bed with Shanann and our argument ensued. After Shanann had passed, Bella and CeCe woke back up. I'm not sure how they woke back up, but they did. It makes the act that much worse knowing I went to their rooms first and knowing I still took their lives at the location. 3) The reason the medical examiner found oxycontin in Shanann's system is because I gave it to her. I thought it would be easier to be with Nichol if Shanann wasn't pregnant.

If the world knew all of that, I'm pretty sure a new petition would be started to have me put to death or I would be killed in prison if I ever got transferred from this institution.

I'm not sure if this was a spiritual visit, but I had a dream Cole was dancing next to the chair in my cell. When she was dancing, one of my folders on the chair started moving and I thought she was in trouble, so I said "Watch out, get away, watch out!" Then I woke up. I'm hoping she comes back! I hope everyone comes to visit me. I'm trying to see if I can clear my head better before I go to sleep to help.

I like that John 10:1-10 passage you sent. I wish I could've had an open ear to hear the Lord calling me back in June/July/August. If we run after sin, we won't hear our Shepherd calling us. I couldn't discern between the good spirits and the evil spirits and that eventually lodged me into a deep pit I couldn't climb back out of.

I pray that you and your family are doing good and I pray that the Lord will keep directing us in His path. Take care & God Bless!

Chris

"The night is far spent, the day is at hand: let us therefore cast off the works of darkness, and let us put on the armor of light."

- Romans 13:12

(4)

Dear Cheryln, 5.15.19

Hello Again! I hope this letter finds you doing well! Thank you for the two songs you sent, "Who You Say I Am" and "Be Still." I'm sure the songs will take on a new meaning once I can hear them with music, although the lyrics are good by itself.

You ask if there's anything I haven't talked about in regards to Nikki, honestly, I'm not sure what I've said and what I haven't, but this is what I know: She has a small group of friends that she didn't tell me a lot about until near the end, She was involved in an abusive relationship a few years before and, after that, she removed most of her social media (not sure if it was the result of that relationship), most, if not all, of her mail was delivered to her Dad's house (not sure if she was hiding from someone), she took medication (never told me what for though). She came over to my house twice, July 4th and July 14th. I didn't have to work July 4th, so I stayed at Nikki's house that morning and missed tons of phone calls from Shanann. When I called Shanann back, she was obviously furious. I went home and decided to stay home the rest of the day which made Nikki upset (I think this was the 1st time she realized in her head that she wasn't #1 in my life). Nikki came over and we went over an eating/protein plan for me. She didn't look around the house much on this visit. On July 14th, we were heading

(2)

back from the Shelby Museum and stopped by my house efore we went to get something to eat. While in the ouse, she was playing with Dieter and he led her upstairs nd she saw a lot of pictures of Bella, Celeste and Shanann (I was downstairs at the time). She came back ownstairs with this frozen, dazed and confused look on her ace (probably now realizing for the first time in her head he family life I lived and the family that would be broken o pieces). We laid on the couch and she said "You have ll this, more than most people, and we are doing this? hy are we doing this? Are you willing to give all this up? Is our relationship that bad?" I said "Shanann and I were ifting apart and that we didn't talk (I'm not sure if I elieved that fully, but I can see the deficiencies in our elationship today)." I also said "Shanann and I were ctively trying to have a baby before we met (Nikki and)" Nikki instantly freaked out about this because she idn't think the relationship could've been that bad if Shanann and I were trying to conceive. Nikki went ut to her truck and sat there for about 30min texting e while I was inside my house. I somehow calmed er down (Nikki repeatedly reminded me I was the only uy she had ever met that tried to fix problems, smooth ut issues and talk about things. Ironically, I never did hat with Shanann. Maybe I thought she wouldn't listen!). fter this, Nikki still invited me over to her house ike nothing had happened and said "I got mad because I hought I could give you a son, and when you told me

(3)

you and your wife were trying, that made me upset."

After all this, we went to the drag races in Bandimere on July 21st and camping July 28th-29th. When I left to go to N.C, she sent me a text saying "Use this time to fix the issues with your wife and enjoy time with your Family." The first night I was there, (the night I gave Shanann the oxycontin) I texted Nikki saying "I wouldn't be able to call, just text" Nikki responded "Why not? Are you with her?" I thought she wanted me to spend time with my family, but obviously she wanted me to make time for her no matter what. The next 8 days I ignored Shanann every night so I could disappear and talk to Nikki For hours.

When I returned to Colorado, I saw Nikki after work (I went to her house in my work truck) and she gave me a key to her place. I saw this as a pretty big step because, what woman gives another man a key to her place without wanting to take a big step in their relationship? I had told her that Shanann and I were going to get a separation, and that the relationship was going to end. Shanann had mentioned the word separation, but she was still actively trying to fix our marriage. I don't know if this day, when I received the key to Nikki's place, was the day I realized I couldn't have my family and her at the same time.

(4)

When I left Nikki's house, I had to hurry home because Shanann and I had an ultrasound appointment. This should've been a joyful time but, instead, I was so overcome with evil and lust, I didn't even let the event register. There was my son (didn't know the gender) on the screen and my beautiful wife on the chair and I could barely hold her hand. Shanann needed a supportive husband and my kids needed a loving father, but I was neither at this time.

Shanann made it a point to bring up the "cold hand holding" and I just told her "my head wasn't in the right place and that I was going to sleep on the couch." Shanann responded "Whatever is going on or whoever she is, you'll never see those kids again" and slammed the door. Once I knew she was asleep, I proceeded to call Nikki while laying on the couch. The next night I would sleep in the basement on that bed and call Nikki as well. I had made up in my mind that my marriage was over without even trying to talk to my wife first. Shanann knew the altercation with my parents had affected me, so she began sending pictures of the ultrasound to my Mom & DAD.

Nikki began telling her friends about me and I deleted my FaceBook because of that (I didn't want her friends looking me up) Deleting my FaceBook was another sign to Shanann that something was up, but she was still wanting to find a way to fix things. She then booked a couple's weekend in the mountains.

(5)

The last time I saw Nikki was August 11th when we went out to eat. I had gotten a babysitter for the night. Nikki talked about different apartments she had found for me that would be big enough for me and the kids. She then talked about how after I found my own place we could move at a slower pace and treat our relationship as a normal relationship. (She said this because we saw each other every night possible in June-July). I didn't talk to her again until Aug 12th, after the birthday party I took my kids to. The rest I think is all in discovery from then on. I hope this sheds some light on that relationship. I'm not sure if that is all common knowledge or not, but that's it regarding Nikki from me. I pray that she has peace now and can find peace in the Lord. Everyone involved in this tragedy has had their life turned upside down and I pray they will seek the Lord with all their heart to get back on the right path.

OK, enough of the Nikki relationship! Let's get to Salvation Night, October 2018! I've been trying to narrow down the day for you and I have an idea! If you can find out when the Kansas City Chiefs played Sunday Night Football in early October 2018, it was that night. I remember watching that game that night. It's weird sometimes what our mind can remember about certain nights and give us some clues.

The pod I'm in is called "RS" and, attached to the cell there's a room with a table, T.V and phone. I've only been in this cell for two days, so all this is very new to me. I'm sitting at the table reading a book when the news comes on around 9:30pm, then I hear my name. I look up and see myself sitting in a courtroom in an orange jumpsuit, never thinking in my entire life I would ever see that image. Then I see a picture of my family on the screen. This is the first time I've seen a picture of my family since August 15th. All the newspaper articles were cut out of the newspaper so I wouldn't see them.

Lockdown was at 10pm and I went in my cell and laid on my bunk in the dark ~~[illegible]~~ with the picture of my family frozen in my head. I see Bella, I see Celeste, I see Shanann.... ~~[illegible]~~ I see their bright, shining faces, their ~~[illegible]~~ radiant cheeks, their beautiful smiles. Now more memories start to flood my brain: Memories of the pool when both girls would jump into my arms and I would fly them around, memories of snowstorms when I would pull the girls around in a sled, memories of the wedding when I saw Shanann walking down the aisle and seeing her stand right in front of me looking absolutely stunning, memories of Cece tackling me everytime I picked her up from school (the smile she gave me when she saw me was priceless), memories of Bella's first time seeing fireworks, memories of being a family.

(7)

These images came at me like tidal waves, flooding my mind with the love that I once had and piercing my soul knowing that they were gone. I longed to hold my family in my arms again, to read one more bedtime story, to give another goodnight kiss, to hold my son for the first time, to sing one more song in the car, to be a Dad, to be a husband... one more time.

I rolled over in my bunk onto my knees and cried out to the Lord, "Please take this pain away, take this guilt. How did I let this happen? How did I let it get this far? This pain is too great for me to handle, to bear alone. I'm sorry for the pain I've caused; please take this guilt, this shame that I feel and help me follow You. Heal my heart, cleanse my soul and help me follow You. Please forgive me! You're my Lord and Savior, and I want to do Your will." At that moment I felt a hand touch the top of my head. It didn't startle me, it didn't scare me, what it did was overwhelm me with so much emotion I couldn't stop crying. That hand that touched me was the Lord's hand and He healed me that night with His divine Spirit. That night changed my life and set me on a course that I will never forget. These verses from Lamentations

(8)

best describes that night: "I called upon Your name, O Lord, out of the low dungeon. You have heard my voice: hide not Your ear at my breathing at my cry. You drew near in the day that I called upon You: You said, 'Fear not'. O Lord, You have pleaded the causes of my soul; You have redeemed my life." (Lamentations 3:55-58).

That was Salvation Night! I pray that everyone can have that same type of experience. My salvation night was only possible because I humbled myself before the Lord and answered His call. The Lord calls us constantly but we don't open ourselves up to let Him in. "Behold, I stand at the door, and knock: if any man hear My voice, and open the door, I will come in to him, and will dine with him, and he with Me." (Revelation 3:20). Our heart is the door and He is always ready to come in!

Hearing the Lord's call is in direct relation to John 11:38-44 when Lazarus is brought back to life. Our souls are ravaged in sin because of the fallen world we live in. None of us do good, not one. When Jesus cried with a loud voice, "Lazarus, come forth", He essentially is calling all of us to do His will. Will you keep your ears sharp so your soul can also be redeemed by answering the Lord's call?

Also, in John 20:11-16, when Mary Magdalene was at the sepulchre and she had mistaken our Savior as the gardener, Jesus said to her "Mary" and then, she said "Master." Jesus opened the eyes of

(9)

her spirit. Her physical eyes could not see, but she answered the call of the Lord and when her "spirit eyes" were opened, she could perceive. Will you open your eyes to the Lord so that you can see the glorious light of salvation?

My hand is starting to get tired, HAHA! Those last two questions I asked in the last two paragraphs were not for you, but for others who haven't accepted the Lord. Feel free to use any of this for the book. I pray that the Lord will use us both as divine vessels to reach countless people all over the world with the words that we shall write. Something that's been on my mind lately, the Lord has been putting this on my heart about the title. What do you think about:

HOPE.
WAIT.
TRUST.
Christopher Watts' Amazing Grace

I just wanted to share that with you and see what you thought. I know I shared a lot of information in this letter and I believe you can use some for my testimony as well. The more questions you ask, the more my gears in my brain start turning.

(10)

I hope this letter finds you in good spirits and doing well. Take care and God Bless!

In Christ,

Chris

"Meditate upon these things; give yourself wholly to them, that your profiting may appear to all."
1 Timothy 4:15

"Humble yourselves therefore under the mighty hand of God, that He may exalt you in due time: casting all your care upon Him; for He cares for you."
1 Peter 5:6-7

Dear Cheryln,

Hello Again! I hope you're doing well! I think Wisconsin weather compares to Colorado weather in that it can vary so much from one day to another. I think Spring lasted for a week, then Summer hit for a day and now it's been a mixture of Fall/Winter the last few days. I will say I'd rather be cold than hot, especially in this little shoebox I'm in! OK, let me go into the Weld County Jail experience:

I arrive at the Weld County Jail the night of August 15th. I get booked, finger printed and my picture taken and then escorted by a deputy and two tactical officers to the unit I'm staying in. When the door to my cell shuts behind me I'm standing there alone in the darkness wondering if this was it; is this my normal for the rest of my life? I lay down in the bunk in my suicide turtle suit (as I'm in their suicide watch pod) and just stare off into the darkness. Nothing is adding up and it feels like none of this can be real. To my astonishment I look in the front corner of my cell and see two dark figures standing there. I thought "OK, this is my eyes playing tricks on me", so I closed them and opened my eyes again and, yet, they are still there. As I focus more intently I can see one is male and one is female. The male is in a black suit and

(2)

he female in a black dress with a Victorian style ıat. Both their wardrobes looked vintage. The faces were sh colored and almost familiar, until the familiar eeling turned into a sure thing. This was my grand-ather and grandmother on my Mom's side. Their faces eing unmistakable now, I almost wanted to move loser to them when their eyes opened in unison. Their yes were as red as blood, like crimson. This eerie eeling came over me as I had four eyes staring ack at me as if piercing my soul in a bad way. The nly problem was that it felt like I was in a trance d had to keep eye contact. I felt like I needed o go over to the both of them but, all of a sudden omething broke the trance. I stopped looking at the air, looked back again and the corner of my cell as empty once again. I obviously couldn't sleep uch after this event, thinking this type of visit ould only get worse if I let my guard down. I tayed on this unit for a week until I was moved o the restrictive housing unit or, "the Hole". The uicide watch pod was quiet, but I soon learned the ole was not the same. As soon as I entered the nit the screams and shouts pierced my soul. Out f the 20 cells I'm sure 90% of them were creaming at me, and the berating remarks ranged from "I'm going to rip your face off" to "Kill Yourself" to "I'm going to F**K your wife in the afterlife". All f these comments felt like daggers hitting my heart.

(3)

This went on for weeks and I basically drew the conclusion that this must be what Hell feels like. The shouting, the pounding on the walls had to stop at some point, right? It eventually did, either by the others losing interest or the fact I wasn't responding to anything they said.

During this time is when I started to read the Bible. I didn't know if I should even pick the Bible up because I thought I was too far gone. I was lost, broken and I even listened to the other inmates informing me the different ways I could kill myself while in my cell. Their words were "If you don't do it yourself, they will do it for you in prison." With these thoughts flowing through my head, I didn't think God could forgive me for what I'd done. But, I picked up the Bible and began reading because there had to be a message in this Book that will help me persevere.

I finished the Bible in about two weeks. Some days were harder to concentrate than others due to the noise in the pod and the horrible letters I would get from time to time. Not all the letters were terrible. There were a few that had encouraging messages and even pointed out Scriptures in the Bible for me to commit to memory. The first that was brought to my attention was 1 John 1:9 "If we confess our sins, He is faithful and just to forgive us

(4)

ur sins, and to cleanse us from all unrighteousness." The
ther was from the Gospel of Luke in chapter 23 when
e describes the account of Jesus speaking with the other
nan on the cross beside Him. And Jesus said "Verily, I
ay to you, Today you shall be with Me in Paradise."
Luke 23:43). Both of these verses show the mercy and
oving-kindness of Christ. The man beside Jesus was a
riminal, condemned to suffer crucifixion, but He still
orgave him because He saw the faith in his heart!
These verses sparked a zealous hope inside me that
carried me through the rest of my time there at the jail.

After about 5 weeks in the Hole I was moved to
S pod to give me a little extra movement (Enter the
salvation Night Story Here). My attorney team would
ome to see me 3-4 times a week and I can't thank
hem enough. They were my only human contact; they
reated me not like a client, but as a friend.
They didn't treat me with hostility, but with
ompassion and would be there in a moments notice
f I was struggling with something. On November 5th
ny attorney team flew my Mom, Dad & Sister out to
alk to me via video monitor because the next day
I was going to plead guilty to all charges. I got to
spend 30min individually with each member of my family.
Those were some hard, heartfelt moments and I
herish the time I was able to spend with them at
hat moment.

After the visit was over, I was swiftly

(5)

moved to another pod. I'm guessing the visit was being watched by other officials in the jail and they felt it was prudent to move me to a more secure location if I was taking a plea deal the next day. This next pod was called "Close-watch" and it was just me and another deputy (hence the name "close-watch"). This was a dry cell and padded and kind of felt like a shoebox as it was only 5.5ft wide. I stayed in this cell from November 6th - November 26th, and the fact that it was just me and another deputy, gave me more opportunity to talk to them. Some could care less about having a conversation with me, but others did. When I was reading my Bible the deputies would ask what part I was reading and then that would spark up a whole conversation about the Word. I was amazed at how much I had retained from reading the Bible and it felt good to talk with someone who is a believer just like me. One deputy went on to tell me about some miracles that had happened in his life; in particular when his sons late grandfather was leaving a single rose in sporadic places just to let his son know he was there with him. I'm not doing the story justice, but Wow! It was spectacular! When I returned from my sentencing hearing on November 19th I was very emotional as you can imagine. The deputy that

(6)

was working saw I was having a hard time holding it together and asked if he could pray with me. I was shocked at this, but completely honored at the same time. Picture it; a deputy in his uniform and an inmate in his oranges, two entities that are usually at enmity with one another, praying through a cell door! Remarkable! After he was done praying, I took over and read Psalm 33 verses 13-22 (what I wanted to read at my sentencing hearing, but I thought it better I didn't) and said a little prayer for my wife and kids and every one affected by this tragedy. I was in tears, he was in tears, it was very moving moment.

In the end, I can look back at each pod I was housed in and relate it to a stage in my faith: 1) Realization - realizing who I am and that I am nothing without God in my life. 2) Sanctification - God was filling my soul with His Word to make me ready to spread His grace and mercy. 3) Salvation - I gave myself, my life and my soul completely to the Lord. 4) Consummation - God has taken absolute control and He is keeping me on the straight path that leads to life everlasting.

The Weld County Jail experience was a rollercoaster; full of ups and downs and twist and turns, but it is also the spot of my Salvation. When Jesus said I have come "to preach deliverance to the captives" (Luke 4:18) that rings true if you're physically captive and/or

(7)

spiritually captive. I went through a lot of dark times in that jail, but Jesus showed me the light at the end of the tunnel. And "that is the true Light, which lights every man that comes into the world." (John 1:9)

My Mom asked me if you could use the letters that I wrote to Bella, CeCe, Nico & Shanann back in December, and I think that will be a good idea. The HLN reporter wanted to use them as part of the documentary to show my character, but I believe God didn't want them used there. He wants the book to be the platform they are used on, so I will give you the green light to go ahead and use them.

You wanted me to give you some detail into the life of me, Shanann & the girls so here we go: It seemed like the perfect life; I had a beautiful wife, two beautiful daughters, a good job, a home.... everything felt like it fit. My life and Shanann's life revolved around Bella and CeCe and we would do anything to make sure they were happy and healthy. We worked as a team the best we could, even when it was evident the girls only wanted me or wanted her. I loved picking them up from school! When I walked into CeCe's classroom our eyes would meet, a huge smile would shine from her face and she would sprint over to me, almost tackling me in the

rocess. Bella would usually be on the playground, so
I would usually have to go into the playset to corral
ve. Once in the car, Bella would find their car ride
snacks, dispose one to Cele and then I would buckle
hem up. The short ride home consisted of a lot of
inging to "Moana", "Frozen" or "Trolls" soundtracks. I loved
hearing them sing! And they loved telling me to stop singing!
I guess my voice wasn't that good. Once home they would
un to Shanan and eat their dinner. Now, shower time!
hey usually got me [scribbled] so wet from the bathtub
hat the shower was a welcome change. They loved washing
their hair like big girls. Afterward, Shanan would come
p and help me lotion the girls up and get their pajamas
on. Then it was off for a snack, a cartoon, brush
heir teeth, inhalers/meds and time for bed. Usually Bella
wanted Shanan and Cele wanted me. Cele picked almost
very book in her room some nights and asked so many
uestions, I loved it! She was such the little character!
Sometimes, Bella would be waiting for me to sing her a
little song (You are my sunshine) and get one extra kiss from
me. Once in bed, Shanan worked on her phone the
est of the night while we watched our shows on T.V.
here wasn't a whole lot of conversation going on, and
hat's my fault, too, for not speaking up. The weekends
usually consisted of getting the girls outside as much
as we could as they were very active. I would take
hem in the backyard to play on their playset, play
some tee ball or pull them around the neighborhood

(9)

in their wagon. At night on the weekend, we would usually take them to the splash pad because they absolutely loved water! When we would go to the pool, it would be a chore to get them to go home! The smiles on their faces were totally worth every second though! As I'm writing this, I can see I didn't put much effort into my marriage other than being the best Dad I could be, and performing my husbandly duties (cleaning, etc.). I did as much as I could to keep the kids from distracting Shanann from her work, that I forgot to focus on her. We did everything as a family. pumpkin patches at Halloween plus all of us wearing costumes, I even wore the costume to the girls' Halloween party at school. Christmas was always fun because I would dress up as Santa and the girls would absolutely love it! Their birthday parties would usually be a little over the top, but we would do anything for Bella and Cece. Shanann and I did go out from time to time; usually for birthdays or anniversaries. My favorite memories of her are the early ones, like: the beach photos we took while the trip where I proposed to her in 2011. Her smile was captivating and we were having a blast. Another would be obviously the wedding. I'll never forget her walking down the aisle, looking flawless, and seeing her look into my eyes when she got up to me and saying "Breathe". She literally took

(10)

ny breath away. That love never died, rather the focus of that love went toward the kids.

I can say with a certainty that I always loved Shanan and always will, but there was always this lingering fear that I would do something wrong. The verse I John 4:18 comes to mind, "There is no fear in love, but perfect love casts out fear..." because how can you fear what you love? Or, how can you love what you fear? The two feelings are at enmity with one another, polar opposites if you will. I seemed to always walk on egg shells around Shanan. There was uneasiness and careful/fearful planning with every step I took. That's not what love should feel like, but I never communicated that to her. When I was with Bella and Cele, being a Dad, there was no fear, just overwhelming love. It could've been just how my personality is structured to be nervous and/or submissive around Shanan, but that's still not how love should be. Finishing off the rest of the verse, "...because fear has torment. He that fears is not made perfect in love" resonates with me because fear is nothing but torment for the soul. That's what the fear eventually did to me; it broke me down spiritually, emotionally and mentally. Was I aware of it? I don't think so. It's like the frog that was put in a pot full of water and, slowly, the water turned to a boil and the frog boiled to death. I didn't see what was happening until it was too late and that mistake cost me the chance to grow old with my family for the rest of my physical life!

Love is a resounding warmth that envelops your entire being. We should all strive for that because fear should never conquer love. Love is from God! When we were made in His image, it was in the image of love and that quality is what will overcome the world!

I think I will end this letter here! I hope you are doing well and your entire family too! Take care and God Bless!

Chris

"Eye has not seen, nor ear heard, neither have entered into the heart of man, the things which God has prepared for them that love Him."

-1 Corinthians 2:9

"If My people, which are called by My name, shall humble themselves, and pray, and seek My face, and turn from their wicked ways; then will I hear from Heaven, and will forgive their sin, and will heal their land."

-2 Chronicles 7:14

"Father, I will that they also, whom You have given Me, be with Me where I am, that they may behold My glory, which You have given me; for You loved me before the foundation of the world."

-John 17:24

(1)

Dear Cheyln, 6.17.19

Hey! I hope this letter finds you in great spirits and growing in God's grace every day. I'm sorry your mountain trip was so soggy, but I know it had to be good to be out in God's creation experiencing His energy, power and blessings. That's where Jesus did most, if not all, of His sermons to the multitude, He could draw from the Father when He was teaching the Gospel.

Thank you for sharing John 15! I think we all have a calling on our lives, some are different than others, but all work for the glory of God. "And we know that all things work together for good to them that love God, to them who are the called according to His purpose." (Romans 8:28). God doesn't "need" to use us, but He "wants" to use us for the growing of His Kingdom and disciples here on Earth. The calling He has on my life is not fully known yet, but slowly it is coming into the light.

In regards to the fruit that we bear, that deals directly to whether we are listening to the mind of the Spirit or the carnal mind. The carnal mind is enmity against God, but the Spirit mind is one with God. Going against God separates us from Him and gets us cut off the branch. Being without the Vine, we go out and venture on our own. That leads to self-sufficiency and pride, which leads to vanity and self-exaltation; all things or traits the carnal mind loves. We go down this road too much and this

(2)

will eventually lead to a life consumed in depression and hoplessness. However, living in the mind of the spirit helps us yield so much fruit that His reservoir of joy inside of us spills out to everyone around us. The more good fruit we bear, the more we manifest a life of Christ in our every day actions. We can leave the darkness that consumed us and reach forth to the light that calls us. Thats my hope for everyone that is stuck in the carnal mindset!

As far as Nichole Atkinson goes, I have nothing against her. She spent a lot of time with Shanann in Arizona and knew that Shanann was upset at me and probably told her about the marital problems. When she didn't hear from Shanann the next day she knew something was up, as she knew Shanann always had her phone. Her actions at my house were one of a concerned friend who believed I had done something, or caused my wife's depression over the weekend. She caused the police to come back a few minutes after they left to search the house and she set up the news crews to come the day after. She was always nice to me when she came over so, like I said, she was just a concerned friend. The YouTube presence I know nothing about. Nicole was a reserved person that Shanann encouraged to put herself out there more selling Thrive. Nicole wasn't as shy as me, but she wasn't as outgoing as Shanann when it came to direct sales. Shanann was her leader and...

Nicole looked up to her.

I never knew anything about the Child Protection Services claims This report about Shanann only being allowed around the kids 90mins a day is something that never was made aware to me. If it was true, I would think I would've been notified. I will admit I was in the dark on a lot of issues, but I just can't see that being veiled from my vision. I guess there is a CPS claim out there, from what my parents tell me and a court date, but I was not in the loop on this if there is any validity. When I worked on the weekends, Shanann was with the kids by herself. She took the kids to school early during the week because she liked to keep a schedule and get the day going early. She used the time alone to work the Thrive business and I would go pick up the girls when I got home from work. There are so many things that don't make sense that people are grasping at that have no precedence in my eyes, but I have been very shielded from much of the information about my case and from the logistics of my marriage. I just can't see this being true.

I do like the head title "Letters from Christopher" with the subtitle being "Hope Wait Trust" I think that will catch the mainstream's attention so they will pick it up. Do you think most of society likes to physically have a book in their hands or download one on their tablet? I never really read books unless

(4)

e was to Bella and Cele.

I don't know if I want anything in the book bout my Dad's struggles. I know he had a hard time with all that coming out in the media and I don't hink he would want all of it re-hashed in the book. That was a tough time in his life and I don't want him to re-live it.

My daily schedule here: 6:15am Standing count (basically o make sure everyone is still alive and counted for). We at breakfast at or around 6:45-7:00am. Depending on the ay we either have showers next or cell-cleanup. Most of my time between 8:00-11:00am is spent reading or praying. My prayers in the morning usually take over a hour because I feel led to pray for everyone I've met in here. I know their struggles and I feel they might not have anyone praying for them on the outside. I also pray for all my friends, family, Shanann's amily, people who have touched my life, people who write me (the bad letters as well) and my wife nd kids. I also thank the Lord for all His blessings and for moving me to a safe place and for everything He is doing in my life. The relationship I have with he Lord is exponential to what it was before. Lunch s at 11:15am and then 12:30pm Standing Count. The time between 12:30pm-4:00pm I spend reading, praying or writing letters. Dinner is at 4:00pm and then recreation s at 4:30pm, five days a week. Another Standing Count is at 5:00pm with dayroom time from 6:00-7:30pm.

I never saw my marriage as a struggle until I met ikki. That temptation brought out any negative perceptions i had concerning my marriage and shut away all the good s well. "I have found whom my soul loves" (Song of Solomon 3:4). oes this mean we have a special person out there made recisely for our soul? Romantically? Only friendship? I can't ay Shannon was my soulmate because we were so different, ut we fit and I love her. There was fearfulness there as nervousness on my part that led to shutting down. never thought it was healthy to argue and I just anted peace in every aspect, I was never an argumentative rson, and that type of peace-keeping made me walk on egg hells to make sure I didn't screw up or do some- hing wrong. She was always so stressed about money that I elt the slightest thing would set her off. That's why tried to do everything I could around the house, utside the house and with the girls I could. That ust created more of a communication barrier that as almost insurmountable. We hardly spoke about anything ith substance and I guess you could say we had fallen to a rut, but didn't acknowledge it. The fact that I ould shut down during an argument was a product of my rsonality. I knew anything I would say would be of o importance, wouldn't contribute constructively and ould only make her angry, even more so than e already was. Even if I did comeback with something in the gument then I knew it would get cut down by whatever e would say next, so I didn't bother. I just stood

(2)

there, avoiding eye contact and nodding like I always would. We didn't argue a lot, but this is how it transpired each time. I guess you could say near the end we were more involved in a successful routine than a relationship because our days were so choreographed. Sure, every relationship needs a plan, but our's was to a tee. We just needed to sit down and express ourselves in a non-judgemental environment to convey our feelings. We, unfortunately never got to do that. She may have not been my soulmate but she's my babygirl, my boo, my wife and my friend. I love her with all my heart.

Going back to the Song of Solomon 3:4 and the question of, if we have soulmates? I love Shanann, my girls, my son, my family and my friends. They will always be a part of my soul. "Nevertheless I have somewhat against you, because you have left your first love" (Revelation 2:4). The One who our soul loves is the Lord (our eternal soulmate) and that will never change.

To Frank and Sandie and Frankie;

I'm sorry for the pain and utter anguish that I've caused your family. This is a tragedy that I never thought could or would occur. Shanann, Bella, Celeste and Nico are four beautiful souls that will live on forever in Heaven and in our hearts. I know you must hate me for what I've done and, honestly, I would be surprised if you didn't. This is a moment in my life that I will never be able to undo and it rips me apart every single day. I see their beautiful faces, their beautiful

(8)

smiles everywhere I look. When I read to them at ight, I can feel them snuggled up next to me like e were at home. I want you to know that I till consider you my Father-in-law, my Mother-in-law and y Brother-in-law, and that I love you all the same. esterday, today and Forever. I pray that one day you an have forgiveness for me ~~[illegible]~~ but, most of all, I ray that you can have compassion on my family. They're urting so bad from this and I know they would love o reconcile if that was something you would allow to appen. I pray every day that both families can meet t the grave site, hold hands, pray and talk about ood times. Share about birthdays and visits and funny FaceTime conversations. I know this prayer hasn't been nswered yet, but I know God is working this request f mine in your hearts. Forgiveness is the start of healing and I pray you can start that process with my family.

You wanted me to write an excerpt into the letters ou received that I wrote Shanann, Bella, Celeste & Nico. I'm not sure what I had written down in those letters so hope this fits in OK; To Shanann, Bella, Celeste & Nico: I love all of you to the moon and back or, s Bella would say, "I love you ALL DAY!" You guys will lways be my shining stars, my light in the darkness nd my guardian angels. I'm so sorry for the pain and error I caused all of you. It rips my heart to pieces knowing what happened. ^Bens^ A husband and a father are true blessings from God. I was blinded from seeing those gifts He bestowed upon me. I hope, when you look down upon me, you don't see the person that hurt you, but the person that loves you. I pray that you say "There's my husband" and "There's my Daddy." I love you all so much and, ~~always~~ remember, you will always be my sunshines.

OK, into Revelation we go. You are correct, we are not mentioned by name in the seven churches. The Churches that are named are all in Asia and part of Paul's Missionary journeys, I believe. Either Paul went there or some of his partners. I think the seven churches reflect the seven continents. The message to each Church consists of a positive commendation and what the church needs to fix. Although the message to Philadelphia portrays they need to fix nothing; "Behold, I come quickly: hold fast what you have, that no man takes your crown." (Revelation 3:11). The message to Laodicea gives no commendation, but all repairs that are needed. The Lord says "Because you are lukewarm... I will spew you out of My mouth. Because you say, 'I am rich, and increased with goods, and have need of nothing'..." (Revelation 3:16-17). The Lord asks the Church of Laodicea to come to Him for salvation so they ~~could~~ could be clothed (because their pride has made them naked) and to see (because they have been blinded by the world and its lusts). I truly believe the United States is the Church of Laodicea. We live by our own excesses and are proud of it.

(5)

Dayroom time is when we can all use the phone, watch T.V., play cards/other games and talk to each other. The rest of the night I spend reading or writing letters until I fall asleep sometime around 11:30pm. As you can see I pray, read and write a lot! My faith in the Lord and the ability He gives me to spread His word consumes most of my day, and I love it. The Lord's presence lets me rest in peace knowing that His grace and love sustains me.

You say the K-9 dogs went crazy in one spot in the basement and I can't think of a physical reason why. I went downstairs that morning (to the basement) to get some trash bags, but that's it. I know dogs can see/feel things humans can't so, maybe, they felt the evil spirits that were in the house. That's the only reason I can come up with why the dogs picked up anything in the basement.

I don't think Shanann took oxycodone or was getting it from Nicole. I know Nicole was doing something in the medical field, but I sincerely doubt Shanann was taking anything. Yes, I only gave Shanann the oxycodone the first night I was at my in-laws. I was obviously not in the right state of mind, but the idea was for her to lose our baby so it would be easier to be with Nikki. It's hard even writing that and I feel like such a monster, but I know those 2½ months was not the person I am today or was before. I'm so thankful the Lord has delivered me from whatever evil was tormenting me and my family. I just wish they were still here.

That is what I pick up when I read about the seven churches. I never had that revelation before you asking me about it. That's what God put on my heart when I asked Him to reveal more of the Book of Revelation to me. I will continue to pray on this to see if this "knowing" came from Him. 30,000 Guillotines?? My goodness! That is absolutely scary! That is such a cruel form of punishment that it would have to be used for the people who don't take the mark of the beast. The days are growing shorter and I don't know how much lower the world can fall before the appointed time is come. All we can do is keep spreading the Word and lead people to Christ. The more people that are led to Christ, the more people will answer the call and/or knock on the door of their heart.

The last ten months have definitely been an up and down rollercoaster of emotions, a crushing experience if you will. But those are the types of experiences God has put in our path to overcome. Not of ourselves to overcome them, but of our faith in the Lord to overcome them. When we encounter tribulations, we often ask, Why? Then, we start to worry how to remedy the issue without looking to God. Worrying is counterproductive and keeps you from experiencing the Lord's blessings. Worrying is a by-product of fear. Fear is a choice, but love is everlasting. That love is from God and God is our Strength. That Strength is what carries us through by faith. "For by grace you are saved through faith, and that not of yourselves. it is the gift of God" (Ephesians 2:8). That faith is the calling inside all of us by God through Jesus Christ. That faith is a fighting faith that pushes us passed the thought of trying to "BE" someone in this world because, through the grace of God, we "ARE" someone in Jesus Christ. When we realize who we are in Christ we can truly say "the winter is past, the rain is over and gone." (Song of Solomon 2:11).

I will continue to reach for the hem of His garment and I will keep praying that all obstacles for this book will fall before the feet of the Lord. "Surely as I have thought, so shall it come to pass; and as I have purposed so shall it stand." (Isaiah 14:24). With God pushing us, we cannot fail. Prayers to you and your family. Take care and God Bless!

In Christ,

Chris

"So shall My word be that goes forth out of My mouth; it shall not return to Me void, but it shall accomplish that which I please, and it shall prosper in the thing whereto I sent it." (Isaiah 55:11)

"For You are my lamp, O Lord; and the Lord will lighten my darkness. For by You I have run through a troop; by my God have I leaped over a wall." (2 Samuel 22:29-30)

(1)

Dear Cheryln, 7.5.19

Hello Again! I hope you're doing well and in great spirits. I didn't see any fireworks last night, but I could hear a number of them being set off around the neighborhood that surrounds the prison. It brough back some good memories of my family from past July 4th celebrations. Twice we were at a cookout and sitting in the front yard of our friend's house when his sprinklers went off during the fireworks! Priceless! I remember in 2015 recording Bella's astonished look watching the firework in Denver. Shanan was nine months pregnant at the time and absolutely glowing. I remember in 2017 the girls were playing with sparklers for the first time. That was a little nerve-racking, but they had a blast! Good memor I will always hang onto during this time of year!

When we spoke on the phone last night you said "I need the Prologue ASAP", so I figured I better get on that. I've been in prayer most of the morning laying on my bunk and the Lord has granted me some wisdom in what to say. Here it goes:

Foreword

Hope... Wait... Trust... Three little words with some mighty heavy significance. "Now faith is the substance of things hoped for, the evidence of things not seen." (Hebrews 11:1) Do you have hope in things you've seen or things you wan that you've seen? Why? Everything that you see is temporary, so why hope in it? If you have hope in this world or in yourself, you've given yourself over to pride. Hope in the world traps your feet in a net, wh

hose who have their hope in Christ safely walk on
ay. "But they that wait upon the Lord shall renew
heir strength; they shall mount up with wings as eagles; they
hall run, and not be weary, and they shall walk, and
ot faint." (Isaiah 40:31). It's hard to wait for anything,
specially since were all impatient creatures in an on-
emand world. We let waiting bring on stress and
nxiety because everything we want, we wanted
esterday. That should be an indication to us all, that
e are waiting on the wrong objective... worldly riches.
Trust in the Lord with all your heart; and lean not
nto your own understanding" (Proverbs 3:5). Trust brings a
hole new avenue to your heart. If you don't have trust
n someone or something, you totally disregard it. But,
f you do, it can bring a calmness to your life
hat is almost Heavenly.

So, what do I hope in? What do I wait on?
What do I trust in? Christ! I had a beautiful
ife. I experienced beautiful love. But I let
temptation steal it away. Darkness can restrain you
rom making the decisions you should. Darkness can
ob you of everything you love. Darkness can blind you
rom everything you hold dear. Darkness can destroy your
soul, but the Light can restore it. That Light is
peace in your heart. That Light is the smile and
aughs you go home to every day. That Light is the
love of God in His Son; a love that stretches
from the east to the west.

(5)

God didn't create us to be robots. He gave us freewill to see what path we would follow and what decisions we would make. Those of you who knew me before this tragedy would say "Nope! No Way! Not in a million years would he go down that path. Those of you who know of me because of this tragedy have formed your opinions; mostly negative, and I don't blame you. I just want you to realize darkness can enter into our lives in any form (another person, an activi a feeling, a thought) and jetasin us down a path we think is right, being blinded by evil, but only leading to turmoil.

The world tries to negotiate for peace, but the peace you're looking for only comes from the Prince of Peace. Striving for a safe, predictable life won't bring you the peace in your heart until you receive Christ there. Life is a tempestuous wind that never seems to back down but, when you have the peace of God, you can be at peace during the storm "For, lo, the winter is past, the rain is over and gone (Song of Solomon 2:11)

Acknowledgments

- Thank you to my Mom, Dad and Sister! No mat what, you've all been by my side and your love for me never stopped. Through the good days and the bad you're all right there to support me in every way. Love you all so much!

* Sorry for the type-o's

(4)

- Thank you Anna for all your support. You reached ut to me and my family ~~[illegible]~~ from the very beginning. ou followed where God was leading you and we have ecome great friends. Your letters, phone calls and visits lways bring a smile to my face. ~~[illegible]~~ Your courage and faith have made a huge impact n my life. God Bless you and your family!
- Thank you Janelle for all your support. You took the hance reaching out to a stranger in another country in ecember and our friendship has grown extensively since. ou've basically become sort of a human diary for me nd you've helped me become stronger as a person. Follow e Lord's path for you and I'll be calling you Dr. Janelle a few years. God Bless you and your family!
- Thank you Cheryln for all your support. You were very ersistent in contacting me, even though I didn't respond. You didn't give up. You listened to the Lord and kept riting me until I listened to what the Lord was telling e, "Write her! She wants to help!" A couple months later and e are great friends and helping each other grow in ur faith. God bless you, your family and everyone at ible League as well!
- Thank you to everyone who has supported me and ritten to me. You've all made a mark on my life hat will last a lifetime. I am in debted to you ll! God bless!
- Thank you to my Lord and Savior for saving my life! Without Your help I would either be

dead or [illegible] surrounded by darkness searching for a way out. "I waited patiently for the Lord; and He inclined to me, and heard my cry. He brought me up also out of a horrible pit, out of the miry clay and set my feet upon a rock, and established my goings." (Psalm 40:1-2). You have taken darkness and turned it into Your marvelous light "that shines more and more to the perfect day." (Proverbs 4:18) I will praise Your name forevermore!

OK, I think that's all I got for now! I pray the Lord keeps guiding us, protecting us and correcting us, so we stay on His path. I will leave you wit a few verses that the Lord brought to my attention. Take care and God Bless!

In Christ,
Chris

"You have granted me life and favor, and Your visitatio has preserved my spirit."

- Job 10:12

"Your sun shall no more go down, neither shall your moon withdraw itself; for the Lord shall be your everlasting light, and the days of your mourning shall be ended."

- Isaiah 60:20

(6)

"And I will bring the blind by a way that they knew not; I will lead them in paths that they have not known; I will make darkness light before them, and crooked things straight. These things will I do unto them, and not forsake them."

- Isaiah 42:16

"You are wearied in the greatness of your way, yet you said not, 'There is no hope'; you have found the life of your hand; therefore you were not grieved."

- Isaiah 57:10

This last verse is great because the interpretation I
erceive out of it is this: "The greatness of your way"
fers to the great obstacles and pain in your life and
et, you said "There is no hope." You are not grieved
ecause the "life of your hand" is with you. That is
our Rock, our Redeemer, our Lifeforce, our Shield.
it's such a beautiful verse!

RELIANCE ON THIS POWER OF ATTORNEY FOR FINANCES AND PROPERTY

Any person, including my agent, may rely upon the validity of this power of attorney or a copy of it unless that person knows that the power of attorney has been terminated or is invalid.

SIGNATURE AND ACKNOWLEDGMENT

Your signature [signature] Date 7.19.19

Your name printed Christopher Watts

Your address: PO Box 700 Waupun, WI 53963

Your telephone number: ______

State of: Wisconsin County of: Dodge

This document was acknowledged before me on

Date ______ by name of principal ______

(Seal, if any)

Signature of notary [signature]

Name of notary (typed or printed) Michael R. Bernstein

My commission expires: 01/27/2021

This document prepared by: ______

LIMITATION ON AGENT'S AUTHORITY

An agent who is not my spouse or domestic partner MAY NOT use my property to benefit the agent or a person to whom the agent owes an obligation of support unless I have included that authority in the special instructions.

SPECIAL INSTRUCTIONS (OPTIONAL)

You may give special instructions in the following space

I authorize Cheryln Cadle to use any and all correspondence I've sent her for the purpose of the book she is writing.

EFFECTIVE DATE

This power of attorney is effective immediately unless I have stated otherwise in the special instructions.

NOMINATION OF GUARDIAN (OPTIONAL)

If it becomes necessary for a court to appoint a guardian of my estate or guardian of my person, I nominate the following person(s) for appointment

Name of nominee for guardian of my estate: ______

Nominee's address: ______

Nominee's telephone number: ______

Name of nominee for guardian of my person: ______

Nominee's address: ______

Nominee's telephone number: ______

Wisconsin Department of Corrections

Governor Scott Walker | Secretary Cathy A. Jess

Mailing Address:
Attention Visitor Processing
Initial Classification Unit
P.O. Box 661
Waupun, WI 53963-0661
Phone: 920-324-6255

PRINT LEGIBLY

OFFENDER NAME	DOC NUMBER	INSTITUTION/CENTER NAME	LIVING CENTER/UNIT
Christopher Watts	674796	Dodge Correctional Institution	Unit 11
OFFENDER SIGNATURE			DATE SIGNED
[signature]			12 30.18

Proposed Visitor - Please Read This Section:

- If you wish to visit with this offender, fully complete the reverse side of this questionnaire. The offender will notify you when the processing of this form has been completed. If you do not wish to visit, please disregard this form.
- Each visitor, including minors, is required to submit a separate DOC-21AA Visitor Questionnaire.
- All questions and check boxes on the reverse side of this form must be answered completely and accurately. Falsified or incorrect information may result in denial of visitation. If form is incomplete or illegible, it will not be processed and will be destroyed.
- If the proposed visitor named on this form is a minor, the legal, non-incarcerated guardian/custodial parent of the minor listed must sign the form.
- All approved minor visitors must be accompanied by an approved non-incarcerated adult that is listed on the offender's approved visiting list.
- This form must be mailed ATTENTION VISITOR PROCESSING at the address listed above. If this form is given or mailed directly to the offender, it will NOT be processed and will be destroyed.
- If you are approved for visiting and are over the age of 16, you will be required to show photo identification upon arrival at the institution. Only the following forms of VALID identification will be accepted.
  - State Driver's License
  - Military/Tribal Identification Card
  - Department of Transportation Picture Identification Card
  - Passport/Visa

DEPARTMENT OF CORRECTIONS
Division of Adult Institutions
DOC-21AA (Rev. 6/2018)

Milton Keynes UK
Ingram Content Group UK Ltd.
UKHW010317010624
443378UK00005B/456